S0-AFQ-593

Counterinsurgency
in Africa

Recent Titles in
Contributions in Military Studies

COUNTERINSURGENCY IN AFRICA

The Portuguese Way of War, 1961–1974

John P. Cann

Foreword by General Bernard E. Trainor

Contributions in Military Studies, Number 167

GREENWOOD PRESS
Westport, Connecticut • London

DT
36.7
C355
1997

Library of Congress Cataloging-in-Publication Data

Cann, John P., 1941–
    Counterinsurgency in Africa : the Portuguese way of war, 1961–1974
/ John P. Cann ; foreword by Bernard E. Trainor.
        p. cm. — (Contributions in military studies, ISSN 0883–6884
; no. 167)
    Includes bibliographical references (p.) and index.
    ISBN 0–313–30189–1 (alk. paper)
    1. Portugal—Colonies—Africa.   2. Portugal—Colonies—History.
3. Africa, Portuguese-speaking—History, Military.
4. Counterinsurgency—Africa, Portuguese-speaking—History—20th
century.   5. Counterinsurgency—Portugal—History—20th century.
6. Angola—History—Revolution, 1961–1975—Campaigns.
7. Mozambique—History—Revolution, 1964–1975—Campaigns.   8. Guinea-
Bissau—History—Revolution, 1963–1974—Campaigns.   I. Title.
II. Series.
    DT36.7.C355   1997
    960.3′26—dc20   96–38260

British Library Cataloguing in Publication Data is available.

Library of Congress Catalog Card Number: 96–38260
ISBN: 0–313–30189–1
ISSN: 0883–6884

First published in 1997

Greenwood Press, 88 Post Road West, Westport, CT 06881
An imprint of Greenwood Publishing Group, Inc.

Printed in the United States of America

For my uncle

LANGBOURNE M. WILLIAMS

CONTENTS

TABLES

FOREWORD

The archetypal small war is more relevant than ever today. Although superpower confrontation and its proxy wars of national liberation are quiescent at the moment, ethnic, religious, political, and economic rivalries remain on every continent. In sub-Saharan Africa particularly, where animosities have been a fact of life throughout recorded history, armed conflict driven by ancient antagonisms and modern political ambitions has again become symptomatic. These struggles largely follow the Maoist prescription of protracted war, always a difficult and insidious threat for any incumbent government to fight and win. And yet there are tried and proven solutions to gaining victory in these circumstances. Dr. John P. Cann provides just such a case study in this work.

Portugal was the first colonial power to arrive in Africa and the last to leave. As other European states were granting independence to their African possessions, Portugal chose to stay and fight despite the small odds for success. That it did so successfully for thirteen years across the three fronts of Angola, Guiné, and Mozambique remains a remarkable achievement, particularly for a nation of such modest resources. Dr. Cann calls attention to this important counterinsurgency campaign, one that was overshadowed by the United States involvement in Vietnam and that is now largely forgotten by non-Portuguese scholars. He dispels the conventional thinking that such a campaign cannot be won, particularly by a country lacking wealth in manpower, treasure, and experience. While the military plays a key role in counterinsurgency, at heart it remains a political struggle. Consequently, the job of the armed forces is not necessarily to deliver an outright military victory, but rather to contain violence, protect people from intimidation, deny guerrillas access to the local inhabitants and their supply of food and recruits, gain the people's confidence with psychological and social initiatives, and through these activities produce enough respect among the insurgent leadership to induce political negotiations.

The Portuguese military accomplished all of these things. Its route to success was not always direct; however, it profited from its mistakes and remained flexible in its thinking. It was able to learn while doing. Unfortunately, in the end Portugal's politicians squandered the hard-won military gains by refusing to come to terms with the insurgents.

Dr. Cann's work is the first comprehensive account in English of how the Portuguese armed forces prepared for and conducted their distant campaign. The Portuguese military crafted its doctrine and implemented it to match the guerrilla strategy of protracted war, and in doing so followed the lessons gleaned from the British and French experiences in small wars. Portugal defined and analyzed its insurgency problem in light of this accumulated knowledge on counterinsurgency, developed its military policies in this context, and applied them in the African colonial environment. The Portuguese approach to the conflict was distinct in that it sought to combine the two-pronged national strategy of containing the cost of the war and of spreading the burden to the colonies, with the solution on the battlefield. Dr. Cann argues the uniqueness of this approach by highlighting it through a thematic military analysis of the Portuguese effort and a comparison with the experiences of other governments fighting similar contemporaneous wars. Since many records of the campaigns were destroyed in Portugal's April 1974 revolution and many more were abandoned in Africa during the decolonization process, Dr. Cann's work draws primarily on his wide-ranging interviews of participants and decisionmakers and on the extensive use of their personal papers. This original material is ably blended with published sources in both Portuguese and English to produce an informative, valuable, and readable account of the agonies and successes in the development of Portugal's counterinsurgency capabilities. Even today Portugal's systematic and logical approach to its insurgency challenge holds valuable lessons for any nation forced to wage a small war on the cheap.

Harvard University   General Bernard E. Trainor
Cambridge, Massachusetts
29 July 1996

PREFACE

The origin of this book can be traced to the time between 1987 and 1992, when I participated in maritime exercises as a naval officer temporarily augmenting the staff of the Commander-in-Chief Iberian Atlantic Area at NATO headquarters in Oeiras, Portugal. Every Portuguese officer with whom I worked during these exercises was a veteran of the African Campaigns of 1961–1974, a lengthy war that was not well known or understood outside of Portugal. There is little written about the conflict in English, and those works that are available are relatively obscure. Consequently, as my interest in low-intensity conflict and guerrilla warfare matured during subsequent assignments, I was offered the opportunity to pursue this topic.

There are invariably two sides to the story of every war, and the Campaigns are no exception. The Portuguese military was faced with the difficult job of winning a "war of national liberation" in an era when it was not politic to retain one's colonial empire. In such a war, victory may be achieved militarily, but more than likely it will be achieved by producing a stalemate in which the government has gained credibility through military and social initiatives and has thereby induced the guerrillas to negotiate. Such an accomplishment is no small feat in a war in which the guerrillas seek a total displacement of authority. The Portuguese military achieved outright military victory in Angola, a credible stalemate in Guiné, and, with additional resources and spirited leadership, could have regained control of northern Mozambique. Unfortunately, Portugal's political leaders remained shortsighted and removed from reality, and the military and social successes were squandered through political intransigence. When victory was within Portugal's grasp, political inflexibility created a frustrated military and a revolution in 1974.

This book is the story of the Campaigns from the perspective of the Portuguese military. It addresses the conflict through a thematic military analysis of the counterinsurgency effort from the time of the Angola uprisings on 4 February and 15 March 1961 until the military coup in Lisbon on 25 April 1974. It describes how Portugal defined and analyzed its insurgency problem, how it developed its own particular military policies and doctrines, and how it applied them in the African colonial environment. Its object is to show how Portugal's national strategy to husband and preserve its meager resources was translated into policies and practices at the campaign and tactical level, and how this strategy was effective in permitting Portugal to conduct a sustained and lengthy campaign in three distant colonies. In following both broad and narrow campaign strategies, Portugal attempted to disrupt the organization of the nationalist movements through the operations of agents and to counter their armed action with appropriate military force and diplomatic pressure. Concurrently, it sought to protect its people from insurgent contact and to win their loyalty by elevating their standard of living and redressing their grievances. These elements, their particular combination, and their style of execution reflect what may be termed a Portuguese way of war. This book seeks to analyze each of these factors, to examine their coordinated and synergistic application, to compare them with other contemporary counterinsurgency experiences, and to emphasize their uniqueness.

Research for the work, conducted between 1993 and 1996, focused on how the Portuguese, through imaginative leadership and management of the Campaigns, fought a three-front colonial war 8,000 kilometers from home for thirteen years on a very limited defense budget. Since many official records on the wars either were destroyed in the 1974 Portuguese revolution or abandoned in Africa upon decolonization, the central research challenge has been to reconstruct events largely through the process of interviewing key participants and decisionmakers. To those who so graciously supported me, I owe a large debt of gratitude.

ACKNOWLEDGMENTS

I wish to thank Professor Patrick Chabal, head of the Department of Portuguese and Brazilian Studies, and Dr. Martin Navias, Department of War Studies, King's College, London, both observant critics, for their skillful guidance and support during the research and writing of this work. Their careful reading of the manuscript immensely improved the quality of the final product, and they have been perfect advisers and ideal friends throughout.

I am most grateful for the assistance and hospitality offered in Portugal by General Joaquim Chito Rodrigues, Director of the Instituto de Altos Estudos Militares (IAEM), and his entire staff, who spent many hours helping me. Particular thanks are due to Colonel Fernando José Pinto Simões, Director of the Library at the IAEM, who along with his staff gave so generously of their time. General José Manuel de Bethencourt Rodrigues, Brigadeiro Renato Fernando Marques Pinto, and Colonel Luís Alberto Santiago Inocentes deserve special thanks for their tireless help in explaining the African political and military environment, for introducing me to the appropriate experts on various unique aspects of the wars, and for reading earlier drafts of this book. General Pedro Alexandre Gomes Cardoso, Presidência do Conselho de Ministros, and his staff; General Jorge Brochado de Miranda, former Chief of Staff of the Portuguese Air Force, and his staff at the Arquivo Histórico da Força Aérea Portuguesa; Colonel Luís Valença Pinto, Commandant of the Escola Prática Engenharia, and his staff; Colonel António Rosas Leitão, instructor at the Academia Militar; and Lieutenant Colonel Aniceto Afonso, Director of the Arquivo Histórico Militar, and his staff, deserve particular thanks for their helpful support.

Deep appreciation goes to my good friend of three decades, Stephen W. Woody, who has taken a personal interest in the success of this volume from its inception and who introduced me to Colonel A. Marques de Carvalho, who in turn was instrumental in helping me at the beginning in Portugal. I owe a particular debt to the many participants in the Campaigns who so patiently helped me to fill in the gaps in information that contributed to a fuller picture. To General José Luís Almiro Canêlhas, General Tomás George Conceição Silva, General Joaquim Miguel Duarte Silva, General Manuel Amorim de Sousa Menezes, Vice Admiral Nuno Gonçalo Vieira Matias, Brigadeiro Hélio Felgas, Colonel Dionísio de Almeida Santos, Colonel Carlos Fabião, Colonel Carlos da Costa Gomes Bessa, Colonel César Augusto Rodrigues Mano, Colonel Luís A. Martinho Grão, Inspector Óscar Cardoso, the Duke of Valderano, and Mr. Colin M. Beer, each of whom provided an invaluable and unique perspective on the wars, I am deeply grateful for their patience and care in helping me to understand the many facets of the conflict. Without exception they gave freely of their time and experience, and I hope that I have done justice to their views.

My research in published sources uncovered a varied array of experts whose advice and counsel proved indispensable. I am indebted to the very professional library staffs throughout the University of London, most particularly to Carole Radanne, whose tireless initiative, knowledgeable assistance, and dear friendship remain an integral part of this book. To Caroline Tyssen of Livraria Galileu in Cascais and to Fritz Berkemeier of Livraria Histórica e Ultramarina in Lisbon, whose encyclopedic knowledge of the literature on Portuguese Africa proved as indispensable as their stimulating discussions, I owe a special debt. Many thanks are due my cartographer, Edward Haile, whose personal interest in Portuguese Africa lent a special dimension to the maps.

Funding of the original research for this work was received from the Department of War Studies, King's College, London, and from the Overseas Research Students Awards Scheme as administered by the Committee of Vice-Chancellors and Principals of the Universities of the United Kingdom, for which I am most grateful.

Finally, I owe a particular debt to my family—Courtenay, Jay, and Jamie—all of whom lived patiently with the domestic chaos of this work.

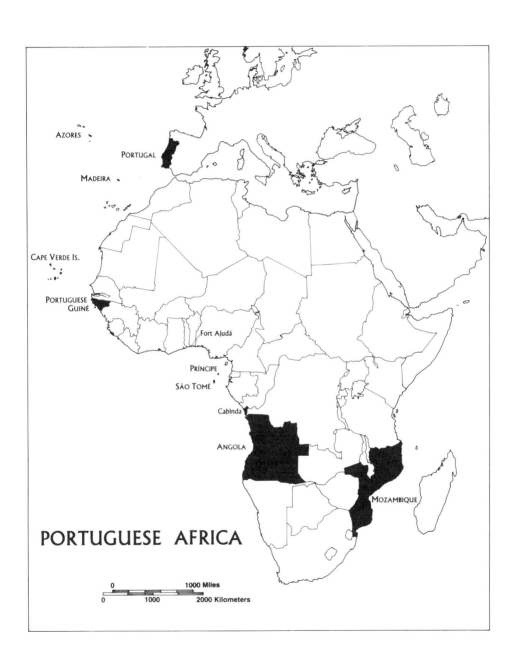

AZORES

PORTUGAL

MADEIRA

CAPE VERDE IS.

PORTUGUESE
GUINÉ

Fort Ajudá

PRÍNCIPE

SÃO TOMÉ

Cabinda

ANGOLA

MOZAMBIQUE

PORTUGUESE AFRICA

0   1000 Miles

0   1000   2000 Kilometers

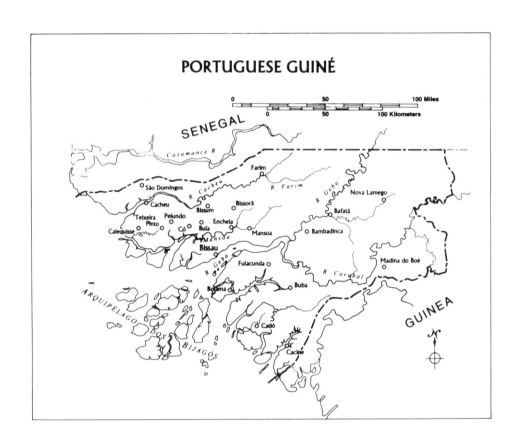

PORTUGUESE GUINÉ

SENEGAL

GUINEA

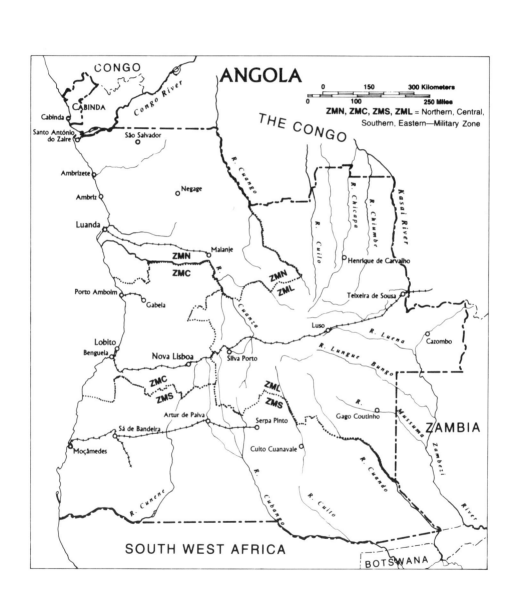

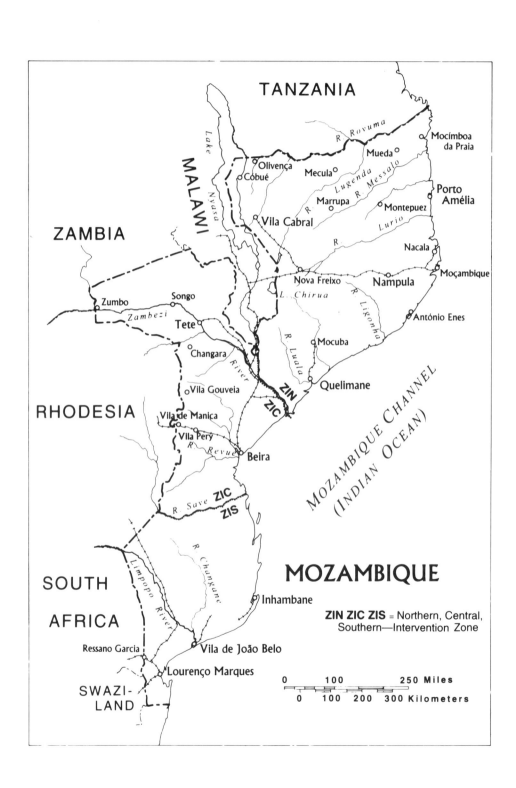

TANZANIA

MALAWI

ZAMBIA

RHODESIA

SOUTH

AFRICA

SWAZI-
LAND

R. Rovuma

Mocímboa
da Praia

Olivença
Cóbué
Mecula
Mueda

Lugenda
R. Messalo

Porto
Amélia

Marrupa
Montepuez

Vila Cabral

Lurio

Nacala

R.

Lake

Nyasa

Nova Freixo
Moçambique

Nampula

Zumbo
Songo
L. Chirua
R. Ligonha

António Enes

Zambezi
Tete
R. Luala
Mocuba

Changara
River

Vila Gouveia

Quelimane
ZIN

ZIC

Vila de Manica
Vila Pery
R. Revue
Beira

MOZAMBIQUE CHANNEL
(INDIAN OCEAN)

R. Save **ZIC**
ZIS

R. Changane

MOZAMBIQUE

Limpopo River

Inhambane

ZIN ZIC ZIS = Northern, Central,
Southern—Intervention Zone

Ressano Garcia
Vila de João Belo

Lourenço Marques

0	100		250 Miles
0	100	200	300 Kilometers

Counterinsurgency
in Africa

1

A REMARKABLE FEAT OF ARMS

Between 1961 and 1974, Portugal faced the extremely ambitious task of conducting three simultaneous counterinsurgency campaigns in Guiné, Angola, and Mozambique. It was at the time neither a rich nor a well-developed country. In fact, it was the least wealthy Western European nation by most standards of economic measure. Thus, for Portugal in 1961 to have mobilized an army, transported it many thousands of kilometers to its African colonies, established large logistical bases at key locations there to support it, equipped it with special weapons and matériel, and trained it for a very specialized type of warfare was a remarkable achievement. It is made even more noteworthy by the fact that these tasks were accomplished without any previous experience, doctrine, or demonstrated competence in the field of either power projection or counterinsurgency warfare, and thus without the benefit of any instructors who were competent in these specialties. To put this last statement in perspective, other than periodic colonial pacification efforts, Portugal had not fired a shot in anger since World War I, when Germany invaded northern Mozambique and southern Angola.

PORTUGAL'S COUNTERINSURGENCY CHALLENGES

The immediate and largest obstacle to conducting the campaigns was the geographic distance that separated Lisbon from its battlefields. Angola, the scene of the initial action in 1961, is located on the southwest coast of Africa. Luanda, its principal city and resupply point, is approximately 7,300 kilometers by air from Lisbon. Guiné, the scene of the second insurgency from January 1963, is located on the west coast of Africa about 3,400 air kilometers south of Portugal. Mozambique was the scene of the third insurgency in September 1964, and its principal resupply airfield of Beira is some 10,300 kilometers from

Lisbon. These distances compounded the problem of logistics and produced an associated strain on transportation resources.

The British were forced to fight in Malaya and Kenya, which from London were about 9,300 and 5,700 kilometers distant, respectively. French Indochina was 10,600 kilometers from Paris, and Vietnam was halfway around the world from the United States. Only Algeria was a close 800 kilometers from southern France. Except for Algeria, all of these insurgencies were far from the home of the defending power. Regarding multiple fronts, only Britain had to face three separate insurgencies simultaneously in Malaya (1948–1960), Kenya (1952–1956), and Cyprus (1954–1983), and in the latter instances had severe difficulty mustering adequate troops for the conflicts.[1] France and the U.S. did not have a multifronted conflict and the associated strain on resources that such a situation would impose. When France had been faced with this problem in 1956 while fighting in Algeria, Tunisia and Morocco were being granted independence. This development removed the problem of multiple fronts for which it did not have sufficient manpower.[2]

Not only were these colonies distant from Portugal, but they were also distant from one another. This separation added another dimension to the conduct of the African campaigns and exacerbated difficulties in the logistical support of Portuguese forces. While Bissau (Guiné) is 3,400 kilometers south of Lisbon, Luanda (Angola) is an additional 4,000 kilometers south of Bissau, and Lourenço Marques (Mozambique) a further 3,000 kilometers southeast of Luanda. For the most modern intertheater transport aircraft in the Portuguese fleet of the time, these distances represented a hard several days' work for both aircrew and machine.

Not only were these territories distant from Lisbon and each other, but Angola and Mozambique were vast by any standard, further complicating their defense. Angola covers 1,246,314 square kilometers, an area which is about fourteen times the size of Portugal or as large as the combined areas of Spain, France, and Italy. Its land frontier with its neighbors of the Belgian Congo (Zaire), Northern Rhodesia (Zambia), and South-West Africa (Namibia) extends 4,837 kilometers. Mozambique, the second largest territory, covers an area of 784,961 square kilometers or about nine times the size of Portugal. Its land border of 4,330 kilometers is shared with Tanganyika (Tanzania) in the north, Nyasaland (Malawi), Northern Rhodesia (Zambia), Southern Rhodesia (Zimbabwe), the Republic of South Africa, and finally Swaziland in the extreme south. Guiné, the smallest of the three, is a tiny tropical enclave about the size of Switzerland. It covers an estimated 36,125 square kilometers, but because of tidal action that affects 20 percent of the country, only about 28,000 square kilometers remain above the mean high-tide mark. This tidal delta and its characteristics further complicated its defense. Its land frontier is about 680 kilometers, of which 300 comprise the northern border with Senegal, and 380 the eastern and southern borders with the Republic of Guinea, both former French colonies.

By contrast, only Algeria was larger, with 2,204,860 square kilometers, about 200,000 of which were economically usable.[3] French Indochina was only 750,874, Malaya 333,403, and South Vietnam 174,289 square kilometers. With the exception of the French in Algeria, no other counterinsurgency campaign was waged over such vast territories as the Portuguese had to address in Angola, Mozambique, and Guiné together, and this factor had a significant bearing on the Portuguese way of conducting counterinsurgency.

Distance was not the only obstacle. Terrain features posed unusual problems as well. Topographically Angola is bordered on the west by the Atlantic Ocean, where a coastal belt runs the length of the approximately 1,650-kilometer shoreline, rising to a central highland 50 to 200 kilometers inland that covers about 60 percent of the country. Further inland there is a plateau rising as high as 1,600 meters. The climate is tropical. Particularly important was the vulnerable frontier between Angola and the Belgian Congo to the north. It is immensely long and consists of over 2,000 kilometers of mountain, swamp, jungle, and elephant grass. The Congo River, which comprises part of the border, remains full of thickly wooded islands which provided excellent cover for guerrillas. Crossings could be made undetected at virtually any point. In this area the Portuguese security forces faced approximately 25,000 guerrillas scattered throughout an area the size of the Iberian Peninsula. The terrain from the border southward was also covered with dense jungle, thick elephant grass eight to ten feet tall, swamp, and mountain. The few roads were beaten earth and were little better than tracks in a limitless ocean of elephant grass, an ideal environment for guerrillas and a difficult one for security forces.

Guiné also has a difficult topography that presented its own set of problems. It can be roughly divided into two distinct geographical areas. The western area is characterized by a forbidding stretch of mangrove and swamp forests covering the coastal inlets and deltas of half a dozen rivers. Tidal action floods these deltas twice daily, submerging land and creating vast tracts of impenetrable swamp. The thousands of miles of rivers and tributaries are obscured from the air by mangroves and thick foliage, making clandestine guerrilla movement simple and its interdiction a difficult military problem. These rivers are navigable deep into the country, providing vital lines of communication. The coast also has many small islands, the most important of which form the Bijagos Islets. The land rises in the northern and eastern interior areas of the country, where the coastal forests gradually disappear as the terrain changes into the sub-Saharan savanna plain of grasslands and scattered, scrawny trees. Elevation does not exceed 300 meters.

Mozambique presents yet a third and different topography. Physically it is largely a 1,000-kilometer-long coastal belt, rising in the north and northwest to forested areas. The vast, open, and sparsely populated northern areas are difficult to police; the wide-ranging, often nomadic, and isolated population is vulnerable to insurgent intimidation and difficult to protect. It shares a tropical climate with Angola.

The population diversity posed yet another obstacle. Angola's population, according to the 1960 census, was 4,830,283, or about four people per square kilometer, which was 95.2 percent black, 3.5 percent white, and 1.1 percent *mestiço* or mixed, and 0.2 percent others. The black population consisted of ninety-four distinct tribes divided into nine primary ethnolinguistic groups, each of which had its own degree of loyalty to Portugal. The population was concentrated in the coastal west and the central plateau. The arid eastern desert and steamy northern jungle were only sparsely populated. It was in these remote areas that the guerrillas operated and posed a severe military challenge.

Guiné had a population in 1960 of 525,437, or an average of fifteen people per square kilometer. However, because of a concentration of the population in the western coastal delta, the figure there rose to 100 people per square kilometer. This situation left the arid eastern half quite remote, with about one person per square kilometer, and it was here that guerrilla infiltration occurred with the least opposition. Ninety-nine percent of the population was black, fragmented into two primary groupings covering twenty-eight ethnolinguistic groups, each exhibiting various degrees of loyalty to Portugal.

Mozambique's population in 1960 was 6,603,653, or about eight people per square kilometer, 97 percent of which was black. This segment was fragmented into approximately eighty-six distinct tribes in ten ethnolinguistic groupings, each with its own conviction of loyalty to Portugal. The north and northwestern regions of open, sparsely populated bush country next to Tanganyika (Tanzania) and Northern Rhodesia (Zambia) were the most vulnerable to guerrilla infiltration. Here the isolated and sparse population was vulnerable to insurgent intimidation from these sanctuary countries.

The mosaics represented in these populations were at once a problem and a source of strength to Portugal because of their varying loyalties both to Portugal and to each other. Portugal was able to exploit these differences to its advantage in that the guerrillas were often from a group that had little in common with other groups. The reverse of this coin was that Portugal found it necessary to adjust its psychosocial program to each group and to tailor its appeal to various and different cultures.

The French faced a similar situation in Algeria, where the 1966 census showed 11,833,000 people concentrated along the northern coast of its 2,332,164 square kilometers, leaving the mountains and the arid desert sparsely populated. The guerrillas operated in both the urban and the rural areas to the extent that there was a population to be won. Territory beyond the coast was forbidding and remote, and was used mostly for transit and concealment. The guerrillas were part of the local Arab population and were as difficult to identify as those in Portuguese Africa.

In Malaya the 10,500,000 population was concentrated in and around the cities, principally Singapore, as the 333,403 square kilometer area was largely jungle. British security efforts were concentrated at the jungle margins, where the Chinese guerrillas could make contact with the Chinese squatter population.

The guerrillas were exclusively Chinese, and once the squatter population was removed to and isolated in the New Villages, identifying the Chinese communists was simplified, as Malays and Chinese are distinctly different in appearance. The guerrillas were confined almost exclusively to jungle concealment, and the military was forced to pursue them in this forbidding and difficult milieu. Of all recent counterinsurgencies this environment most parallels that of the Portuguese in Guiné and northern Angola.

Indochina represented a similar concentration of people, the small rural populations of Laos (3,000,000 estimated) and Cambodia (7,000,000 estimated) were evenly scattered over 236,800 and 181,035 square kilometers, respectively. This dispersion yielded a low thirty-eight people per square kilometer for Laos and twelve for Cambodia. The bulk of Indochina's population was concentrated along the coast, with North Vietnam's 21,150,000 (1970) population in the eastern portion of its 158,750 square kilometers, and South Vietnam's 17,400,000 (1971) living in the southern delta and eastern coastal regions of its 174,289 square kilometers. In the Mekong Delta population densities ranged from 750 to 2,000 people per square kilometer. This situation was a constant problem in that with these high densities, indiscriminate use of firepower by any security force was bound to endanger the population, and consequently, the government's cause. For both France and the United States the war was concentrated along the coast of Vietnam, where the guerrillas tended to blend easily with the population and presented a difficult problem in separating the two.

Each of these counterinsurgency sites had its own characteristics, some similar to those of Portugal and others not. The difficulties that each security force faced varied considerably, but in no case did a force face an enemy scattered over three widely separated and distant fronts in such difficult terrain with a population of such varied demographics, a situation largely unique to the Portuguese conflict and one that imposed enormous demands on its defense machinery.

THE MILITARY BALANCE

On 15 March 1961 approximately 5,000 poorly armed men crossed the northern border of Angola at numerous sites along a 300-kilometer strip and proceeded to create mayhem. This number is thought to have been increased to as much as 25,000 through forced recruiting.[4] These incursions and attacks were instigated by Holden Roberto, who had founded the nationalist movement of the UPA (*União das Populações de Angola*, or Union of Angolan Peoples) in the mid-1950s based on the transborder Bakongo population and the premise that Angola should be fully independent. He had been influenced by events in the Belgian Congo, where violence against the whites had delivered independence, had held the view that a militant approach was required with the Portuguese, and had acted accordingly. The death toll in the first week was estimated at 300 whites and 6,000 blacks, and this figure is thought to have risen to about 500 whites and perhaps 20,000 blacks by the time that the force was checked by local militias of farmers and loyal blacks.[5]

Portuguese forces in Angola at the time numbered 6,500 troops, of which 1,500 were European and 5,000 locally recruited. They were spread across Angola in various training roles and unprepared to repel a full-scale invasion. Equally unprepared was the Portuguese war machine, which was unable to bring troops to the area in appreciable numbers until 1 May 1961, and it took until 13 June to reoccupy the first small administrative post of Lucunga.[6]

The Portuguese armed forces at the time numbered 79,000, of which the Army accounted for 58,000, the Navy 8,500, and the Air Force 12,500, with a defense budget of $93 million. Compared with others who had fought or were fighting counterinsurgencies, Portugal's armed force was physically small and underfunded. Britain had an armed force of 593,000 and a defense budget of $4,466 million. With conscripts France had an armed force of 1,026,000, the greater part of which was fighting in Algeria, and a defense budget of $3,311 million. The United States had an armed force of 2,489,000 and a defense budget of $41,000 million.[7] Alongside these powers Portugal had meager resources. Britain's manpower was 7.5 times that of Portugal, and its defense budget 48 times. France was about the same multiples, and the United States was 32 times in manpower and 441 times greater in funding. In summary, Portugal's armed force was dwarfed by those who had fought or were fighting counterinsurgencies.

Portugal's commitment at the time was to NATO and the majority of its forces were in Europe. By the end of 1961 it had moved 40,422 of its European troops to the three colonies, a figure that represented about half of its armed force. At the end of the conflict in 1974, Portugal had an armed force of 217,000, of which 149,000 or 69 percent were located in the three African theaters.[8] Its defense budget had grown to $523 million, almost six times the earlier figure, but it remained meager in comparison with the three other powers.

Portugal faced an intimidating array of insurgent organizations. These forces were in the beginning quite fragmented, but to the extent that they could mend their relationships with one another, they presented a solid and formidable front. In Angola at the commencement of the war the primary opposition was centered in three nationalist movements. The first was the *Frente Nacional de Libertação de Angola* (FNLA), or the National Front for the Liberation of Angola, which was frequently referred to by its old initials of UPA and had an active force of about 6,200 men based in the Belgian Congo. This number remained largely unchanged throughout the war. The second was the *Movimento Popular de Libertação de Angola* (MPLA), or the Popular Movement for the Liberation of Angola. The MPLA operated from various sites until 1963, when it settled in Congo (Brazzaville), the former Middle Congo of French Equatorial Africa. The bulk of its effective force moved to Lusaka in Zambia in 1966 to open an eastern front and is estimated to have been about 4,700 strong from that time until 1974. Finally, the UPA/FNLA breakaway movement of *União Nacional para a Independência Total de Angola* (UNITA), National Union for the Total Independence of Angola, was formed in 1966 with only about 500 fighters.[9]

In Guiné the only credible movement was the *Partido Africano da Independência da Guiné e Cabo Verde* (PAIGC), African Party for the Independence of Guiné and Cape Verde, which began to field a force in 1962 and built it to about 5,000 regular troops and 1,500 popular militia by 1973. In Mozambique the *Frente de Libertação de Moçambique* (FRELIMO), Mozambique Liberation Front, began with a disorganized force of uncertain strength and by the early 1970s had an active force of 7,200 regulars and 2,400 popular militia.[10]

The internal struggles within these movements frustrated their effectiveness throughout the campaigns in all of the theaters. Leadership in the MPLA changed hands three times in its early years and blunted its capability to wage war until 1966, when it found an opportunity to open an eastern front from the sanctuary of Zambia. Splitting the headquarters between Lusaka and Brazzaville also hampered its direction. While the UPA/FNLA continued under Holden Roberto, his "foreign minister," Jonas Savimbi, broke away to form UNITA, creating a disruptive crosscurrent in its momentum. Also Roberto married into the family of his host nation's president and became more attracted to a comfortable life in Leopoldville than the rigors of aggressively leading a nationalist movement. Eduardo Mondlane, the founder of FRELIMO, was assassinated in 1969, and PAIGC founder Amílcar Cabral was assassinated in 1972, both in part because of internal power struggles that were fostered by the activities of the Portuguese secret police. These leadership changes altered the posture of both movements. In these cases polarization against the Portuguese was the result of each successor's strategy to reduce internal party friction.

Despite these shortcomings, 27,000 insurgents spread over the three theaters was a problem for Portugal in that it was difficult to prevent their entry, and once across the border, it was difficult to locate them. Their ability to cross the long, unpatrolled borders in the remote areas of Africa and to make contact with the population represented a dangerous threat. In no other modern insurgency was there such a multiplicity of national movements across such a wide front in three theaters.

In contrast, Britain's security forces at the height of the 1948–1960 Malayan emergency numbered 300,000 police and British and locally recruited troops in 1952, and faced Chinese communist guerrillas numbering 8,000, giving a numerical superiority of 37.5 to 1. In Kenya from 1952 to 1960 British security forces numbering 56,000 faced 12,000 Mau Mau terrorists, a ratio of 4.6 to 1. In Cyprus from 1955 to 1959 British security forces of 24,911 faced 1,000 EKOA guerrillas, a ratio of 25 to 1.[11] The nearly 400,000 French troops in Algeria faced 8,000 FLN guerrillas at the close of 1956, a ratio of 50 to 1.[12] The United States in its Vietnam experience held a ratio of 4 to 1 prior to 1964,

and in 1968 it had elevated to 8.75 to 1.[13] Portuguese security forces of about
149,000 faced 27,000 guerrillas at the close of the war in 1974, giving a
nominal superiority of almost 6 to 1, although this ratio was increased somewhat
through local militias.   Nevertheless, few contemporary insurgencies went
against such odds.   That Portugal believed it could overcome the numerical
shortcoming through its own particular strategies and undertook to do so with
military success makes this counterinsurgency unique.

THE ECONOMIC EQUATION

The fact that Portugal was prepared to initiate and sustain a comparatively
large military campaign was impressive in that it appeared to have few national
resources for such an undertaking.   By European standards Portugal did not
have a powerful economic engine that could readily support a large and distant
military venture.   Compared with its Southern European peers both on the eve
of the war and a decade later, Portugal showed strong economic growth, but
nevertheless failed to displace its neighbors in its peer group rankings.   The
most helpful comparison is seen in Table 1.1, which lists the per capita gross
domestic products (GDP) of these countries and their changes over the
1960–1970 period.

Table 1.1
Per Capita GDP in U.S. Dollars

Country	1960/61	1970	Percent Change
Greece	364	1,090	199
Spain	274	1,020	272
Yugoslavia	246	650	164
Portugal	270	660	144

None of these countries was, however, undertaking a major counterinsurgency campaign.   Members of this club were Britain, France, and the
United States.   Alongside these counterinsurgency campaigners Portugal's
economy was truly anemic and raised serious doubts about its ability to mount
any such military enterprise.   Portugal's GDP on the eve of the war in 1960 was
$2.5 billion.   Britain's at $71.0 billion was twenty-eight times Portugal's.
France's at $61.0 billion was twenty-four-fold greater.   The U.S. economy at
$509.0 billion was 203 times greater than Portugal's.   When these numbers are
reduced to per capita GDP, which is an indicator of the ability of wealth to be
generated and taxed to support a war, Portugal's relative economic weakness is
so apparent as to call into question its ability to mount and wage any war.
Given the statistical shortfall in resources that Portugal faced in conducting
its counterinsurgency, it would have to adopt strategies different from those of
the Britain, France, and the United States.   It would have to address these
serious limitations by devising ways to work around them and to avoid their full

impact on its ability to wage war. There were two key elements that underpinned Portugal's effort in this sphere. The first was to spread the burden of the war as widely as possible, and the second was to keep the tempo of the conflict low enough so that the expenditure of resources would remain affordable. The counterinsurgency practices that Portugal adopted and that reflected these two national policies in conducting the campaigns can be termed the Portuguese way of war.

In the first instance the burden would be spread to the colonies. Portugal's capacity to support a distant military campaign perforce must include the large and dynamic economies of Angola and Mozambique. These additions, which are not reflected in the cited figures, are important in that they supplied a significant share of the military budget and manpower for the wars. At the beginning of the conflict in 1962, European Portugal's GDP was $2.88 billion. To this figure must be added the $803.7 million GDP of Angola, a similar $835.5 million for Mozambique, and $85.1 million for Guiné.[14] This fuller picture reveals a nation with a GDP of $4.6 billion and alters the equation of wealth significantly. It also reveals why Portugal had such a strong commitment to its colonies.

Also during the 1961-1974 period the economies of Angola and Mozambique were growing rapidly at 11 percent and 9 percent, respectively. Table 1.2, compiled from various official sources, traces the overall expansion.

Table 1.2
National and Per Capita GDPs, 1962–1970

Colony	GDP (millions of U.S. dollars)			Per Capita GDP (U.S. dollars)		
	1962	1965	1970	1962	1965	1970
Angola	803.7	1,099.0	1,888.5	161	210	333
Mozambique	835.5	1,213.4	1,872.0	121	165	228
Guiné	85.1	97.6	125.8	166	194	258

With the exception of Rhodesia and the Republic of South Africa, per capita GDP in Portuguese Africa during the wars exceeded that of all other countries in sub-Saharan Africa.

In 1965, some four years into the war, the defense budget amounted to 48 percent of European Portugal's national budget. Comparatively this allocation was greater than that of any other European nation, Canada, or the United States. The next highest was the United States at 42 percent, followed by the United Kingdom at 34 percent. However, observers tended to overlook the contribution that the colonies made to their own defense. The addition of colonial resources enabled Portugal not only to reach an apparently high level of expenditure but also to sustain it over thirteen years. The three colonies contributed approximately 16 percent of the defense budget over the term of the conflict.[15] This contribution, along with the inclusion of the colonial economies in the broader consideration, meant that Portugal was spending only about 28 percent on the average, of its national budget on defense and reached a peak of 34 percent in 1968.[16] These percentages reflect a more readily sustainable expenditure and place it proportionately equal to similar national defense budgets. It should also be noted that a great portion of the defense budget was allocated to social programs that benefited the population in the areas of health, education, and agriculture, and contributed directly to the planned economic expansion in Portuguese Africa. Thus while the fiscal resources were seemingly modest from a traditional perspective, in fact they were adequate for the low-technology campaign Portugal envisioned.

If the colonies were thought to contribute relatively modestly to the defense budget, they conversely shouldered an increasingly important manpower burden that gradually replaced metropolitan Portugal's soldiers with African ones. The population of continental Portugal in 1960 was 8,889,392, and that of the three African colonies was aggregately 11,959,373. The potential of the African population to supply troops was thus about a third greater than that of European Portugal.

Local recruitment began at modest levels in 1961, when it represented 14.9 percent of the forces in Angola, 26.8 percent in Mozambique, and 21.1 percent in Guiné. By the end of the wars in 1974, and with the expansion of the security forces into militia and other paramilitary organizations, Africans represented fully 50 percent of the force in Angola, 50 percent in Guiné, and 54 percent in Mozambique.[17] This shift accelerated following 1968, for after seven years Portugal had exhausted its European manpower pool and increasingly sought recruits from the larger colonial pool. While there were problems inherent in this shift, such as the low educational level of the recruits, these shortcomings were addressed with enough success to mold an effective fighting force. Officially the troop level exceeded 149,000 men in the three theaters of operations; however, with the consideration of paramilitary forces, the level approached twice that number. Official records of these forces were difficult to maintain at the time, and following the conflict were largely lost or destroyed.[18] Thus, only approximations can be made. Nevertheless, the impact of using this broader manpower pool for recruiting enabled the Portuguese armed forces to maintain adequate force levels almost indefinitely. This unique capability was critical in extending the conflict for thirteen years, and is developed in Chapter 5.

THE PORTUGUESE WAY OF WAR

The Portuguese had had the benefit of earlier British, French, and U.S. experiences in the twentieth century prior to 1961 and proceeded to develop their military policies accordingly. Their early adoption of the counterinsurgency principles was relatively straightforward, and this point will be developed fully in Chapter 3. Portuguese uniqueness came in their understanding of the struggle and adaptation to it at the theater level and in successfully converting national strategy to battlefield tactics. With comparatively few resources and no army trained in this type of fighting initially, Portugal had to improvise. While it anticipated employing the standard types of counterinsurgency operational practices, it also sought innovations that were able to utilize the unique terrain and demographic characteristics in each of its three theaters. The concept might be borrowed from others and modified so extensively as to be nearly unique, or it might be purely Lusitanian. Some of the broader challenges and solutions characterizing the Portuguese way of counterinsurgency warfare are listed below.

- The complete reorientation of the entire Portuguese armed forces from a conventional force to one for counterinsurgency, thus focusing this resource on a single campaign
- The realignment in recruiting for this force to the indigenous colonial manpower pool to a degree not seen in modern times, thus allowing the colonies to shoulder a substantial portion of this burden
- The shift to small-unit tactics and associated training based on experience in the wars, thus matching Portugal's force with that of the insurgents and keeping the tempo of fighting low and cost-effective
- The implementation of an economic and social development program that raised the standard of living of Portuguese Africans, and in doing so, largely preempted insurgent arguments and raised the ability of the colonies to shoulder part of the war burden
- The extensive psychological operations that rationalized the Portuguese presence in Africa to the population.

Despite the retarded state of Portugal's economy, the enormous geographical challenges, and an unprepared armed force, Portugal felt confident that it understood the job at hand and could overcome these difficulties. Out of this national self-confidence Portugal developed its own style of counterinsurgency warfare through a synthesis of the experience of similar conflicts and of its own experience in Africa since the fifteenth century. The application of this systematic thinking to the threat posed by the nationalist movements was made with both a view to the national strategy of containing the cost and spreading the burden, and addressing the battlefield situation. Forthcoming chapters will topically examine the Portuguese military's understanding of these problems and its search for solutions to them. It will be argued that the Portuguese developed their own unique way of fighting in executing their national strategy and the practices that followed from it—the Portuguese way of war. In order to highlight this Portuguese way, it will be compared thematically with other contemporary counterinsurgencies, and this categorical silhouetting will emphasize the uniqueness. The fact that Portugal lost the war because it failed to find a political solution to the conflict does not negate its military achievements and the fact that they may still hold lessons for others in future conflicts.

NOTES

1. Bruce Hoffman and Jennifer M. Taw, *Defense Policy and Low-Intensity Conflict: The Development of Britain's "Small Wars" Doctrine During the 1950s* (Santa Monica: Rand Corporation, 1991), 6–7, 38.

2. Alf Andrew Heggoy, *Insurgency and Counterinsurgency in Algeria* (Bloomington: Indiana University Press, 1972), 158. Even with the single front of Algeria, France was forced to rely on conscription.

3. Robert Aron, François Lavagne, Janine Feller, and Yevette Garnier-Rizet, *Les Origines de la Guerre d'Algérie* (Paris: Librairie Arthème Fayard, 1962), 176.

4. Willem S. van der Waals, *Portugal's War in Angola 1961–1974* (Rivonia: Ashanti Publishing, 1993), 64.

5. René Pélissier, *La Colonie du Minotaure, Nationalismes et Révoltes en Angola (1926–1961)* (Orgeval: Editions Pélissier, 1978), 657–660; van der Waals, 58–61.

6. Estado-Maior do Exército (EME), *Resenha Histórico-Militar das Campanhas de África (1961–1974)* [Historical-Military Report of the African Campaigns (1961–1974)] (Lisbon: Estado-Maior do Exército, 1988), Vol. II, 27.

7. Institute for Strategic Studies, *The Military Balance* (London: Institute for Strategic Studies, 1960), 11–13.

8. Institute for Strategic Studies, *The Military Balance* (London: Institute for Strategic Studies, 1974), 25; *Resenha Histórico-Militar das Campanhas de África (1961–1974)*, Vol. I, 261.

9. Neil Bruce, "Portugal's African Wars," *Conflict Studies*, no. 34 (March 1973): 19.

10. Ibid., 22.

11. Hoffman and Taw, 38.

12. Alistair Horne, *A Savage War of Peace: Algeria 1954–1962* (Harmondsworth: Penguin Books, 1987), 113, 382; Heggoy, 157.

13. Frank N. Trager, "Military Requirements for a U.S. Victory in Vietnam," in *Viet-Nam: History, Documents, and Opinions on a Major World Crisis*, ed. Marvin E. Gettleman (Greenwich: Fawcett Publications, 1965), 347.

14. Ministry of Foreign Affairs, *Portuguese Africa: An Introduction* (Lisbon: Ministry of Foreign Affairs, 1973), 76.

15. Joaquim da Luz Cunha, et al, *África: A Vitória Traída* [Africa: Betrayed Victory] (Lisbon: Editorial Intervenção, 1977), 58.

16. Ibid., 61.

17. Ibid., 130, 159; *Resenha Histórico-Militar das Campanhas de África (1961–1974)*, Vol. I, 259–260.

18. General José Manuel de Bethencourt Rodrigues, interview by the author, 9 November 1994, Lisbon.

2

COMMITMENT TO THE *ULTRAMAR*

Portugal's commitment to the defense of its colonies, or the *ultramar*, had its origins in their economic promise and in Dr. António Salazar's inflexible African policy in the face of domestic and international opposition to Portugal's African empire. Portugal had been in Africa since 1497, which on the eve of the wars amounted to over four and a half centuries, longer by far than any other colonial power. With the progressive decline of its trading position in the Indian Ocean beginning in 1578, the loss of its colony of Brazil in 1822, and the missed opportunity of a coast-to-coast possession in austral Africa in 1890, Portugal's colonial empire was left with only the potential of the large but incompletely developed colonies of Angola and Mozambique. These colonies in Portuguese minds held the promise of a renewed prosperity and greatness. Further, with the heritage of having been Portuguese for so long, their ownership was to be defended at all costs. For this small European nation, the importance of the colonies was captured in an editorial by Dr. Marcello Caetano in *O Mundo Português* (Portuguese World) that appeared in 1935: "Africa is for us a moral justification and a *raison d'être* as a power. Without it we would be a small nation; with it, we are a great country."[1] In this concept of empire Dr. Salazar sought to dispel the world image of Portugal as a small country. The growth of revolutionary climate in the *ultramar* during the 1950s clashed with this philosophy and the country's refusal to break the colonial bond and to decolonize. By the end of the 1950s local grievances in the colonies had reached dangerous levels. The creole elite were humiliated and the subject of discrimination. The peasants suffered from forced labor and crop cultivation. The "winds of change" were blowing through Africa, but the Salazar regime refused to consider holding democratic elections or decolonizing. Dr. Salazar and Portugal's intransigence in these matters were reinforced by additional circumstances that unfolded during 1961 to solidify the Portuguese position and underpin its war effort. This chapter explains the deep commitment of Portugal to its colonies, the local reaction to dissatisfaction with the status quo there, and the effect of the immediate 1961 chronology in hardening Portugal's colonial stance such that it was to choose protracted armed conflict over other alternatives and maintain that position for years to come.

THE PROMISE OF OVERSEAS WEALTH

Portugal had always looked overseas for its prosperity, having initially found it in the Indian Ocean and later in Brazil, and on the eve of the wars in 1961 potentially in the African colonies, although the latter remained largely unfulfilled. Nevertheless, these African possessions were viewed as a vehicle for the renewed greatness of a former era, and as such, attracted a commitment beyond any previously demonstrated economic value. This earlier era had begun in 1497, when Vasco da Gama rounded the Cape of Good Hope, discovered Mozambique, and established trading contacts in India. Portugal proceeded to develop this new route unchallenged in the short term. Great wealth had awaited the European nation that could directly tap the source of Eastern goods, and Portugal succeeded in this challenge. The trade was immensely profitable, and wealth poured into Portugal on an unprecedented scale. The Portuguese defeated both the European and Muslim challenges to their new monopoly and proceeded to establish a systematic arc of enclaves strategically ringing the Indian Ocean. These bases commanded both the sources of trade as well as the sea routes themselves. As the Portuguese secured their dominance in this area, so profits from their localized trade as well as the Cape route increased accordingly. Portugal reached its height of power and influence during the first half of the sixteenth century. Its decline can be marked from June 1578 and its disastrous North African campaign in which King Sebastião and his army were destroyed in four hours by Moroccan forces at Al-Ksar al-Kebir.[2] The might of Portugal was wasted with this disaster, and the next year Portugal's great epic poet and inspirer of nationalistic sentiment, Luís Vaz de Camões, wrote to a friend from his deathbed in Lisbon, "All will see that so dear to me was my country that I was content to die not only in but with it."[3]

While leaving an indelible imprint on the European perspective of the world, the Portuguese had exhausted themselves in the process. They were never able to regain their sixteenth-century stature, and from that period until 1961 Portugal experienced an irregular path of decline with episodes of partial recovery. As a nation, the Portuguese have historically looked back on this time, which they call *O Século Maravilhoso* (The Marvelous Century), and longed to regain the former height of glory and greatness. Although this first empire was short-lived, it created a permanent nostalgia that gave Dr. Salazar a "vibrant chord of imperial grandeur" around which to rally colonial support.[4] In the period between 1497 and 1578 the Portuguese had established a new concept of empire based on a mastery of the ocean routes. Trade, not territory, was the prime objective. Portugal was unable to sustain such a grand enterprise with its very limited resources, particularly in manpower, and when Spain annexed it in its depleted state between 1580 and 1640, this trade dominance was effectively lost. When Portugal recovered its independence in 1640, it was a wonder that it retrieved so much of its overseas holdings as well, particularly Brazil. As spices were the single most lucrative commodity of the sixteenth century, so Brazilian sugar replaced them in the seventeenth century. When West Indian sugar production threatened to supplant that of Brazil, gold was discovered there in 1694. In 1728 diamonds were discovered. The revenue from this colonial wealth maintained the continuity of Portuguese prosperity until Brazil declared its independence in 1822. It was the memory of Brazil and the wealth that it had provided that generated a twentieth-century hope for a similar prosperity from the African colonies. This Brazilian model, where "Portuguese language and culture were firmly entrenched," became a far more influential guide for the development of Angola and Mozambique than *O Século Maravilhoso*.[5] These two colonies were seen on the eve of the wars potentially as modern-day Brazils and the prized keys to renewed prosperity and greatness. This view was both part of a strong nationalism that had cemented a peculiar alliance of class and political forces loyal to Dr. Salazar and an increasing component of Portugal's expanding post-World War II economy. In the 1950s the colonial economies exhibited steady growth and were no longer a financial burden on the *metrópole*. This colonial expansion and economic momentum, as viewed in 1961, supported the case for their retention.

Elusive domestic prosperity also reinforced the commitment to the African colonies and their economic promise. Metropolitan Portugal from the earliest times remained economically underdeveloped and was dependent on overseas commerce and colonial wealth to maintain more than a subsistence standard of living. Lisbon in the first half of the sixteenth century was a spectacularly opulent city, yet Portugal as a whole did not produce enough goods to feed and clothe its population at the time, and staples had to be purchased abroad. Slaves were imported from the Guinean Coast to supply labor while rural Portuguese emigrated to western Spain in search of employment. The wealth of Lisbon seemed useless to the population at large. As Portugal had never developed a domestic economy of any consequence during the years of plenty, there was no alternative to the stagnation at home when the wealth from abroad evaporated. Portugal's economy persisted at subsistence levels, and because it was so weak, it failed to participate significantly in the industrial revolution of the nineteenth century. This signal failure made the promise of Africa increasingly important.

Portugal began the nineteenth century with such an anemic domestic economy that it could not convert the raw materials of its colonies into manufactured goods to the same degree that its European trading partners could. With the loss of Brazil and access to its readily salable commodities, Portugal was left to survive on its weak economic capability. Its trade patterns during this period give insight on its problem. Portugal's share of trade with its main European partners was a mere 1.20 percent in 1820 and experienced a steady erosion through the century to 0.78 percent in 1899. Its relatively small share of world trade declined from 0.88 percent in 1820 to 0.53 percent in 1899. While world trade was expanding tenfold during this span, that of Portugal only expanded sixfold from a very small base. It is instructive to note that the greatest relative increase in worldwide trade during the nineteenth century occurred with the 80 percent expansion in the 1850–1860 decade. Portugal lagged the averages with a 60 percent performance, while its European trading partners were beating the average with a 100 percent increase during the period.[6] Because Portugal was not developing its economic engine, it was unable to employ the resources of its colonies on any appreciable scale and to exploit any relative trading advantage in international commerce.

The colonies may have had potential, but Portugal was unable to capitalize significantly on their promise in the traditional mercantilist sense to the betterment of its overall economy. Clarence-Smith explains that through poor colonial policies "the colonies became less important to the metropolis in economic terms [between 1910 and 1926], and colonial decline contributed to the downfall of the [republican] regime" in 1926 and the subsequent emergence of Dr. Salazar.[7] In Portuguese eyes they nevertheless continued to hold the ultimate potential for prosperity in their underdeveloped state. While the long-held hope of regeneration had never materialized, Dr. Salazar sought it in his colonial policy. He moved decisively to reinforce economic links between the *ultramar* and the *metrópole*, and on the eve of the wars the African colonies appeared finally to be realizing their true promise. It was at this point that Portugal deeply believed in its African colonial potential.

DR. SALAZAR AND THE COLONIES

Dr. Salazar saw the colonies as an important part of Portugal's ability to emerge from the fiscal chaos of the previous republican government. If Portugal was to rediscover itself, then it would have to reestablish its identity. Dr. Salazar thus sought to promote a new imperial consciousness. It could not be born in an atmosphere of ignorance and disinterest. Consequently, it was based on the Portuguese ideology of imperial greatness with which everyone was familiar. This mentality was defined in terms of three elements: geography, heroism, and trade. The first element was supported by the notion that the Portuguese flag flew over vast territories spreading over three continents and making a small European state the third largest colonial power after Britain and France. The second lay in the discoveries by Portugal's epic sailors and warriors during *O Século Maravilhoso*, and the third focused on the hardships that the Portuguese people had endured in carving the hidden riches from remote lands and establishing centers of production and profit there. Dr. Salazar viewed the colonies as a vehicle to give Portugal stature in a world where the preceding republican government had removed all such standing with the number and volatility of its administrations. He attempted to create a colonial mentality within the Portuguese people by drawing on the sense of achievement in *O Século Maravilhoso* and relating it to the present colonial ownership. Dr. Salazar's vision embodied a sense of unity between the *ultramar* and the *metrópole* that had genuine foundations in national heritage and psychology and past colonial policy.

The modern-day origin of this psychology can be traced to the British ultimatum of 1890. In the last two decades of the nineteenth century, with the industrial machinery of the European economic powerhouses running competitively at full throttle, there occurred a spontaneous "scramble for Africa," a frantic rush to establish colonial claims. This "scramble" was prompted by an increasing awareness in Europe about Africa coupled with a speculative search for new opportunities by Europe's more prosperous powers. Approximately 80 percent of the territorial acquisitions in Africa during this time were made by the three most industrialized nations of Europe: Britain, France, and Germany. Despite Portugal's long-standing presence there, it was squeezed in the competitive race and in its search for a solution to its economic development crisis. Its confrontation with Britain over its coast-to-coast colonial ambitions in joining Angola and Mozambique through austral Africa potentially to form a second Brazil became a face-off that was to seal Portuguese national will and serve as a significant basis for the Salazar appeal to defend and retain the colonies in 1961.[8]

On assuming power in 1933, Dr. Salazar had initially put the colonies on hold until he could get control of the national budget and navigate the country through the depression. By 1937 he had established the colonial development fund, which would be financed primarily through colonial budget surpluses and other colonial monopoly profits. This measure enabled Portugal and its colonies to participate in the economic emergence from the depression of the 1930s and in expansion associated with World War II. These programs were designed largely to improve colonial infrastructure and were in step with Dr. Salazar's neo-mercantilistic view of the empire. His theoretical aim was to construct a form of autarky that allowed Portugal to develop its economy without the use of foreign investment, thus reducing the potential for any foreign obligation or intrusion. Dr. Salazar was provincial in character and temperament despite his sophisticated education. In fact, he was so suspicious of foreigners and resistant to change that he refused U.S. aid under the Marshall Plan following World War II. The error in judgment was so apparent that he reversed himself. He held the view that foreign sources of funding could dwarf Portugal's investment at home and in its colonies, and that any such change, even for the sake of progress, would threaten both the economic and political status quo. This isolationist doctrine of self-reliance was unrealistic in a postwar system of increasing interdependence between states; however, Dr. Salazar saw any change as a potential threat to the forces that kept him in power. With economic freedom would come the desire for political freedom.

The initial rigidity of Dr. Salazar's position softened as he gained an understanding of the impact that foreign capital could make on Portugal's domestic and overseas economies. This softening allowed a significant but belated development of colonial industries. Expertise and supporting funds came from established firms for any significant or complicated undertaking, particularly mining. Belgian (diamond mining), British (railroads), and U.S. (oil exploration) investments dominated and were largely exempt from exchange controls. They strengthened and stabilized the colonial economies in the years between 1945 and 1961, deepening Portugal's economic reliance on the colonies and its commitment to defend them. In 1961 private foreign investment accounted for about 15 percent of gross fixed capital formation in the *ultramar* and had grown to almost 25 percent in 1966.[9] By 1961 the colonies had finally become an economically worthy possession. Basil Davidson described the importance of this colonial goal: "Now it was that the colony [of Angola] began to deliver for the first time on any scale...its exports began to play a critical part in saving from deficit the general Portuguese balance of payments with the rest of the world; as with Mozambique, this became Angola's principal 'national role.' "[10]

By 1961 Portugal's economy had shifted from a partial autarky under orthodox economic practices to a fledgling but rapidly growing industrialized one. The shift away from an agriculturally based economy in the *metrópole* and the *ultramar* meant that there was a decreasing dependence on peasant labor and its attendant policies. As the *metrópole* developed in this direction, so the first moves were made to foster complementary development in the colonies. Mining, oil exploration and refining, textiles, and cashew processing were in place by 1961, and other basic industries were in the planning stages. These activities reflected a break with the past and a new Salazar policy fueled by colonial promise. Education received renewed and expanded attention, as literate workers with skills were in increasing demand. The paranoia regarding foreign investment had evaporated, and French, German, U.S., and South African participation in the economy was welcomed. The gathering momentum of the colonial economies continued to accelerate well past 1961 and became a welcome support for the political element in the counterinsurgency campaigns. The colonies were thus developing into substantial economic engines in their own right, and not only were their citizens beginning to benefit individually but Portugal itself was also reaping substantial rewards from this growing prosperity. Their historic potential was being realized, a fact that reinforced their long-time importance to Portugal and Dr. Salazar's commitment of the nation to their defense.

COLONIAL RESISTANCE TO DR. SALAZAR'S VISION

At the time when Portugal's colonial commitment was being strengthened, local resistance within its African population was increasing. During this period the democratized European powers in Africa were freeing their colonial possessions in step with the post-World War II trend. This development put increasing pressure on Dr. Salazar to move in line with the Western European forms of government and to allow the Portuguese colonies to do so as well. Revolts and the war enabled Dr. Salazar to exploit a tide of Portuguese nationalist fervor in preserving the status quo and his personal regime. Consequently, the nationalist resistance and its challenge to his colonial vision had the effect of reinforcing Portugal's commitment rather than the opposite. While the economy was deemed important, Dr. Salazar's personal position of authority was overriding.[11] Further, his hatred and mistrust of communism played an important role. He was mindful of the Western powers' impotence to contain the economically bankrupt but politically ascendant communism.[12] In a speech to army and naval officers on 6 July 1936, Dr. Salazar described communism as "systems of ideals which are literally systems of crime" and was so convinced of the threat of this ideology that he believed "Western civilization is at stake."[13] His worst fears were realized when Daniel Semenovich Solod, the "brilliant organizer and expert in the tactics of infiltration and subversion," was assigned to Guinea in 1960.[14] Ambassador Solod had established an impressive reputation for increasing Soviet influence in the Middle East and North Africa, and now began to work on the Portuguese colonies and to nurture their long-standing dissident undercurrent of nationalism.

The nationalist movements and their military wings of guerrillas that challenged Portugal's ownership of its colonies had their origins in the 1930s. The emergence of modern-day black opposition to Portuguese rule began with the repressive practices of the *Estado Novo* toward any form of dissent, particularly political. This attitude extended from the *metrópole* to the colonies. Resistance began slowly, as there was a practical barrier to any such opposition in the ethnic and social fragmentation of the overseas nonwhite community. Without strong leadership there would be no nationalist movement able to gain the necessary momentum in reconciling these divergent viewpoints and crystallizing resistance to the Salazar regime. Local African grievances were long-standing and had come to the fore during the early twentieth century with the influx of white settlers and abusive labor practices. This indigenous resentment was publicly evident in 1932 when an independent Mozambican newspaper, *O Brado Africano* (The African Cry) slipped through Salazar's censorship and published a scathing editorial titled "Enough." Thereafter this feeling was never far below the surface, and the apparent calm was illusory.

Following World War II, nationalist sentiments grew among the *mestiços* (mixed-race peoples) and *assimilados* (mostly *mestiços* who were legally assimilated to Portuguese culture). However, these groups were largely urban and thus did not represent the greater population. As they were located in cities, they were in a hostile environment for two reasons: the majority of their opponents, the white population, lived in cities, and the PIDE (*Polícia Internacional de Defesa do Estado*, or International Police for Defense of the

State) operated most effectively there. Consequently, they were either short-lived or dormant.[15] By 1956 the young Marxists of the Angolan Communist Party contributed to the formation of the MPLA. The MPLA developed roots among Luanda's urban and largely radical intellectuals, among its slum dwellers, and to a lesser extent, eastward from the capital among the Mbundu, Angola's second largest ethnolinguistic group, and the Chokwe people. These urban roots were composed largely of *mestiços*, who controlled the party. The movement had little in common with the rural peasants of the east and south of Angola and made little effort to gain their true devotion. In December 1956 the initial MPLA manifesto was openly published in a direct frontal assault on the government. Predictably the PIDE reacted adversely, and a number of the MPLA leaders were forced to flee into exile. From 1957 onward PIDE action was so successful "that the nationalists were not able to maintain more than the most rudimentary organization inside the colonies and could not communicate with those cells that did exist."[16] The parties were forced to conduct their affairs from neighboring states and were deeply influenced by their foreign connections.

The presidential election in May 1958 gave all of Portugal some opportunity to express its dissatisfaction with the status quo. Elections under the Salazar regime as a rule were perfunctory, colorless, cosmetic affairs with foreseeable results. In 1958, however, Humberto Delgado's high-profile and emotionally charged challenge to Salazar's candidate, Admiral Américo Tomás, excited all of Portugal. This taste of partial suffrage awakened dissatisfaction within the *mestiços* and *assimilados*, and a number of small parties were formed in Angola, only to be shattered through arrests in March, May, and July of 1959. As the PIDE systematically wrecked the MPLA organization, it became progressively weaker and isolated from its leadership that was now abroad. In this deteriorating position it supported an uprising in February 1961 that stood no chance of a lasting success. It was doomed to be transient, for it occurred in Luanda, center of Portuguese police and military strength, and the MPLA had no constituency or bases elsewhere among the rural population.

The MPLA in exile established itself initially in Leopoldville and aligned itself not only with other independent African nations and their socialist philosophy but also with the communist bloc, including the Italian and French communist parties. The leadership was consequently familiar with the communist theory in wars of national liberation and organized itself accordingly. The MPLA found that it was in competition with the other prominent Angolan nationalist group at the time, the UPA, for acceptance as the leading representative of the Angolan people. In 1962 the MPLA formed its military wing, EPLA (*Exército Popular de Libertação de Angola*, or Popular Army for the Liberation of Angola), to project its influence into Angola. This nascent force numbered between 250 and 300 young men who had undergone military training in Ghana and Morocco. The EPLA sought to expand the conflict with this force across Angola's northern border and penetrate the entire country, publicizing the MPLA manifesto. Recruiting proved to be difficult because of ethnic rivalries, and military action was thwarted by the competing UPA. The UPA through its influence with the Congo leadership forced the MPLA to leave Leopoldville in 1963 and reestablish itself in Brazzaville, from which it was difficult to conduct a campaign in Angola. As a result northern Angola proved to be barren, and it was not until 1966, with the opening of the second front from Zambia, that some success would come to the MPLA. The most consequential development from the Portuguese perspective was the capture in July 1963 of various 35mm films which described the MPLA's military doctrine of revolutionary warfare. It paralleled the Maoist creed by reiterating that the movement was a people's war and that the struggle would be protracted.[17] The first priority would be indoctrination and organization of the masses, and next the establishment of rural bases and resistance areas.[18] This doctrine would serve the MPLA until 1974, and as we shall see in future chapters, the Portuguese correctly anticipated this guerrilla approach.

The UPA was formed in the mid-1950s from a number of small groups with conflicting goals by Barros Nekaka, who in 1958 passed leadership to his nephew Holden Roberto. UPA strength rested in the rural populations of the Bakongo ethnolinguistic region of Angola. These people straddled the border between the Belgian Congo and Angola and extended into Cabinda and the French Congo, the boundaries of the ancient Kongo kingdom. Roberto unequivocally held the view that not just the Bakongo kingdom or some other entity but all of Angola must be freed. An ardent anticolonialist, Roberto had been born in Angola but had lived his adult life in the Belgian Congo. He had been educated in the Baptist Church missionaries and employed in the Belgian colonial economy as an accountant between 1941 and 1949. Northern Angola was an area that had become more politically aware in the 1950s through white settlement, Baptist missionary influence, and an easy access to the developing political activities of the Belgian Congo. Roberto thus felt a close kinship with the peoples immediately across the border. The UPA was able to develop a following there because of the relatively open frontier, and this loyal cadre became the basis for the uprising in March 1961. Portuguese presence in this area took the form of *chefes do posto* (heads of posts) and administrators, as opposed to PIDE, and these officials were so sparse that it was physically impossible for them to maintain anything but the most casual control over their districts.[19]

While Roberto was relatively well educated, he was a member of the Bakongo ethnolinguistic group, was not a *mestiço*, and consequently did not share their more European cultural perspective. He was also tribally oriented in contrast to the nontribal declarations of the MPLA. Consequently, the personality and leadership philosophy of the UPA contrasted clearly with the MPLA and its sophisticated *mestiço* leadership, which was left-wing, intellectual, and acculturalatively Portuguese. Funding and support also glaringly contrasted, the MPLA actually being linked with the Eastern bloc.

The UPA received financial support from the American Committee on Africa and from various African governments, preponderantly that of Leopoldville.[20] Accordingly they were never able to resolve their differences and join forces effectively.

When the Belgian Congo became independent on 30 June 1960, its government began to give Roberto practical assistance, including permission to establish a radio station and a training camp within its borders. This sanctuary was an important facet of UPA operations in its early years. Roberto had witnessed the long series of Congolese crises that had begun with the violent political rioting on 4 January 1959 and had led to the accelerated Belgian push toward Congo self-government and independence in eighteen months. By December 1960 he believed that just as the Belgians had quickly grown weary of armed conflict, so would the Portuguese when it was initiated. He consequently used his Congo sanctuary and the porous common border to set the stage for an end to relative colonial tranquillity for Portugal.

The UPA formed its military wing, the ELNA (*Exército de Libertação Nacional de Angola*, or Army of National Liberation of Angola), in June 1961 after the March attacks did not achieve a Portuguese withdrawal. Roberto was its commander-in-chief and its other two leaders were Portuguese Army deserters, Marcos Xavier Kassanga, its chief of staff in Leopoldville, and João Batista, its operational commander in Angola with headquarters near Bembe. This leadership was ineffective. Roberto was so autocratic that he would accept little more than arms and money. Without training, the ELNA "set a demoralizing example of politico-military incompetence and indiscipline."[21] The South African Defense Force vice-consul in Luanda noted that the ELNA "involved itself in military activities in the narrowest sense...but avoided contact with the Portuguese security forces as far as possible."[22] The training was so poor that despite the expansion of the ELNA to about 6,200 troops, their deportment at such camps as Kinkuzu in the Congo was cause for alarm.[23] Andreas Shipango, South-West Africa Peoples Organisation representative in Leopoldville, made an appraisal during a 1963 visit: "With representatives from a number of other liberation movements, I visited Holden Roberto's training camps near the Angolan border with a view to sending our young men there. But the atmosphere in Roberto's training camps was very bad, and I could not recommend such a course."[24]

This lack of direction caused great rifts in the UPA leadership. Despite the UPA reorganization in March 1962 to include additional groups, to rename itself FNLA, and to establish a government in exile named GRAE (*Governo da República de Angola no Exílio*, or Government of the Republic of Angola in Exile), little of substance was accomplished. A frustrated Jonas Savimbi, Roberto's "foreign minister," formally broke with the UPA/FNLA in July 1964 and eventually formed the third nationalist movement in Angola, UNITA. The next year Alexandre Taty, "minister of armaments," after challenging Roberto in an unsuccessful coup, defected to the Portuguese in Cabinda with a substantial number of his followers. John Marcum described the situation as it existed in 1963: "Whether by the inaction or heavy hand of shortsighted leadership, one opportunity after another was lost, one potential source of support after another was alienated."[25] The political crosscurrents within the UPA/FNLA, the lack of training for ELNA cadres, and major competition from MPLA and UNITA activities reduced the UPA/FNLA to a spent force within two years of initiating the conflict.

Roberto followed no sophisticated guerrilla creed other than the initiation of violence in the hope that the Portuguese would become weary with it and capitulate. There was only a weak military program unsupported by political indoctrination. There was no talk of winning the population to the UPA/FNLA point of view, which was simply that Angola should be an independent country with Roberto as head of state. The approach was amateurish and ineffective alongside that of PAIGC and the work of its founder, Amílcar Cabral.

Aside from Angola, there were nationalist movements associated with Guiné and Mozambique that prior to the events of 1961 were hoping to negotiate concessions with the Portuguese on self-determination. In Guiné efforts by local nationalists to organize began in the early 1950s. The PAIGC was founded in September 1956 by local *assimilados* and educated Cape Verdeans. Its initial political organization prompted an aggrieved dockworkers' strike on 3 August 1959, which ended in a violent disaster when it was broken with excessive military force. Fifty workers were killed, and the incident became known as the "Pidjiguiti dock massacre." PAIGC leadership quickly realized that peaceful protest would not achieve its objective of self-rule and independence. Accordingly, it shifted its strategy to one of clandestinely organizing the rural population for an insurgency.[26] PAIGC had learned hard lessons in 1959 well ahead of the MPLA and UPA/FNLA experiences of 1961, and had shifted its approach accordingly. It was not prepared to begin guerrilla war in Guiné until January 1963, when all of the elements for success were in place, including firm sanctuaries in adjacent countries.

The driving force behind the PAIGC was Amílcar Cabral, who was born in Guiné of Cape Verdean parents. Cabral was an agronomist by profession, having been educated in Lisbon, served the Portuguese administration in Guiné (1952–1955), and worked for various agricultural institutions in the *metrópole* (1955–1959) with research trips to Angola. His political awareness came at an early age and matured during his academic time in Lisbon. While influenced by Marxist-Leninist ideas of the time, Cabral was primarily a nationalist and developed his own variant of both the PAIGC political message and its associated military dimension. In his own words: "It is good [for all nationalist movements] to remember…that regardless of how similar are their struggles and their enemies to one another, national liberation and social revolution cannot be exported. They are…the products of local and national forces. While somewhat influenced by external factors, they are largely determined and tempered by the particular culture of a country's people and its unique local characteristics."[27]

It was in this context that Cabral began to prepare the political landscape for guerrilla warfare.

Following his experience in the Pidjiguiti dock demonstration, Cabral realized that the Portuguese would not negotiate and that an armed struggle was the only way to achieve PAIGC ends. Cabral had received no known military training and had little interest in such affairs prior to 1959. It is possible that he had some such exposure during his visit to China in 1960, and certainly Chinese influence was seen in the training of his guerrilla army. It was known that elements of PAIGC also underwent courses in guerrilla warfare and subversion in Algeria, Russia, and Czechoslovakia.[28] Notwithstanding this lack of military experience, the mantle of undisputed commander and tactician fitted him well, and his imagination and flexibility were evident in the conduct of his campaign.

Cabral became quite attuned to the requirement for population indoctrination and keenly aware of the need to bridge the gap between the urban intellectual and the traditional Guinean. His two-year preparation of the political battlefield was classic in its effort to draw the population together in a common ideology that would transcend tribal and ethnic divisions. His investigation into local grievances was the most thorough of any of the nationalist movements. Cabral faced a difficult task in convincing the population that they were being oppressed. The land, for instance, already belonged to the peasants and was generally village property. Guiné had no concentration of foreign settlers who were seemingly exploiting the population. In Cabral's own words: "We were not able to mobilize the people by telling them: 'The land to him that works it.' Because here land is not lacking.... We were never able to mobilize the people on a basis of the struggle against colonialism. This yielded nothing. To speak of the struggle against imperialism yielded nothing between us.... This proved the necessity of having each peasant find his own formula to mobilize for the fight."[29] He thus sought to couch his revolutionary message in terms that would address the daily concerns of the rural population: "Remember always that the people do not fight for ideas, for things that only exist in the heads of individuals. The people fight and they accept the necessary sacrifices. But they do it in order to gain material advantages, to live in peace and to improve their lives, to experience progress, and to be able to guarantee a future to their children."[30] This approach was far more fruitful than comparable activities in Angola.

Cabral met and worked closely with MPLA leaders and established his exile headquarters in Conakry, the capital of the ex-French Republic of Guinea. From here he conducted his campaign against the Portuguese. The other prominent nationalist movement in Guiné was FLING (*Frente de Luta pela Independência da Guiné*, or Front for the Struggle for the Independence of Guiné). Led by Benjamin Bull, J. Fernandes, and H. Labery, it was an amalgamation of a number of smaller movements and was given sanctuary in Senegal on Guiné's northern border. Again as in Angola, the philosophies of the leaders of these two movements were so disparate that there was little common ground for agreement and cooperation, although Cabral worked hard to compromise.

Following the unsuccessful employment of autonomous guerrilla groups in the first year of the conflict, Cabral held the Cassacá Congress in February 1964 to reorganize the war effort and establish a national army in the FARP (*Forças Armadas Revolucionárias de Povo*, or Revolutionary Armed Forces of the People). His organization was so effective that, as we shall see in future chapters, the Portuguese copied it in 1968. Because the Portuguese had shown that they were not going to negotiate, Cabral's only option was to win in the field. He thoughtfully assembled and implemented the proper elements of guerrilla warfare, particularly that of political indoctrination, to achieve PAIGC ends.

In Mozambique there were a number of exile, very small, nationalist organizations prior to 1961. The Portuguese government made every effort to dampen the spirit of nationalism in its formative stages; however, there were at any one time perhaps half a million Mozambicans, or about 10 percent of the population, working in neighboring countries. This group was exposed to new political ideas and in the period 1958-1960 began to organize themselves into associations with the goals of social contact, self-help, and ultimately national politics. The first true nationalist organization was UDENAMO (*União Democrática Nacional de Moçambique*, or the National Democratic Union of Mozambique) and was established in Southern Rhodesia in October 1960, moving to Dar-es-Salaam in February 1961. Two additional groups of note appeared at the time, MANU or UNAM (*União Nacional Africana Moçambique*, or Mozambican African National Union), depending on the English or Portuguese conformation, and UNAMI (*União Nacional do Moçambique Independente*, or National Union of Independent Mozambique). Both MANU and UDENAMO set aside their differences and attended the 1961 conference in Casablanca, where the nationalist movements in the Portuguese colonies consolidated their front to become a coalition. Subsequently, in September 1962, elements of MANU, UNAMI, and UDENAMO were united in FRELIMO (*Frente de Libertação de Moçambique*, or Front for the Liberation of Mozambique) at the urging of Julius Nyerere, the Tanganyikan leader, making it the strongest and most important movement.

Dr. Eduardo Mondlane assumed its leadership. He, too, absorbed the lessons of 1961 and was not prepared to launch a guerrilla war until some three years later in September 1964, after his small army was trained. Mondlane, in coming late to the nationalist movements against Portugal, was very much influenced by the trend in Angola and Guiné. His organization initially developed similarly to the PAIGC and experienced the same sort of problems in subordinating military operations to political leadership. His doctrine paralleled that of the MPLA and particularly of the PAIGC with its emphasis on political indoctrination, and it was along these lines that he sought to conduct his military campaign. Mozambicans had already tried peaceful demonstrations with the same consequences as occurred in Angola and Guiné. At Mueda in 1960 reputedly about 500 Africans were killed in a demonstration. FRELIMO felt that armed struggle was the only answer, as Portugal would not grant self-determination and would destroy those who demonstrated for political freedom.[31]

Political expression was forbidden both in the *ultramar* and in the *metrópole* except in the narrow context of the Portuguese staged elections every four years. The airing of grievances or liberal political views attracted a heavy hand from the authorities. In the case of the 1959 strike by the Pidjiguiti dockworkers, the PAIGC had hoped that it would lead to negotiations with the authorities and a redress of grievances. When this traditional procedure failed, Cabral had no choice but to seek an alternative in guerrilla warfare with the goal of opening negotiations or ultimately of gaining control of the country. The same can be said for the MPLA and its earlier flight from Angola in 1956 and 1957.

Peasant populations are not normally a revolutionary force, and such was the case in Portuguese Africa.[32] They are conservative by nature and find security and comfort in the routine of their lives and the socioeconomic institutions that govern them. Change is resisted and outsiders are viewed with suspicion. The guerrillas of the various nationalist movements in Portuguese Africa represented change that the populations were not prepared to accept readily. Thus, despite the justified grievances of Portugal's black African citizens, overall they appeared to be loyal to Portugal and to suspect the activities of the nationalists. This apparent support reinforced Portugal's commitment to the colonies and their people. As Portugal entered 1961, its internal confidence in its position was as strong as ever. There occurred, moreover, a series of events that had the cumulative effect not only of reinforcing this attitude but of hardening it into an irreversible course of war. These events began with the affront of the attacks in the north of Angola and continued with an attempted coup against Dr. Salazar in an effort to moderate the country's position toward the demands of the nationalist movements. This failure alongside the message from the United Nations served to silence moderate voices. The final blow was the debacle of Goa, which made any further loss unthinkable. Each of these and its role in moving Portugal to war is examined below.

ANGOLA UPRISINGS OF 1961

The Angola uprisings and the immediate events served as a warning of things to come and prompted Portugal to think more clearly about defending its colonies. Sporadic agitation and unrest had occurred throughout 1960 at the time when Portugal began to realize the rich economic potential of Angola and Mozambique. Yet European troop strength in Angola numbered under 1,000 in early 1958, and was reinforced only to about 3,000 by mid-1960.[33] Overall strength was 8,000, of which at least 5,000 were African troops.[34] These forces, while scattered throughout Angola, were confined to the larger towns and accustomed merely to administering subjective rule.[35] This modest order of battle was hardly adequate to face the uprisings in early 1961.

The opening challenge was made by the MPLA in Luanda on 4 February 1961 by a truly aggrieved group armed only with clubs and knives and driven by a frustration with their treatment. They entered the capital and attacked a number of police installations, a prison, and the radio station in an attempt to have fifty-two political prisoners released. Seven policemen and forty of the group were killed. During the funeral for the policemen, shots were fired on the mourners, and whites attacked blacks in a display that incensed Portugal. The prison was suicidally attacked again on 10 February. Government forces overreacted in quelling the disturbance because of the strong emotional feelings that had accumulated in Luanda. Several hundred Africans were killed indiscriminately, their bodies being left to rot in the streets as a warning sign to aspiring revolutionaries. The events gained international attention and put Portugal firmly on the U.N. agenda. Race relations remained polarized in Luanda and would take years to rebuild. The MPLA instigated the mob action with little planning or consideration of the consequences. Picking the capital with its troop and secret police concentration was an unfortunate choice, and the MPLA was quickly destroyed inside Angola.

These events were a prelude as well as a warning of further trouble. On 15 March 1961 shortly after the MPLA episode, the UPA seized on the confusion and launched a multipronged attack in northern Angola with a flood of 4,000 to 5,000 armed men. Approximately 700 European farms plus additional trading settlements and government posts were overwhelmed.[36] This mob laid waste to whatever was in their path and killed men, women, black, white, young, and old. It was a senseless act of violence with only an amorphous political aim rather than a military campaign with a political goal. Roberto did not understand the difference. All of Portugal was shocked at the horror.

This savage foray occurred in an area demarcated by the Congolese frontier, the Kwango river, the Malange-Luanda railroad, and the Atlantic Ocean. The attackers pushed nearly to Luanda. Military leaders faced a situation in which

over 100 administrative posts and towns, in three districts of northern Angola from the Congo border to within 30 miles of Luanda, the capital, had been either wiped out, taken, or paralysed by African nationalist groups; over 1,000 Europeans were dead, and an unknown number of Africans; the economy of north Angola was crippled; communications were largely cut or damaged; and thousands of Portuguese refugees were camped in Luanda, or on their way back to Portugal. The internal situation in Angola was rapidly and sensationally projected to a large international audience over several months.[37]

For a month Portugal and Angola seemed paralyzed and unable to act. Equally, the insurgents were incapable of sustained military engagement. Civil militias were formed, and loyal Africans armed. It was this patchwork of civil-military defense and its frenetic activity that brought UPA momentum to a halt.

Formal military reoccupation began on 13 May and was intensified as troops arrived from the *metrópole*. During the July-August period approximately 20,000 reinforcements landed in Angola. These troops behaved emotionally as they bombed and strafed areas that had not been affected by the uprising. This indiscriminate terror did enormous damage to Portuguese credibility and to race relations, and drove over 150,000 refugees into the Congo over the next nine months.[38] On 7 October, General Deslandes, the governor-general, announced that reoccupation was complete and that mop-up policing would begin. It has been estimated that 500 Europeans and about 20,000 local people died in this jacquerie.[39] This series of events deeply shocked all of Portugal and hardened its colonial commitment and the restoration of order in Angola. To the Portuguese it was unthinkable that such lawlessness should be tolerated, and a strong, uncompromising reaction to the nationalist behavior was widely supported. These events with their horror also diverted domestic attention from Dr. Salazar's political vulnerability.

THE COUP OF 1961

Dr. Salazar's vulnerability had been revealed in the Delgado challenge of 1958 and its strong message that it was time for Portugal to move toward democracy. The colonies were seen by many as a liability in that their ownership under the current arrangement represented a major obstacle in Portugal's joining the European Economic Community and in trading with Third World nations.[40] The strength of this view was manifested in the coup of 13 April 1961, which was probably the closest that Salazar came to being removed. The 1960 debacle in the Belgian Congo prompted heated debate in the Portuguese Supreme Council for National Defense (*Conselho Superior de Defesa Nacional*) about the security of its overseas territories. Colonel Kaúlza de Arriaga was notably vociferous in saying that the *ultramar* forces should be augmented, particularly in Angola. He was opposed by General Botelho Moniz and by fellow Colonels Almeida Fernandes and Costa Gomes, who advocated a dose of the "winds of change" for the colonial situation.[41] The uprisings themselves acted to bring the differing opinions into focus. Virtually the entire defense staff decided that a motion of no confidence in Dr. Salazar should be made at the approaching meeting of the Council on 8 April. Dr. Salazar, tipped to the plans by Colonel Arriaga, did not attend the meeting. As an alternative the plotters had asked President Tomás to dismiss Dr. Salazar. Tomás indicated that he would not dismiss the "greatest statesman of the century after Churchill." By then Dr. Salazar had identified the plotters, and on 13 April the relevant participants were detained. The inevitable reshuffle ensued in which Dr. Salazar assumed the defense portfolio, and no change in policy was brooked.

Dr. Salazar had managed over the years of his rule to control and manipulate the military through a strategy of co-optation and "divide and rule."[42] Military pay was poor, and to advance in pay and promotion, ambitious officers were removed from the immediate military environment by posting them to lucrative and prestigious special positions. Normally these were at high levels of government in both the *metrópole* and the *ultramar*, and it was these postings, promotions, and pay that Dr. Salazar controlled. Allegiances were ambivalent. This undermining of traditional military bonds enabled Dr. Salazar to create mistrust and fear within the armed forces to his advantage. Until the 1974 revolution when the coup participants did not "chicken out," the Salazar regime would be safe from a military coup, and despite its enormous reservations and latent moral indignation, the armed forces would be forced to honor his commitment to the colonies and to fight his war in Africa.[43] With this event it became evident that the purpose of colonial policy was now to preserve the Salazar regime. The alternative colonial options had been neutralized, and commitment to war reinforced through destruction of the coup. These events accented Portugal's increasing international isolation.

U.N. REVERSAL OF 1961

Portugal's international isolation had been growing ever since it had joined the United Nations in 1955 following a number of vetoes by the Soviet Union. There had been pressure building from the members of that body for it to grant self-rule to its colonies. This agitation had been fed by the newly independent states joining the United Nations and by the writings of several authors highlighting the human abuses in Lisbon's policy toward the colonies, most notably the Galvão report. Captain Henrique Galvão, chief inspector of Colonial Administration, wrote a report in 1947 describing the labor conditions in Angola and warning against their continuance.[44] Dr. Salazar had the report banned and in 1952 arrested Captain Galvão on treason charges. This incident gained international attention. Portugal also refused to submit the periodic technical reports on its colonies, as required by the United Nations for nonself-governing territories. While the other colonial powers were unhappy in disclosing facts about their colonies, they complied. Portugal attracted additional attention in its refusal.

In 1955 a group of nations advocating colonial independence with the support of the Soviet Union orchestrated the passage of a resolution condemning colonialism as a violation of human rights and the U.N. Charter. In response Portugal claimed that it had no colonies, as all of its overseas provinces were part of a single state with one constitution. It also claimed that the United Nations had no competence in this matter as it was an internal affair. The issue was debated for four years, and finally on 15 December 1960 the U.N. General Assembly, again pushed by this group and the Soviets, ruled against Portugal. Portugal saw itself as victimized and refused to accept the resolution. The NATO alliance became Portugal's ally before the United Nations in preventing a catastrophe; however, this support began to fray in 1961.[45] Following the uprising, the UN Security Council convened in May and June to discuss among other agenda items the events in Angola. The United States under President John F. Kennedy reversed support in this forum and sided with the Soviet Union in condemning Portugal's African policy. This event was an enormous blow to Dr. Salazar, who criticized the United States for voting with the Soviet Union in the face of historical opposition to Soviet diplomatic and military activity. Portugal thus was destined to become a semi-pariah state, politically isolated along with its colonial neighbors, South Africa and Southern Rhodesia, and was forced to fight the ensuing war hobbled by this isolation. It felt beleaguered and viewed its position as neither understood nor appreciated. This ostracism served to harden its commitment to its colonies. Portugal believed that it was acting properly and responsibly and had nothing of which to be ashamed. It proceeded accordingly to defend its sovereign territory and interests.

THE COLLAPSE OF GOA

This beleaguered colonial position was reinforced by the actual loss of the Indian colonies in what was an act of war that Portugal was powerless to prevent. The events surrounding Goa in 1961 again hardened Portugal's position by providing Dr. Salazar with a nationally distressing event to coalesce the population for war. While Portuguese Indian territory was relatively small at 4,194 square kilometers, the Indian government's seizure was a blatant act of aggression against another state. Portugal had three trading enclaves there: Goa, Damão, and Diu. The fledgling Indian government had threatened to take these properties in the late 1940s, as it considered them an affront. Britain's Prime Minister, Winston Churchill, along with the United States, forcefully intervened to moderate Indian ambitions. Later Prime Minister Nehru, emboldened by the outbreak of armed revolt in Angola, made some very peremptory demands of the Portuguese.[46] When it became clear that Dr. Salazar did not intend to relinquish the territory and refused to negotiate, India massed 30,000 troops, supported by tanks, aircraft, and warships, on the borders of the three territories. Governor-General Vassalo e Silva could defend his territory with only about 3,000 ill-equipped troops without air cover or air defense, 900 Goan police, and an old frigate. On 11 December, Dr. Salazar attempted to invoke the Anglo-Portuguese Treaty without success. Great Britain had since 1954 refused to help, saying that the 600-year-old alliance had clear limitations, particularly since a member of the Commonwealth was involved. Britain no longer needed Portuguese ports for the transit to its colonies, and Portugal no longer needed the protection of the dwindling British navy. New alliance structures, such as NATO, had clearly replaced the Anglo-Portuguese Treaty in both intent and practice.

Dr. Salazar gave instructions that resistance must last at least eight days to mobilize international support. Should that not be forthcoming, then "total sacrifice" must be made to save Portuguese honor. Indian forces invaded in the morning of 17 December, and Vassalo e Silva capitulated in the pointless struggle on 19 December, far short of eight days and total sacrifice. Vassalo e Silva and the other officers involved were dismissed from the army in 1963 in what appeared to be an effort to shift blame for the loss of Portuguese India to the military and to set an example for officers in similar future situations, such as the approaching colonial wars. The military at large was resentful at the unjust punishment and at making soldiers the scapegoats for civilian mistakes. The armed forces carried into the African campaigns this "ominous message that the government was prepared to manipulate and sacrifice them in hopeless missions and to court-martial virtually all survivors."[47] General António de Spínola, who was to be the Commander-in-Chief of Portuguese forces in Guiné (1968–1972), the Deputy Chief of the General Staff (1972–1974), and the first President of the new government following the revolution in 1974, described the anxiety permeating the entire Portuguese military on the eve of the African wars: "India is a clear example of what we fear. Never was its inevitable loss believed possible. And yet when the tragedy happened, the Nation's attention was immediately focused on the narrow aspect of military conduct. The Armed Forces were accused of not having defended India heroically; when, in reality, no matter how effective its defense, India would have fallen in only a matter of days."[48] The punishment for the leaders of the Indian garrison carried the broad message that there would be no turning back from the government's decision to defend the colonies. Dr. Salazar's commitment to preserving his regime was unswerving in its purpose, and the events in Goa served to push Portugal further down the road to war.

Portugal's commitment to the defense of the *ultramar* had its origins in a search for the renewed greatness of an earlier era as espoused by the Salazar government's vision of empire. The modern-day African colonies had largely been an irregular economic and political burden until the eve of the wars, and until after World War II had held only a promise of any substantial economic benefit. Political opposition to Dr. Salazar was tolerated neither at home nor in the *ultramar*. The long-standing abuses of Portugal's African populations thus created widespread dissatisfaction with no outlet. Between the intransigent Salazar and an aggrieved African population an explosion was inevitable. When it happened in 1961, the events in Angola along with the coup, the isolation in the United Nations, and the seizing of Goa pushed Dr Salazar to solidify the commitment of the Portuguese people to defend the colonies and preserve his regime. This national commitment was a reflection of his own personal commitment and his propensity to brook no opposition, particularly from seemingly upstart nationalist movements and elements of his military. So strong was this feeling that it defied any voice of reason and foreclosed any retreat or compromise over African affairs. Portugal's armed forces and treasure were thus pledged in full as the ultimate manifestation of this promise to make the colonial system work in Dr. Salazar's concept of empire.

NOTES

1. Marcello Caetano, "Editorial," *O Mundo Português* [Portuguese World], 2 (1935): 218.

2. William C. Atkinson, "Introduction" to Luís Vaz de Camões, *The Lusiads*, trans. William C. Atkinson (Harmondsworth: Penguin Books, 1952), 19–20. King Sebastião's force totaled some 15,000 foot and 1,500 horse with 9,000 campfollowers. Five hundred vessels were required to transport the force. Eight thousand were killed, 15,000 were taken prisoner and sold into slavery, and perhaps 100 eventually reached the safety of Portugal.

3. Ibid., 20.

4. W. Gervase Clarence-Smith, *The Third Portuguese Empire 1825–1975: A Study in Economic Imperialism* (Manchester: Manchester University Press, 1985), 1. The author argues that while politicians and colonial ideologues were able to play strongly on this vibrant chord of imperial grandeur throughout the history of the Third Portuguese Empire (1825–1975) by recalling the great days of the discoveries and Asian conquests, the Portuguese citizens themselves were never unanimous in their attitudes toward Portuguese Asia, and many saw it as a hollow triumph that drained the country of resources and left it impotent in its defense against Spain.

5. Ibid., 2. The author argues that Brazil was a far different enterprise than the earlier Asian experience in that it had provided raw materials and in turn Portugal had supplied manufactures. It also had been a colony of settlement rather than one where "immigrants died of tropical diseases and melted into the local population."

6. Michael G. Mulhall, *The Dictionary of Statistics*, 4th ed. (London: George Routledge and Sons, 1909).

7. Clarence-Smith, 116.

8. Ibid., 83–85. See also H. V. Livermore, *A New History of Portugal* (Cambridge: Cambridge University Press, 1966), 305–306; "Great Britain's Policy in Africa" by an African Explorer, *The Times* (London), 22 August 1888, 8; and Eric Axelson, *Portugal and the Scramble for Africa 1875–1891* (Johannesburg: Witwatersrand University Press, 1967), 211–213. Portugal had launched expeditions by Serpa Pinto, Capelo, Roberto Ivens, and Henrique de Carvalho between 1877 and 1885 to explore its claimed territory in Central Africa, and thus from the de facto perspective viewed itself as already in possession of this land. Consequently, following the treaties with Germany and France resulting from the Berlin Conference of 1885 on the ownership of Africa, Portugal published the "Rose-colored Map" (*Mapa Cor de Rosa*), which showed Angola and Mozambique united in a coast-to-coast colony. Britain took strong exception, and in June 1887 Lord Salisbury stated that the British would "not recognize Portuguese sovereignty in territories not occupied with sufficient forces to maintain order." Portugal proceeded with its colonial expansion plans. On 11 January 1890 Salisbury demanded Portugal's immediate withdrawal from the questioned area and backed the demand with the threat of force. Portugal withdrew accordingly in great humiliation. This action became known as the "Ultimatum," and its consequences were to make Mozambique a coastal colony with no hinterland and British territory landlocked with no outlet to the sea. Mozambique remained separated from Angola by between 500 and 700 kilometers, and Portugal's ambition of a grand, coast-to-coast colony unrealized. The depth of this humiliation cannot be overemphasized. Colonialism was the center of national discourse

for almost a century following, and the country as a whole developed the notion that every portion of national territory was sacred. Portugal had long-established trading interests in the area questioned and felt totally cheated. If one views the territory that was lost to Britain and its imperial developer Rhodes from a twentieth century perspective, it is easy to understand that the hinterland wealth of the Rhodesias and the Belgian Congo, when connected to the Atlantic and Pacific outlets of Angola and Mozambique, would have given Portugal a second Brazil. The magnitude of this loss became a Portuguese preoccupation and steeled its national attitude in the absolute sacredness of its remaining territories abroad.

9. L. H. Gann, "Portugal, Africa, and the Future," *Journal of Modern African Studies* (March 1975): 2–3.

10. Basil Davidson, *In the Eye of the Storm* (Garden City, N.Y.: Doubleday, 1972), 124.

11. Clarence-Smith, 193. Internal and external pressures to democratize Portugal and put it in step with Western Europe had increased since World War II, and Salazar's rule had become tenuous in the late 1950s.

12. Hugh Kay, *Salazar and Modern Portugal* (London: Eyre and Spottswoode, 1970), 69, 133. The author argues that even in England communism had become "the rallying cry of the revolutionary instincts of our age" and had done so "by power of words, by sheer bluff, perhaps by the voluptuousness of contrast." It was largely the success of communist "evangelism" that made Salazar so suspicious of it.

13. Dr. Salazar quoted in Ibid., 133.

14. Ibid., 238.

15. John A. Marcum, *The Angolan Revolution, Vol. I, The Anatomy of an Explosion (1950–1962)* (Cambridge, Mass.: MIT Press, 1969), 347–351. Marcum lists some fifty-nine groups affecting Angola alone beginning in the 1940s and either merging with one another or vanishing by 1962.

16. Malyn Newitt, *Portugal in Africa: The Last Hundred Years* (London: C. Hurst & Co., 1981), 190.

17. Willem S. van der Waals, *Portugal's War in Angola 1961–1974* (Rivonia: Ashanti Publishing, 1993), 103. Dr. Neto is quoted: "If the enemy presently possesses more forces than we do, and this is so, then it is correct that we should prepare for a protracted war. The misconception that we should be able to execute a war of rapid decisions should be removed once and for all."

18. Região Militar de Angola, *Supintrep No. 19: Guerra Revolucionária* [Supplemental Intelligence Report No. 19: Revolutionary War], July 1963, Luanda, quoted in van der Waals, 103.

19. Douglas L. Wheeler and René Pélissier, *Angola* (London: Pall Mall Press, 1971), 167. The authors cite as an example the Congo district in 1960. For its 37,000 square miles it had fourteen *concelhos* (basic urban or semi-urban administrative unit) or *circunscrições* (basic rural administrative division) and thirty-seven posts, for an average of 725 square miles per administrative division. This presence would hardly be effective in controlling a frontier, as the posts would be dozens of miles apart. Large numbers of people could and did cross undetected.

20. Hélio Felgas, "Angola e a Evolução Política dos Territórios Vizinhos" [Angola and the Political Evolution of the Neighboring Territories], *Revista Militar* (December 1965): 706.

21. van der Waals, 96.

22. Ibid., 97. The author argues that Portuguese propaganda and social work among the refugees in Angola persuaded most of these displaced people to move into controlled settlements. This development deprived ELNA of popular support. ELNA had concentrated on military action in a human desert and on preventing MPLA infiltration. It had neglected to indoctrinate, organize, and win recruits among refugees returning to Angola and thus missed an opportunity to undermine Portuguese authority. Consequently no ELNA internal political infrastructure was established in Angola. Portugal gained the upper hand and maintained superior momentum until 1974.

23. Neil Bruce, "Portugal's African Wars," *Conflict Studies*, no. 34 (March 1973): 22.

24. Sue Armstrong, *In Search of Freedom* (Gibraltar: Ashanti Publishing, 1989), 71.

25. John A. Marcum, *The Angolan Revolution, Vol. II, Exile Politics and Guerrilla Warfare (1962-1976)* (Cambridge, Mass.: MIT Press, 1978), 113.

26. Patrick Chabal, *Amílcar Cabral* (Cambridge: Cambridge University Press, 1983), 56-57.

27. Amílcar Cabral, *Guiné-Bissau—Nação Africana Forjada na Luta* [Guiné-Bissau—African Nation Forged in Struggle] (Lisbon: Publicações Nova Auora, 1974), 39.

28. Hélio Felgas, *Os Movimentos Terroristas* [The Terrorist Movements] (Lisbon: Privately printed, 1966), 57.

29. Amílcar Cabral, *Textos Políticos* [Political Texts] (Porto: Edições Afrontamento, 1974), 19-20.

30. Amílcar Cabral, *Palavras de Ordem Gerais* [Speeches on Overall Methods] (Bissau: PAIGC/Secretariado Geral, 1976), 34.

31. Eduardo Mondlane, *The Struggle for Mozambique* (London: Zed Press, 1969), 125.

32. Gerald J. Bender, "The Limits of Counterinsurgency: An African Case," *Comparative Politics*, 4, no. 3 (April 1972): 357.

33. Douglas L. Wheeler, "The Portuguese Army in Angola," *Modern African Studies*, 7, no. 3 (October 1969): 430.

34. Douglas L. Wheeler, "African Elements in Portugal's Armies in Africa (1961-1974)," *Armed Forces and Society*, 2, no. 2 (February 1976): 237.

35. Estado-Maior do Exército, *Resenha Histórico-Militar das Campanhas de África, Vol. II, Dispositivo das Nossas Forças Angola* [Historical-Military Report on the African Campaigns, Vol. II, Disposition of Our Angolan Forces] (Lisbon: Estado-Maior do Exército, 1989), 63-65.

36. René Pélissier, *Le Naufrage des Caravelles: Etudes sur la Fin de l'Empire Portugais (1961-1975)* [The Shipwreck of the Caravels: Studies on the End of the Portuguese Empire (1961-1975)] (Orgeval: Editions Pélissier, 1979), 147.

37. Douglas L. Wheeler, "The Portuguese Army in Angola," *Modern African Studies*, 7, no. 3 (October 1969): 431.

38. René Pélissier, *La Colonie du Minotaure, Nationalismes et Révoltes en Angola (1926-1961)* [The Colony of the Minotaur, Nationalist Movements and Revolts in Angola (1926-1961)] (Orgeval: Editions Pélissier, 1978), 658.

39. Ibid., 657-660; van der Waals, 58-61.

40. Clarence-Smith, 193. The author argues that by 1968 the Portuguese economy was turning decisively from the colonies toward Europe. Portugal in the course of the 1960s and early 1970s became a booming and aggressive "newly industrialized country" and was described as a "Taiwan of southern Europe."

41. Douglas Porch, *The Portuguese Armed Forces and the Revolution* (Stanford: The Hoover Institution Press, 1977), 38.

42. Douglas L. Wheeler, "The Military and the Portuguese Dictatorship, 1926-1974: 'The Honor of the Army,'" in *Contemporary Portugal*, ed. Lawrence S. Graham and Harry M. Makler (Austin: University of Texas Press, 1979), 199.

43. Porch, 26.

44. Captain Henrique Galvão, *Report on Native Problems in the Portuguese Colonies* (Lisbon: Ministry of the Colonies, 1947).

45. Joaquim Moreira da Silva Cunha, *O Ultramar, a Nação e o "25 de Abril"* [The Overseas Provinces, the Nation and the "25th of April"] (Coimbra: Atlântida Editora, 1977), 13-14.

46. Richard Robinson, *Contemporary Portugal* (London: George Allen & Unwin, 1979), 103. Nehru announced that India was "not prepared to tolerate the presence of the Portuguese in Goa, even if the Goans want them to be there."

47. Porch, 36.

48. António de Spínola, *Portugal e o Futuro* [Portugal and the Future] (Lisbon: Editoria Arcádia, 1974), 235.

3

O EXÉRCITO NA GUERRA SUBVERSIVA: PORTUGUESE COUNTERINSURGENCY DOCTRINE ON THE EVE OF WAR

In anticipation of the wars the Portuguese Army General Staff (*Estado-Maior do Exército*) began to write its counterinsurgency doctrine, *O Exército na Guerra Subversiva* (The Army in Subversive War), in 1960. This chapter will review the origins and methodology of this effort and analyze the doctrine in terms of its relevance and applicability to the colonial situation that the Portuguese faced in the 1958 to 1963 period. The process and its result are also compared with similar contemporary thinking by Britain, France, and the United States.

ORIGINS OF PORTUGUESE DOCTRINE

Dr. Salazar was particularly sensitive to the vulnerability of the Portuguese colonies in Africa to nationalist movements and had been so since the end of World War II. He had witnessed the British experiences beginning in 1946 with Palestine and extending to Malaya, Borneo, Kenya, Cyprus, and a host of smaller colonies. He was acutely aware of the French experience in Indochina and the war that was then being fought in Algeria. And finally, the liberating of much of Africa from its former colonial masters held grave warning signals for Portugal.

This sensitivity was reinforced by a very deep and ingrained anticommunist Cold War stance by Portugal. Dr. Salazar had sent a volunteer force in 1938 to fight on the anticommunist side of Generalissimo Franco in the Spanish Civil War, and was of the common view following World War II that with the German bulwark dismantled, an unchecked Soviet Union would engulf Europe. Portugal's place was alongside the democratic nations that had won the war, and a collective security arrangement was the only logical way to contain the threat. This defense position prompted the intense study of Soviet policy, particularly that of sponsoring insurgent proxy wars, both by the general staffs of the various

armed services and in the senior staff officer courses in Lisbon at the Institute
of Higher Military Studies (*Instituto de Altos Estudos Militares*, or IAEM).[1]
This institute remains the premier forum for the study of defense issues in
Portugal. By the late 1950s Fidel Castro's rise in Cuba and the British and
French insurgency experiences, among others, were included in the IAEM
curriculum.

The IAEM was founded in 1911 as the Central School for Officers (*Escola
Central de Oficiais*, or ECO) with the purpose of preparing officers to be
promoted to captain, major, and colonel. In 1927 it was installed in the Palácio
Real de Caxias outside of Lisbon, and its curriculum was expanded to prepare
officers for staff duties and for promotion to general officer. At the same time
it also assumed the related task of supporting the unification of military doctrine
by acting as a center for its study. In 1937 with the merging of the *metrópole*
and the *ultramar* defense establishments, the name was changed to the Instituto
de Altos Estudos Militares, and it was assigned the mission of preparing staff
officers through the General Staff Course (*Curso de Estado-Maior*, or CEM),
senior officers through the Course for the Promotion to Senior Officer (*Curso
de Promoção a Oficial Superior*, or CPOS), and general officers through the
Course for High Command (*Curso de Altos Comandos*, or CAC) for their
portending duties.   In 1958 the IAEM was moved to new, expanded
headquarters in Pedrouços, a suburb west of Lisbon.[2]

The creation of modern doctrine in the Portuguese military followed the
merging of the *metrópole* and *ultramar* defense organizations and their further
reorganization, which included the creation of the Portuguese Air Force in 1952.
These changes were begun in 1937 and required more than two decades to effect
with their completion in 1960. Prior to 1950 the management of military affairs
relating to national defense was coordinated in the political sphere through the
routine conduct of government affairs.   There was no elaborate defense
hierarchy to oversee and plan military force structure and activities in
accordance with an established national policy. Beginning in 1950, joint
operational activity of the armed forces was channelled through the Chief of
Staff of the Armed Forces and the various Commanders-in-Chief, and after 1956
the Prime Minister and the Minister for National Defense were supported by a
defense hierarchy, including ministers for the various service arms.[3]

Until this reorganization was completed, defense policy and force structure
were promulgated in the form of decrees. Doctrine, on the other hand, was
developed by the General Staff of the Army, or by the headquarters of the
military region of each colony. There was a single navy, and later one air
force, so a single doctrine for these forces extended servicewide. In 1938, for
example, Decree 28 520 ordered a study of the military mission in the colonies.
On its completion in 1939 and in accordance with its recommendations, Decree
29 686 fixed the composition of colonial forces in time of peace and remained
in effect until 1953.[4] Prior to that time the colonial forces were the province
of the governor of each colony and the Minister of the Colonies and not the

command hierarchy in the *metrópole*. These colonial armies were led by officers and sergeants assigned from the *metrópole*, and their troops were largely recruited and trained locally. It had been important at one point to have separate armies for each colony and its defense; however, with the advent of improved communications and command and control practices after World War II, it proved unnecessarily cumbersome. These forces and their guiding doctrine underwent major changes on Portugal's joining NATO and followed the U.S./NATO conventional war doctrine. This doctrine addressed the conventional-force-defense-of-Europe war and Portugal's contribution to it. It did not properly address subversive war.[5]

Portuguese doctrine was basically an authoritative, approved description of how to perform a task and was developed in several ways. Service institutes, such as the IAEM; certain commands, such as the Headquarters, Military Region of Angola; and professional journals, such as *Revista Militar* (Military Review), *Boletim Militar do Exército* (Military Bulletin of the Army), *Boletim do Estado-Maior* (Bulletin of the General Staff), *Jornal do Exército* (Journal of the Army), *Revista da Armada* (Naval Review), and *Revista do Ar* (Air Review); all contributed both formally and informally to the production and dissemination of doctrine. The doctrine itself was written by the General Staff of the Army, Navy, or Air Force, as appropriate, and promulgated by that body. The institutes and schools were particularly important, as they were stewards of the doctrinal memory and presented the approved way of doing things to the officer corps that passed through their instruction as students. The propagation of doctrine depended on cycling the officers through the institutes so that the abstract concepts presented in manuals were understood and practiced in the field, making them a part of accepted procedure and thinking. In the event of war and the actual employment of doctrine under combat conditions, the institutes served as an agent for adjusting doctrine based on this experience. Military reversals would thus theoretically result in a corrective modification to doctrine.

The IAEM had concentrated its efforts prior to 1961 on doctrine for conventional war in accordance with Portugal's role in NATO and the feared conflict in Europe.[6] This traditional focus, however, had not been to the exclusion of insurgency and counterinsurgency warfare, for a substantial amount of material had been accumulated on the topics. The Portuguese armed forces had for a number of years studied the development of subversive war as simply a form of popular revolt that was sporadic and isolated but not in the mainstream of worthy security topics. Following World War II, the number and severity of insurgencies increased to the point that insurgency became the most prevalent form of conflict in the world. As nuclear war was an unlikely event in Portuguese eyes and one in which it would have only an indirect participation, it seemed appropriate for Portugal to prepare for the reality of a subversive war that would most likely require the mobilization of large numbers of its troops and other national resources.[7]

GROUNDWORK FOR SUBVERSIVE WAR

The Portuguese Army took a number of initiatives in the 1950s that laid the groundwork in preparing for the conflict and in formulating its doctrine. The first occurred in 1953, when the IAEM conducted a course of eight weeks for fifty-three officers known as the *Curso de Estado-Maior de Pequenas Unidades* (Staff Course for Small Units). This course was also known by the nickname of *"Curso dos SS,"* from the word *secção* or section, a small unit being a "section of a section." It was designed to prepare officers for staff functions at the battalion and regimental level. The course was remarkable at the time for its innovation within the Portuguese Army and had its roots in the composite experience of officers who had primarily attended U.S. Army schools in the United States or visited U.S. Army units in West Germany. With the initiation of this course, the Portuguese Army began to build small, well-prepared staffs to support the battalion and regimental commanders. From that year onward the preparation for small unit staffs was incorporated at the CPOS as well as the course for promotion to captain, which was given at the various practical schools of the Portuguese Army.[8] While the *Curso dos SS* was not especially designed for subversive warfare, it proved to be very important after 1961 and throughout the African Campaigns of 1961-1974.[9]

During 1958 and 1959 the Portuguese Army sent five officers to the Intelligence Centre of the British Army at Maresfield Park Camp, Uckfield, Sussex, to attend intelligence courses at the School of Military Intelligence.[10] These courses contained a strong component of subversive warfare, as the British were heavily influenced by their experiences in Malaya, Kenya, and Cyprus. On their return two of these five officers, Captains Pedro Cardoso and Renato Marques Pinto, were appointed as instructors at the IAEM. Captain Cardoso brought with him from England a manual, *Keeping the Peace (Duties in Support of the Civil Power)*, which was rapidly translated by him and his fellow Captains Marques Pinto and Remígio dos Santos.[11] The volume generally treated insurgency as a communist-inspired problem progressing from subversion to a seizure of base areas, and incorporated the lessons from the British experience in Malaya. It did not acknowledge that nationalist movements might be motivated by a simpler and more straightforward desire for independence, and the lack of this aspect reinforced the Portuguese theory of a communist conspiracy. With the completion of this translation, which served as a text, the problems of subversive warfare and the support of civilian authorities were introduced into the staff courses of 1958-1959. While there had been earlier study of subversive warfare theory as part of the Soviet policy curriculum, this initiative marked the beginning of practical instruction in the problems of subversive warfare to the officer corps at large and shifted the course from the nearly exclusive focus on conventional warfare.[12]

In 1959 a mission of six officers under Major Joaquim Franco Pinheiro was sent to Algeria. These officers spent fifteen days at the Centre d'Instruction de

Pacification et Contre-Guerrilla at Arzew in Oran province, where they took a stage of instruction with some 200 French officers. Founded in 1956, the Center ran an arduous twelve-day program, normally accommodating 250 reserve officers who had been recalled to active duty, and attempted to prepare them for their command positions in Algeria. Following this instruction, they were sent two to each of the three French corps stationed throughout Algeria for one month. On their return to Portugal, they produced a voluminous report of their experiences in and observations of insurgency or subversive warfare. The overwhelming message in this account was that the Portuguese Army must make the most urgent preparations to fight an insurgency.[13]

This sense of urgency was reinforced on 6 December 1960, when the "Congress of 81" communist countries concluded its three weeks of deliberations in Moscow. The meeting was widely publicized and followed closely by those with a vested interest in the politics of developing nations. The last such meeting had been held in 1957 and had hosted only thirteen countries. The proceedings of this latest meeting were published in *NATO News* (*Nouvelles de l'OTAN*) and later extracted in an analysis in the May 1961 issue of *Revue Militaire Générale*. Subsequently French Army General Jean Valluy made a detailed study of the meeting declarations, which appeared in the October 1961 issue of *Revue Militaire Générale*. The implications of these declarations were known to the Portuguese in December 1960, and worrisomely they announced the targeting of a number of countries for subversive activities. Portugal and its colonies were foremost on the list.[14] They asserted that the way to change Portugal's dictatorship was to disturb the colonial situation, and presented a plan to topple the authoritarian government of Dr. Salazar and to separate Portugal from its colonies. This plan was to be implemented simultaneously with the support of African nationalist organizations advocating the independence of the Portuguese colonies and by the infiltration of Portuguese universities with elements supporting this notion of colonial independence and espousing the communist doctrine.[15] As far as the strategy for colonial independence went, the newly independent nations being created from the former colonies of Belgium, Britain, and France were to be subverted and used to encircle and isolate Portugal's colonies, thus denying them friendly borders and local support. This formula was designed to produce a debilitating colonial war for Portugal, a war that would both liberate the colonies and topple the anti-communist regime.

With respect to the other arm of Soviet strategy, Portugal's military leadership believed that Portugal could cope with the military situation initially, but as the wars expanded, its armed forces would need to recruit large additional numbers of temporary junior officers (*milicianos*) from the universities. Thus, the appropriately indoctrinated university graduates would in the meantime be entering government and particularly the military service and making their new views felt. The plan then called for these forces to combine to create an opportunity for the installation of a communist government in Lisbon.[16] The ultimate aim was to replace the Salazar regime, which had refused even to establish diplomatic ties with the Soviet Union, with a government friendly to the communist sphere. While the Portuguese authorities were largely concerned about the nationalist movements associated with their African possessions and the threat that they represented, this declaration of support for them and the direct threat to the Portuguese government and its policies were sources of concern even in its reemphasis of known Soviet intentions. The normal passivity of this forum had been replaced with an aggressive posture. As Portugal was sensitive about its colonial situation, this noisy and threatening display, which had included a disturbing speech by Nikita Khrushchev on "wars of national liberation," was seen as a direct challenge.

At the same time Lieutenant Colonel Artur Henrique Nunes da Silva, who was working in the Operations Branch of the Army General Staff and was also an instructor for the CEM, had read the report on Algeria and the French documents that accompanied it. This development was propitious, as Lieutenant Colonel Nunes da Silva had been a student of the two-year "Cours Supérieur de Guerre" at the Ecole Supérieure de Guerre in Paris from 1958 to 1960. In his final year there he had a cycle of "Guerre Subversive." When he returned to Portugal in the summer of 1960 as a major, he was well acquainted with the French doctrine and had assumed new duties both as an instructor at the IAEM and as a staff officer on the General Staff of the Army.[17] He took these materials to the IAEM immediately following the 6 December 1960 meeting of communist countries. Working with the 1961–1962 CEM class of about thirty officers and using current additional information and documents, principally from the Headquarters, Military Region of Angola, he produced the publication *Apontamentos para o Emprego das Forças Militares em Guerra Subversiva* (Notes on the Employment of Military Forces in Subversive War).[18]

Lieutenant Colonel Nunes da Silva had the support of the IAEM, where traditionally the best minds in the Portuguese armed forces were sought as instructors. The instructors were mobilized with the approval of the Army Staff Headquarters to support the development of the new counterinsurgency doctrine and to supervise and coordinate the staff work performed by the co-opted students. Virtually all of these instructors had served in the colonial armies and consequently represented a wealth of experience in Africa.   Each also represented a specialty of warfare that would be required there: intelligence, tactics, engineering, and logistics. The experience and skill of these instructors was to give the doctrine a full orientation toward the *ultramar* and the special requirements for the likely wars that would be fought there.   Many of the instructors were later to become noteworthy figures through their contributions to Portugal's military effort in its colonies. On completion of this work, Lieutenant Colonel Nunes da Silva moved the project to the Army General Staff, where frenetic activity accompanied the now urgent need for a specialized and comprehensive doctrine. The doctrinal manual *O Exército na Guerra Subversiva* (The Army in Subversive War) was produced by the Army General Staff with support from the IAEM in stages until its completion in 1963.[19]

DEVELOPMENT OF *O EXÉRCITO NA GUERRA SUBVERSIVA*

Lieutenant Colonel Nunes da Silva and the staff assigned to assist him in writing *O Exército na Guerra Subversiva* began with the information that had been assembled from various sources in the 1958–1960 period. This material included the essential elements of the British and French doctrines and renditions of their experiences in Malaya, Kenya, Indochina, and Algeria, and a modest amount of U.S. material.

Between 1945 and 1960 Britain had conducted campaigns in Palestine, Malaya, Kenya, and Cyprus. Except for Palestine, these post-World War II campaigns were successful. The conduct of these operations had not been based on formal doctrine but rather on certain principles of English common law and policing experience:

1. Disorders were suppressed with a minimum of force,
2. Successful counterinsurgency had depended on a close cooperation between all branches of the civil government and the military, and this coordination had been the responsibility of a single individual,
3. Successful counterinsurgency had depended on good intelligence, and its gathering and collation had been coordinated under a single authority,
4. Successful counterinsurgency had called for the adoption of highly decentralized, small-unit tactics to defeat irregulars.[20]

Eventually these principles were brought together in a comprehensive strategy in 1960, when all were incorporated into a formal doctrine.[21] But until that time doctrine was individually crafted for each campaign after a lengthy apprenticeship. Drs. Hoffman and Taw argue in their study on British counterinsurgency doctrine that the two primary factors in British experience that expanded the cost of insurgencies significantly were (1) the belated identification or recognition of hostilities and the opportunity that this delay gave to the insurgents in gaining an unopposed foothold and developing their momentum, and (2) handicapping government counterinsurgency troops through a lack of proper "small wars" training and equipment.[22] The Portuguese, too, saw these lessons in the British experiences and sought to avoid these pitfalls in part by developing a written doctrine ahead of their anticipated conflict.

When Captains Pedro Cardoso and Renato Marques Pinto took the staff intelligence course at Maresfield Park Camp in 1958–1959, the British experiences in counterinsurgency were just beginning to be part of the curriculum in the various service schools. After over a decade of counterinsurgencies the British Army had finally come to realize that doctrine had to be formulated and taught. Given the unsettled situation in Portuguese Africa, these officers were attentive to the British experiences and absorbed its lessons keenly. The Portuguese Army General Staff knew that Portugal had little time before it must fight a campaign to retain its overseas possessions, and that it must fight its war correctly from the very first shot, if it were to succeed and contain the cost in doing so. If Portugal were forced to fight without a doctrine to guide its forces, and had to develop from scratch the necessary tactics that capitalized on the advantages accruing from the specific situations in each colony, then it would face a more difficult struggle with reduced chances of success. The British provided guidance, and their influence on Portuguese thinking was apparent in the development of *O Exército na Guerra Subversiva*. The British theater doctrines for Malaya (1952) and Kenya (1954) were key references for the Portuguese Army General Staff.[23] These doctrines embodied the principles of minimum force, civil-military cooperation, intelligence coordination, and small-unit operations that had proved so successful in British imperial policing. These principles fit the Portuguese Army's desire to develop an effective and inexpensive approach to counterinsurgency that was appropriate both to its means and to the circumstances in its colonies. This reasoning greatly influenced the development of the Portuguese way of war, in which a cost-effective and sustainable approach was adapted to its African Campaigns.

The French, like the British, had had a successful history of pacification prior to World War II, but since then counterinsurgency doctrine had been built on lessons of defeat. Following France's debacle in Indochina (1946–1954), the concept of revolutionary war or *guerre révolutionnaire* was formulated by a group of officers whose experiences there led them to seek methods of countering anticolonial wars. This list included the prominent commanders and senior staff officers General Lionel-Max Chassin, Colonel Lacheroy, and General Nemo, and the noteworthy junior officers Hogard, Poirier, and Souyris.[24] These officers wrote prolifically on the topic, and their theories were widely debated but not readily accepted in the French staffs or service schools that wrote and taught doctrine.

The central theme of *guerre révolutionnaire* theory lay in the argument that an inferior force could defeat a conventional army if it could gain the tacit support of the population in the contested area. These theorists had also witnessed the strength that a truly unified politico-military command gave to the enemy VietMinh insurgents and argued that this structure must also exist in a counterinsurgent force. These assertions were reinforced by their own experiences with civil-military responsibilities in Indochina. These officers had also felt the impact of psychological warfare and had become convinced that this dimension could be exploited to reinforce the ideological cohesion of government civil and military forces and to counter the enemy's ideology. The French doctrine also addressed intelligence coordination and small-unit operations, but omitted the British principle of minimum force. Although the French, too, had limited resources, the cost sensitivity of the British was not a conscious part of the doctrine's thinking. With this concept of *guerre révolutionnaire*, modern counterinsurgency reverted to the *tache d'huile* (oil spot) principle that Marshal Lyautey and his contemporaries had successfully applied over half a century earlier. The only difference was that the political techniques and military solutions to the problem of civil-military cooperation had been revised for modern times. From the mid-1950s this doctrine provided the theoretical framework for France's effort to retain Algeria.

By the time that Major Franco Pinheiro and his five colleagues visited Algeria in 1959, *guerre révolutionnaire* was the French de facto doctrine, although it had not at that time been promulgated in an official document. They saw parallels between Algeria and Portuguese Africa and assiduously recorded the French problems and solutions in the Maghreb. They were particularly intrigued by French psychological operations and saw an immediate benefit in their application to Portuguese Africa.[25] *Guerre révolutionnaire* espoused a sense of urgency in its approach to counterinsurgency, and it was this sense of immediacy that Major Pinheiro and his associates transmitted on their return to Lisbon.

The U.S. contributed little to Portuguese counterinsurgency thinking and the development of *O Exército na Guerra Subversiva*. Despite the attempts of the U.S. Army to establish staffs to oversee this doctrinal need in the years following World War II, the fragmented lives of these bodies resulted in a loss of continuant thinking on counterinsurgency. The irregularity of this work was reflected in the subsidiary manuals on counterguerrilla operations prior to 1960, which were *FM 31-20 Operations against Guerrilla Forces*, published in 1951, and *FM 31-15 Operations against Airborne Attack, Guerrilla Action and Infiltration*, published in 1953; both were flawed in that they discussed counterinsurgency in the framework of conventional war.[26] These doctrines were never able to reconcile the principle that counterinsurgency operations were based on protecting the population, and this premise went against the massive application of firepower in a conventional war. While they are listed as references in *O Exército na Guerra Subversiva*, they contributed little useful thinking on the Portuguese Army's anticipated problems in Africa. U.S. doctrinal literature during the 1950s was slow to materialize, and when it did, tended to consider counterinsurgency as an adjunct to conventional war.[27] President Kennedy's advent caused some modification in this position, but it proved difficult to effect any change in the U.S. Army's stance.

Coincident with the activities of Lieutenant Colonel Nunes da Silva, the Center for Instruction in Special Operations (Centro de Instrução de Operações Especiais, or CIOE) was established by the Portuguese Army at Lamego on 16 April 1960 to teach counterinsurgency (countersubversion) tactics to its personnel. Both the CIOE and the IAEM became forums for exploring and developing the strategies and tactics that would be most effective against an insurgency in the Portuguese colonies. Another valuable work and the most prominent private publication of the time on subversive war, *Guerra Revolucionária* [Revolutionary War], also appeared through Army sponsorship, explained the modern basis for subversive war from the Portuguese perspective, and provided the foundation for writing *O Exército na Guerra Subversiva*.[28]

Its title and content were heavily influenced by the French *guerre révolutionnaire* theory.

As the doctrine was being developed, it was also being taught and refined. Each of the five sections was first released in a preliminary version and applied experimentally in Angola. The preliminary sections were also taught in the Practical Schools of Arms, particularly that of the Infantry. It was here that small-unit tactics were developed and the proper combat equipment identified. Their contribution to the elements of the doctrine were important not only as lessons learned from experiments and teaching but also from the experience of veterans returning as instructors from combat in Angola. The Military Region of Angola (RMA) also offered the experience of its officers and the intelligence that it had gathered to the General Staff of the Army. From the opening months of the conflict the RMA had gathered valuable information on the behavior of the guerrillas, their order of battle, and Portuguese infantry tactics that had proved most effective against them. This experience was not only integrated into the doctrine but also made part of the curriculum at the practical schools for those being mobilized for duty in the colonies.[29] Throughout this process the Portuguese Army was attempting to compress the usual time required to develop a counterinsurgency doctrine, a process that normally represented a refinement of fighting experience from varied sources over many years. It was now at war and urgently needed such a document. Consequently, it worked feverishly to generate this valuable guidance.

The original product, *O Exército na Guerra Subversiva*, began with the national policy and rationale for the deployment and use of the Portuguese armed forces to attain the political objective of maintaining the integrity of its empire. In spite of contrary doctrines and practices that, following World War II, had spread everywhere, it reflected the Portuguese politico-strategic philosophy of holding its widely dispersed territories as an indissoluble, traditional empire.[30] It can be inferred from this statement that Portuguese national policy was one of survival and endurance. These goals were also reinforced with the use of such terms as "sovereignty," "national unity," "national integrity," and "economic patrimony," which appeared in Portuguese writings and propaganda and mirrored Dr. Salazar's vision of empire.[31] The empire was seen as a heritage and a promise of a richer future. In Portuguese eyes any fragmentation would not only betray the past but would reduce the empire to a modest European country. This potential catastrophe was to be avoided at all costs. The national policy of endurance also was in step with the campaign strategy of keeping the conflict low-key and inexpensive, so that Portugal could sustain the war for a long period and outlast the guerrillas.

Portugal's countersubversive grand strategy evolved from this policy of maintaining the empire with all of its promise and considered the operational, social, administrative (logistical), and technological dimensions of war in fashioning its three-pronged effort:

1. Military action would maintain order in the colonies and defeat the insurgents in combat (operational),
2. Diplomatic efforts would seek to nullify the activities of Portugal's adversaries, strengthen ties with its allies, and forge new alliances, and while not accepting the legitimacy of the terrorist organizations, seek to open a dialogue with them toward a peaceful solution that did not compromise Portuguese sovereignty,
3. Socioeconomic development within the colonies would improve the lot of the colonial population and make it feel a part of greater Portugal (social).[32]

From the foregoing it is clear that the Portuguese saw the military and social aspects dominating among these four dimensions of war. The administrative (logistics) would present a severe challenge to the Portuguese Army with its long lines of communication; however, the ability to support Portuguese troops on the battlefield and to maintain their consequent operational flexibility was never anticipated to be an insurmountable problem. As guerrillas fight a low-technology war, the Portuguese Army saw the technology aspect as only a minor factor, and consequently it was not treated in the doctrine. *O Exército na Guerra Subversiva* is a reflection of this grand strategy at the tactical level, and the topics treated in its five volumes are analyzed in the following sections according to the broader dimensions of war.

O Exército na Guerra Subversiva is a tactical doctrine with portions of military and operational doctrine bridging gaps to provide understanding of the instruction being given. This structure provides at times a panoramic view of counterinsurgency to support its more specific aspects and illustrates that the Portuguese Army understood and possessed the tools to implement the elements of textbook counterinsurgency doctrine. The volume follows a logical sequence from the soldier's perspective in that it opens with a statement of the purpose of the war and the principles of insurgency (subversive war) and proceeds to explain the field techniques required to defeat the guerrillas and help the soldier survive. The Portuguese soldier is told emphatically that he is the key to winning the population and gaining its confidence in Portugal over that of the guerrillas. Equally important and following from the psychological theme, the soldier is told of the need for military support to civil authorities and his role in this aspect of the war for the loyalty of the population. The doctrine is examined below according to the dominating military, social, and logistical dimensions of war as applied to counterinsurgency.

NATURE OF INSURGENCY AND COUNTERINSURGENCY

O Exército na Guerra Subversiva begins with a description of the principles of subversive and countersubversive war, and relates them to the unique considerations of the *ultramar*. Insurgency or subversive war represented to the Portuguese soldier an entirely new and different type of conflict, one that required a nearly complete reorientation of Portugal's armed forces. Hence the opening didactic was designed not only as an orientation in subversive war but also as a convenient reference. This entire section appears to be based on the earlier referenced publication *Guerra Revolucionária*. It also reflected adjustments to accommodate the particular situation in Portuguese Africa. In their subversive war the Portuguese saw no promise of compromise in an enemy that sought a total displacement of authority.[33]

Prior to the beginning of the Portuguese African Campaigns, insurgencies generally followed the prescriptions developed by Mao Tse-tung in China and expanded by General Vo Nguyen Giap in Vietnam.[34] This insurgency warfare doctrine and its execution were studied and analyzed by the Center for Political and Social Studies in Lisbon and subsequently became available in 1963 as a publication titled *Subversão e Counter-Subversão* (Subversion and Counter-Subversion).[35] This document described this Third World phenomenon as evolving in five phases:[36]

I   *Preparatory phase* or preparation of subversion
II   *Agitation phase* or the creation of a subversive environment
III *Terrorism and guerrilla action phase* or the consolidation of the subversive organization
IV   *Subversive state phase*, corresponding to the creation of bases, a rebel government, and pseudo-regular forces
V   *Final phase* or general insurrection and regular war.

The study also provided the caveat that subversive campaigns develop along widely divergent lines, and that the phases may overlap and blend together. There was rarely a clear break between phases.

Because of this overlapping of phases, the Portuguese Army departed from traditional thinking on the topic, as described above, and lumped the various phases of an insurgency into two larger phases, the pre-insurrection and the insurrection phase:[37]

Portuguese Armed Forces		Traditional View	
I	Pre-insurrectional phase	I	Preparatory phase
		II	Agitation phase
II	Insurrectional phase	III	Terrorism and guerrilla action phase
		IV	Subversive state phase
		V	Final phase

As the differences between the traditional Phases I and II are more theoretical than real, the Portuguese Army elected to combine them into a single, clandestine, pre-insurrectional phase. For the same reason the overt activity of the traditional Phases III, IV, and V were combined into a single, insurrectional phase. This simplification was designed to make the soldier's understanding of insurgency or subversive war easier. This approach has enormous merit in that treatment from the government's viewpoint is not altered by the academic classification but rather ruled by practicalities. The clandestine organization of an insurgency could easily be part of the normal undercurrent of dissention within any society and as such is not directly a military responsibility. Once the use of violence is injected, however, it becomes something very different. This stark contrast, as opposed to a blend, is reflected in the Portuguese military's recognition of the problem and accordingly its application of solutions. Its counteraction is not necessarily linked to each of the five phases but rather concentrates on the broader two. Countersubversion in the pre-insurrectional period is centered on preventive measures, and in the insurrectional period on reclaiming the population and destroying the insurgent infrastructure. In the second phase Portuguese doctrine calls for activities on the military, psychological, social, and political fronts.

The soldier's relations with the population that he is protecting is stressed constantly throughout the document, and particularly in this opening section. While this emphasis is not uniquely Portuguese, it is not generally highlighted to this degree in writings on counterinsurgency theory and practice. The Portuguese soldier is encouraged "to influence [the population] through his presence, calming the population and acting as a preventive measure against the growth of subversion."[38] He is also told that he is part of a psychosocial operation (*acção psicossocial*) in which his military and civilian skills should be used voluntarily to help the population. "The military forces thus have an important role to play despite acting uniquely in preventing subversion and in remaining alert to armed bands or attacking guerrillas."[39] This emphasis on the Portuguese soldier's having a calming effect on the population reinforced the national strategy of keeping the conflict low-key, and indeed calm, and thus inexpensive. His presence was designed primarily to gain the confidence of the local population and follows the British principle of minimum force in counterinsurgency. It contrasts with the initial French practice called *ratissage* or "raking over," which terrorized the Algerian population. It also contrasted with the U.S. practice of conducting counterinsurgency as a subset of conventional war. The massed firepower that had served the U.S. Army well in winning World War II and Korea was both expensive and inappropriate for a conflict in which the enemy mixed with the people and both became targets under conventional war practices. The indiscriminate use of firepower endangered the population and terrorized the very audience that the government was trying to win. Both of these styles also tended to remove the soldier from meaningful contact with the population and thus reduced his effectiveness in gaining its confidence and in winning its loyalty. The Portuguese sought to win militarily and to do so in a subdued, low-key, affordable way.

THE MILITARY DIMENSION

The military dimension is the most detailed portion of the doctrine and is aimed almost exclusively at providing a guide for the conduct of light infantry, small-unit patrols. It is a revision of the *Guia para o Emprego Táctico das*

Pequenas Unidades na Contra Guerrilha (Guide for the Tactical Employment of Small Units in Counter Guerrilla Warfare), issued as a trial in 1961.[40] The "Guide" is a detailed tactical doctrine that was one of the earlier pilot sections tested in the field. It was rushed into service following the uprisings of 1961 and reflected the very thorough groundwork done by the Portuguese Army General Staff to prepare Portugal's troops for a "form of warfare in which most irregular warriors excel and in which regular troops are almost invariably seen at their worst."[41]

The military dimension is tactical, which provides the main body of doctrinal instruction and furnishes a common foundation on which to base plans. Such doctrine normally appears in the form of training and field manuals and is widely disseminated within the armed forces. It supports the tactical level of war, which is the world of combat and is focused on defeating the enemy at a particular time and place. This work builds on the comprehensive treatment given the methods of the insurgent and the principles of warfare used to counter his threat. The topic is addressed in two phases. The first is a compilation of the most important elements of tactical doctrine relating to the preparation and execution of the more typical operations of small units in countersubversive war. The second details these operations in the simplest terms, an important factor in communicating with the soldier.

The entire focus of this military dimension centers on the uniqueness of counterinsurgency. While the armed forces must be prepared to fight with professional skill and dedication, they must do so in a nontraditional and innovative manner, one that avoids the conventional tactics likely to harm and thus alienate the population surrounded by the fighting. This requirement is neither easy nor simple in that it requires conventionally trained troops to modify their tactical practice in ways that run counter to much of their training. This product is the result of the early pilot programs at the CIOE and the doctrinal research done by the IAEM and the RMA, and fully addresses this dilemma. It equally aims at keeping the tone of the conflict low-key to avoid frightening the population. The military contribution is to subdue violent activity and to provide security so that the political process of winning the population can occur. Their organization and training will have to be tailored to the unique task of counterinsurgency, and specialized troops employed as necessary.[42] "So, a total adaption must be made, not only in operational methods but also in the structuring of suitable tactical units—organization, equipment and instruction—so that we can be poised at the opportune time in the area or actual location of the enemy."[43]

The instruction is related well to the strategic objectives in that it explains how the soldier through his tactical actions fits into the campaign goals of protecting the population and reducing the insurgent's access to it. It further explains how the guerrilla operates and stresses the importance of why he must be denied access to the population. Guerrilla contact with the population was to be prevented at all costs, and the Portuguese commanders and soldiers were very sensitive to guerrilla initiatives with the people.[44]   It also reflects the national strategy of keeping the operations subdued and low-key, not only for the cost containment but to avoid terrorizing the population.

THE SOCIAL DIMENSION

As the military dimension talked about the nature of the war and told the soldier how to kill guerrillas and stay alive, so the social dimension talked about his relationship with the population and civil government and the messages that were being carried to the people both in Portuguese Africa and the neighboring countries.   This dimension is important both tactically and strategically, and accordingly receives considerable treatment, as it is a prime consideration in all aspects of counterinsurgency.

When faced with an insurgency, a government must respond as promptly and as positively as possible, particularly to redress grievances. Its response should address the root causes of the insurgency with a clear plan supported by a range of social, economic, legal, and administrative measures in addition to military activity. The words of General Sir Frank Kitson remind us that "insurgency is not primarily a military activity," and thus the Portuguese government's response could not be exclusively military.[45]   The Portuguese authorities identified the social dimension as the key to retaining Africa and consequently oriented their doctrine and the soldier's duties in this direction.   "National mobilization must not then rely exclusively on the armed forces, but absolutely on a country's every resource: teaching and education, hygiene and health, public works and communications, agronomy and veterinary medicine, industry and mining...each and every one must be, as with the military, a force mobilized to intervene in the struggle when and where needed."[46] Writers of the Portuguese doctrine divided the social dimension into two parts, the Army's support of civil efforts and the promotion of these activities through a program of psychological operations.

The support for civic action was initially limited and focused on "providing intelligence, reinforcing police operations or acting in cooperation with them in maintaining order, guaranteeing control of the population, and assuring the maintenance of essential services, when necessary."[47] The initial thrust was to use the military to maintain law and order, and the doctrine consequently stresses as its central theme the support of and coordination with all of the elements of the Portuguese civil arms, which were initially identified as police forces but later expanded to cover all civil authority.[48] As insurgencies are primarily wars for the people's loyalty, there were aspects besides the suppression of violence that demanded attention. The military was to effect a new psychosocial program, a program in which Portuguese soldiers provided not only local protection from insurgent intimidation but the manpower to build schools, teach in the schools, drill wells, and initiate basic medical, health, and sanitation services. This effort required coordination not only across common civil-military disciplines, such as the medical services, but also between every level within such a dichotomy.[49] This coordination was a particularly foreign concept and practice for the normal soldier, who regarded his duties primarily in the conventional war context of killing the enemy. It was thus vital for the doctrine to explain these aspects of counterinsurgency to him, as his awareness of and participation in civil-military measures was the key to victory within the population. The originators of the French *guerre révolutionnaire* theory had witnessed the strong civil-military coordination in the Indochinese insurgents and felt that it must be matched from the counterinsurgency side as well. The Portuguese Army had seen the benefits of this strong civil-military coordination on its visits to Algeria and its observation of *guerre révolutionnaire* principles in operation. In its doctrine the Portuguese Army adapted these French principles to its operation and reflected them in its doctrine.

Colonel Carlos da Costa Gomes Bessa commented on reorienting the Portuguese soldier to civil support, based on his later experience in implementing the doctrine as a staff officer responsible for civil-military coordination: "for the various organs which constituted the countersubversive structure there were civil and military principals responsible at their respective levels."[50] Colonel Gomes Bessa also stressed the importance of having not only an interlocking relationship but also a positive, cohesive one: "With respect to civil-military collaboration, which is indispensable to the proper functioning of a countersubversion structure, more than the organization, all depends on the attitude and training of the people for the task of their respective functions, and is the reason for which their selection is the most important determinant factor."[51] Colonel Gomes Bessa described the problem-solving process in this relationship as being one in which no problem was considered too difficult to solve and that it was the preferred method to make decisions at the lowest possible level, as it was here that people would be immediately affected and benefit most.[52] Elevating the decisionmaking to those without an immediate interest might evoke the wrong solution. Indeed, the process should begin at the level of the local commissions (*comissões locais*) that had direct contact with the population, as they were "in a better position to understand, capture and transmit the true concerns and aspirations" of the people.[53] These commissions proved a valuable tool as a local-level vehicle for political participation in countering the insurgent's promises. Through this process the doctrine was expanded to include the following broad programs in the Army's psychosocial operations:

- Social: —Education
          —Sanitary assistance
          —Economic development in agriculture and cattle husbandry
          —Local infrastructure improvements
- Communications
- Self-defense of localities and villages.[54]

The process in civil-military coordination was initially focused on augmenting the various police functions, as law and order were the primary concerns. The perspective was later widened from security concerns to include an extensive range of social programs and the need for a plan with a single point of responsibility and effective coordination at every level to achieve a unity of effort. Portugal, in making dramatic changes in the treatment of its African population, instructed the soldier in his duties and explained his role in the social dimension.

The second aspect of the social dimension was Portuguese psychological operations (PSYOP, or in Portuguese, APSIC officially, or *Psico* unofficially), which were designed to promote the Portuguese sociopolitical efforts to the target audience of the African population in Portuguese Africa and its neighboring states. The Portuguese also saw PSYOP as an important tool of warfare in that if an opponent's attitude can be influenced favorably, then his physical resistance will diminish. With this effect in combination with other military, diplomatic, or social operations, PSYOP acts as a "force multiplier" by enhancing the result of those operations on the target.[55] The nationalist movements and their soldiers were key targets of Portuguese PSYOP. The Portuguese also designed PSYOP to support the other elements of their counter-subversive strategy and became accomplished in this science.

At the outbreak of hostilities several PSYOP dynamics were apparent. First, prior to 1961 there was only a small PSYOP department in the Portuguese Army. In the 1958–1959 period the missions to Algeria observed the French application of PSYOP and saw immediate application to the *ultramar*. The reports of these officers and their experience with the Service d'Action Psychologique et d'Information (SAPI) in Algeria were thus the beginning of the Portuguese competence in this field.[56] SAPI had been established by Colonel Lacheroy in April 1956 and was a powerful agency for spreading the *guerre révolutionnaire* doctrine.

The French position was that "proper psychological measures could create and maintain ideological cohesion among fighters and their civilian supporters."[57] The Portuguese also believed this premise valid and elected to begin with their soldiers and expand the appeal to the population through them. The most effective medium in targeting the African people was the Portuguese soldier who was in daily contact with the population. The Army was to be during the wars "a psychological 'weapon' of overwhelming value both defensively and offensively."[58] Accordingly, PSYOP doctrine and principles were included in his instruction from the earliest stages of the war. The soldier's understanding of the PSYOP process was vital to its successful application, and his continuing awareness was emphasized through reports and writings that were circulated regularly in all of the military zones.

THE LOGISTICAL (ADMINISTRATIVE) DIMENSION

This dimension of administrative and logistic support is the preponderant factor in the efficiency of military forces in any campaign. As Colonel P. D. Foxton, a British Army logistician reminds us: "It is logistics which moves armies to where they can fight. It is logistics which keeps weapon systems firing and maintained. Indeed, so important is logistics that it features as a principal factor in almost every soldier's appreciation of the task facing him, and in the plan that is finally made."[59] Within NATO, logistics is defined as the science of planning the movement and maintenance of forces.[60] These are essentially unglamorous activities generally lumped together by most armies under a catch-all title of "administration" or "administration and logistics." They comprise such functions as transportation, supply, medical evacuation and hospitalization, and other smaller services. In grand wars logistics are the limiting factor to any campaign. In low-intensity conflict they are not normally as vital, causing Major General Julian Thompson, Royal Marines, to observe, "[Low-intensity operations] provided few examples where logistics played an important part in their success, or otherwise."[61] In this campaign, however, they were vital to Portugal in fighting a counterinsurgency as far as 10,300 kilometers from home.

Portugal believed that in subversive war this support was doubly important for two reasons:

- Morale of the troops assumes a much more elevated role in this environment and is thus more fickle in regard to the functioning of support,
- The level of this morale affects troop relations with the population and vice-versa, and thus the psychosocial program.[62]

Consequently, the characteristics of subversive war in Portugal's case confer special relevance on administration and logistics as a factor of success in the conduct of operations. The topic is so complex that a subsequent chapter is devoted to examining the unique aspects of this support.

TIMELINESS AND IMPORTANCE OF
O EXÉRCITO NA GUERRA SUBVERSIVA

The Portuguese Army's development of its counterinsurgency doctrine is a reflection of Portugal's overall sensitivity to its colonies and their vulnerability, and to its role in their defense. The advent of wars of national liberation with their Cold War undercurrent heightened this Army responsibility. The embroilment of France in Algeria (1954–1962) and of Britain in Malaya (1948–1960), Kenya (1952–1960), and Cyprus (1955–1960) further served as strong warning signals. Accordingly, the Portuguese Army began its earnest work in 1960 and accelerated this effort in the months just prior to and during the opening of the Campaigns.

The Portuguese Army had had a long history of and experience in African operations and knew the vagaries of the terrain and populations well. It had studied the theory and principles of subversive war for the better part of a decade and sought the French and British perspectives on this type of conflict to refine its own understanding. As it proceeded to write its doctrine for the coming wars, it drew heavily on the experiences and theories of these two colonial allies.

In neither of the foregoing cases was there a formal counterinsurgency doctrine on which the Portuguese Army could model its projected work. Although the British published theater doctrines for Malaya (1952) and Kenya (1954), and these volumes were valuable to the Portuguese, the War Office did not issue a formal counterinsurgency doctrine until 1960. In France there was a substantial amount of material written on *guerre révolutionnaire* and its application to Algeria, but the French Ministry of the Army also did not issue an official written doctrine until 1960.

The Portuguese Army assiduously gathered material from those militaries fighting counterinsurgencies, sifted through the information for its application to the portending conflict in Portuguese Africa, and created a timely doctrine for the Portuguese soldier. The concepts and practices in the preliminary doctrine were tested in the beginning months of the conflict in Angola and earlier at the CIOE in Lamego. Refinement and formal publication occurred in 1963, less than three years after the process had begun. The Portuguese Army through this methodology sought to avoid the lengthy and expensive problem that the British had faced in Malaya, Kenya, and Cyprus, in which troops sent to fight an insurgency arrived "not knowing what it was all about" and had no doctrine to guide them.[63] It had devoted considerable and thorough research to the type and style of counterinsurgency operations appropriate to Portuguese Africa, always appreciating the value of and need for effective and inexpensive tactics. As a result, *O Exército na Guerra Subversiva* is a counterinsurgency doctrine that was appropriate both to Portugal's means and to the circumstances in Africa that it faced and was delivered in time for the conflict. The basic tenets of this prewar doctrine and thinking remained valid throughout the Campaigns, and as we shall see, these principles influenced and guided the entire Portuguese war effort.

NOTES

1. Estado-Maior do Exército, *Subsídios para o Estudo da Doutrina Aplicada nas Campanhas de África (1961–1974)* [Aid to the Study of Doctrine Applied in the Campaigns of Africa (1961–1974)] (Lisbon: Estado-Maior do Exército, 1990), 28.

2. Staff of the Instituto de Altos Estudos Militares, *O Instituto de Altos Estudos Militares* [The Institute of Higher Military Studies] (Lisbon: Instituto de Altos Estudos Militares, 1987), 8–11.

3. Kaúlza de Arriaga, "Portuguese National Defense the Last 40 Years and in the Future," lecture delivered on 20 October 1966, Lisbon.

4. Estado-Maior do Exército, *Resenha Histórico-Militar das Campanhas de África (1961-1974)* [Historical-Military Report of the Campaigns of Africa (1961-1974)] (Lisbon: Estado-Maior do Exército, 1988), Vol. I, 176.

5. Kaúlza de Arriaga, *Guerra e Política* [War and Policy] (Lisbon: Edições Refrendo, 1987), 119.

6. *Regulamento de Campanha* [Principles of Campaigning] (series), (Lisbon: Estado-Maior do Exército, 1954).

7. Arriaga, 119-120.

8. Practical Schools of the Army: Infantry at Mafra; Engineers at Tancos; Artillery at Vendas Novas; Cavalry at Torres Novas and Santarem.

9. Brigadeiro Renato F. Marques Pinto, correspondence with the author, 6 September 1995, Oeiras.

10. Pedro Cardoso, *As Informações em Portugal* [Intelligence in Portugal] (Lisbon: Instituto da Defesa Nacional, 1980), 106.

11. *Keeping the Peace (Duties in Support of the Civil Power)* (London: Her Majesty's Stationery Office, 1957). This manual was originally published in 1949 and was obsolete from the start, although the War Office did not see fit to revise it until 1957.

12. Marques Pinto correspondence, 6 September 1995.

13. Ibid.

14. Jean Valluy, "Au Sujet du Manifeste des 81," *Revue Militaire Générale* (October 1961): 282.

15. Jean Valluy, "Acerca do Manifesto de Guerra Fria" [About the Manifesto of the Cold War], trans. and ed. E. Q. Magalhães, *Boletim Militar* (Região Militar de Angola) (15 February 1963): 27; Arslan Humbaraci and Nicole Muchnick, *Portugal's African Wars* (New York: The Third Press, 1974), 40-41. The authors quote Amílcar Cabral's citation of an Armed Forces General Staff report of the Psychological Section No. 15 dated September 1971 and showing the results of the Soviet policy: "The proliferation of anti-government organizations and the agitation that they create leads to an unsuitable psychological climate which, by affecting the activities of students, affects the country, which seems troubled and does not know what to do to lead its children back to the right path...In the metropolis generally, the population continues to show little interest in the war overseas and ignores the efforts being made by the armed forces. The student masses remain vulnerable to pacifist propaganda."

16. Colonel Luís Alberto Santiago Inocentes, interview by the author, 2 September 1994, London. General unrest at the universities began in 1960, and by the fall of 1961 there were open demonstrations against military activity in Angola. The Soviet aim was to achieve optimally a negative attitude in the student population and minimally a passive attitude.

17. Marques Pinto correspondence, 13 November 1995, Oeiras. Major Nunes da Silva was promoted to Lieutenant Colonel in November 1960.

18. Marques Pinto correspondence, 6 September 1995; Inocentes interview, 18 March 1994. Colonel Inocentes was enrolled in the CEM from 1959 to 1962 and worked on the subversive warfare doctrine.

19. Estado-Maior do Exército, *O Exército na Guerra Subversiva* [The Army in Subversive War], 5 vols. (Lisbon: Estado-Maior do Exército, 1963; revised, 1966).

20. Bruce Hoffman and Jennifer M. Taw, *Defense Policy and Low-Intensity Conflict: The Development of Britain's "Small Wars" Doctrine During the 1950s* (Santa Monica: Rand Corporation, 1991), vi, vii; Thomas R. Mockaitis, *British Counterinsurgency, 1919–1960* (London: Macmillan, 1990), 13–14.

21. *Army Field Manual* (Series), British Army General Staff (Year).

22. Hoffman and Taw, vii.

23. *The Conduct of Anti-Terrorist Operations in Malaya* (Kuala Lumpur: Federation of Malaysia, 1952); *A Handbook of Anti-Mau Mau Operations* (Nairobi: Government of Kenya, 1954).

24. Peter Paret, *French Revolutionary Warfare from Indochina to Algeria: The Analysis of a Political and Military Doctrine* (London: Pall Mall Press, 1964), 7.

25. General José Luís Almiro Canêlhas, interview by the author, 3 April 1995, Lisbon. General Canêlhas went to Algeria in the second group of observers of the 1959–1960 period.

26. Department of the Army, *FM 31-20 Operations Against Guerrilla Forces* (Washington: Government Printing Office, 1951); Department of the Army, *FM 31-15 Operations Against Airborne Attack, Guerrilla Action and Infiltration* (Washington: Government Printing Office, 1953).

27. Andrew F. Krepinevich, Jr., *The Army and Vietnam* (Baltimore: Johns Hopkins University Press, 1986), 39.

28. Colonel Hermes de Araújo Oliveira, *Guerra Revolucionária* [Revolutionary War] (Lisbon: Privately printed, 1960). The author visited Algeria alone prior to the 1959 mission of Major Franco Pinheiro and returned to duties as the Professor of Geography and Military History at the Academia Militar, where he gave five lectures on revolutionary war. These lectures were edited and published as this volume under the patronage of the Ministry of the Army.

29. *Subsídios para o Estudo da Doutrina Aplicada nas Campanhas de África (1961–1974)*, 138.

30. Ibid., 34.

31. Douglas L. Wheeler, "The Portuguese Army in Angola," *Modern African Studies*, 7, no. 3 (October 1969): 426.

32. Joaquim Moreira da Silva Cunha, *O Ultramar, a Nação e o "25 de Abril"* [The Overseas Provinces, the Nation and the "25th of April"] (Coimbra: Atlântida Editora, 1977), 31–32.

33. General José Manuel de Bethencourt Rodrigues, interview by the author, 9 November 1994, Pedrouços (Lisbon).

34. Mao Tse-tung, *On Guerrilla Warfare*, trans. Samuel B. Griffith II (New York: Frederick A. Praeger, 1961); Vo Nguyen Giap, *People's War, People's Army* (New York: Frederick A. Praeger, 1962).

35. Joaquim António Franco Pinheiro, Hermes de Araújo Oliveira, and Jaime de Oliveira Leandro, *Subversão e Counter-Subversão* [Subversion and Countersubversion], Estudos de Ciências Políticas e Sociais No. 62, Junta de Investigações do Ultramar

(Lisbon: Centro de Estudos Políticos e Sociais, 1963)

36. Joaquim António Franco Pinheiro, "Natureza e Fundamentos da Guerra Subversiva" [The Nature and Fundamentals of Subversive War], *Subversão e Counter-Subversão* [Subversion and Countersubversion], Estudos de Ciências Políticas e Sociais No. 62, Junta de Investigações do Ultramar (Lisbon: Centro de Estudos Políticos e Sociais, 1963), 24–25.

37. *O Exército na Guerra Subversiva*, Vol. I, Chapter I, 11–15.

38. Ibid., Vol. I, Chapter II, 19.

39. Ibid.

40. Estado-Maior do Exército, *Guia para o Emprego Táctico das Pequenas Unidades na Contra Guerrilha* [Guide for the Tactical Employment of Small Units in Counter Guerrilla Warfare], Part 1, *O Exército na Guerra Subversiva* [The Army in Subversive War] (Lisbon: Estado-Maior do Exército, 1961).

41. Col. Charles E. Callwell, *Small Wars: A Tactical Textbook for Imperial Soldiers* (London: Her Majesty's Stationery Office, 1896; reprint, London: Lionel Leventhal, 1990), 125.

42. Jaíme de Oliveira Leandro, "As Acções Contra-Revolucionárias e a sua Técnica" [Counter-Revolutionary Operations and Its Technique], *Revista Militar* (January 1963): 54–55.

43. Hermes de Araújo Oliveira, "A Reposta à Guerra Subversiva" [The Response to Subversive War], *Subversão e Counter-Subversão*, Estudos de Ciências Políticas e Sociais No. 62, Junta de Investigações do Ultramar (Lisbon: Centro de Estudos Políticos e Sociais, 1963), 55.

44. Brigadeiro Renato F. Marques Pinto, interview by the author, 30 March 1995, Oeiras.

45. Frank Kitson, *Bunch of Five* (London: Faber and Faber, 1977), 282.

46. Hermes de Araújo Oliveira, "Guerra Subversiva: Subsídios para uma Estratégia de Reacção" [Subversive War: Information for a Strategy of Response], *Revista Militar* (November 1964): 672.

47. *O Exército na Guerra Subversiva*, Vol. IV, v.

48. Ibid., Vol. IV, Annex A, 1-5.

49. Ibid., Vol. IV, Chapter I, 1.

50. Carlos da Costa Gomes Bessa, "Angola: A Luta Contra a Subversão e a Colaboração Civil-Militar" [Angola: The Fight Against Subversion and Civil-Military Collaboration], *Revista Militar* (August–September 1972): 421.

51. Ibid., 424.

52. Colonel Carlos da Costa Gomes Bessa, interview by the author, 18 November 1995, Lisbon.

53. Gomes Bessa, "Angola," 427.

54. Ibid., 435.

55. Glenn Curtis, *An Overview of Psychological Operations (PSYOP)* (Hurlburt Field, Fla.: USAF Special Operations Command, 1990), 2.

56. Estado-Maior do Exército, *Resenha Histórico-Militar das Campanhas de África (1961-1974)* [Historical Military Report on the African Campaigns (1961-1974)] (Lisbon: Estado-Maior do Exército, 1988), Vol. I, 397.

57. Paret, 7.

58. *O Exército na Guerra Subversiva*, Vol. III, vi.

59. P. D. Foxton, *Powering War: Modern Land Force Logistics* (London: Brassey's, 1994), 2.

60. *The North Atlantic Treaty Organization: Facts and Figures* (Brussels: NATO Information Services, 1989), 253.

61. Julian Thompson, *The Lifeblood of War: Logistics in Armed Conflict* (London: Brassey's, 1991), xiv.

62. *O Exército na Guerra Subversiva*, Vol. V, v.

63. Hoffman and Taw, 1, 20.

4

PORTUGUESE ORGANIZATION, EDUCATION, AND TRAINING FOR COUNTERINSURGENCY

In 1960 the Portuguese Army along with the entire defense establishment had completed a reorganization begun in 1937 and designed to modernize its structure. The purpose of this lengthy evolution had been to unify the defense organization and place the Portuguese armed forces on a conventional war footing with their NATO partners. Portugal was now faced with a new and different type of war that required immediate adjustments if it were to prevail over the nationalist movements and their military arms of guerrillas. The luxury of a two-decade leisurely reorganization could not be afforded. Portugal would have to restructure its military forces, and train and educate them in record time to become an effective counterinsurgency force that could meet the immediate challenge of a "war of national liberation." This chapter selectively describes this reorganization and the search for solutions in implementing these wholesale changes. It compares this adjustment with that of other armies fighting contemporary counterinsurgencies as a measure of the Portuguese achievement.

MILITARILY UNPREPARED *ULTRAMAR*

Prior to 1950 Portugal had in effect two distinct armies. The primary force was stationed in the *metrópole* and was the one on which the country depended for its defense and which was the responsibility of the Ministry of War. The other consisted of forces stationed in the *ultramar* and was the portfolio of the Ministry of the Colonies. In 1950 the responsibility for the entire armed forces was unified under the Ministry of National Defense, and the Ministry of War became the Ministry of the Army on an equal standing with its Navy and Air Force counterparts. This change and subsequent ones occurred as a result of Portugal's post-World War II integration into NATO and the influence that the alliance had on its military thinking. The move at this level also began in 1953 from the "*Tipo Português*" methods to those of the "*Tipo Americano*".[1] This shift in organizational philosophy was reflected in a reshaped army, and as 1961 approached, it grew to look very much like the U.S. force structure, a conventional army trained and equipped to fight Soviet forces in Europe.

These reorganizations and expansions had had the effect of modernizing the Portuguese armed forces within the limits of national resources and had laid the foundation for the further expansion required to conduct the African Campaigns of 1961–1974.[2] This modernization included construction of an improved national infrastructure and acquisition of new weaponry for use in Europe as part of the NATO commitment. It also had the effect of developing the proficiency of Portugal's armed forces in the operational processes of waging modern war. The gains in new skills, equipment, and facilities put them on a par in force quality with the other front-line NATO militaries. This focus was European at the expense of the colonies.

After World War II and prior to the incidents of 1961 the troop disposition in Angola and the other colonies had been reduced to very modest numbers, and on 31 December 1960 there were approximately 6,500 military personnel in the colony, 1,500 European and 5,000 locally recruited troops.[3] In Guiné and Mozambique figures for this date are unavailable; however, one year later there were 4,736 troops in Guiné (3,736 European and 1,000 locally recruited troops) and 11,209 troops in Mozambique (8,209 European and 3,000 locally recruited troops).[4] In all cases the great majority of these were employed in local security and the recruiting and training of African and local European soldiers. They were consequently scattered throughout the territory of each colony rather than concentrated in any area of potential trouble. Further, the military commanders in each of the three theaters could not have brought these forces together quickly in countering a local threat because of the vastness of Angola and Mozambique and the difficult terrain of Guiné. The limited capability of infrastructure to serve military mobility requirements in each of the three colonies further inhibited any rapid concentration of troops. It cannot be surprising that these small numbers dispersed so widely in each theater were unable to defend Angola or any other territory successfully against the likes of the March 1961 attacks. The most telling fact in the Angola incident was that following these assaults seventy-seven days elapsed until Battalion 88 under the command of Lieutenant Colonel Pinheiro arrived on 31 May at Damba, a city in the center of the devastation, and assumed responsibility for securing an area of 12,000 square kilometers.[5]

The Portuguese proceeded to reinforce Angola throughout the year, as well as Guiné and Mozambique, in anticipation of additional trouble. By the end of 1961 there were 49,422 military personnel in the three colonies, and the jacquerie had been subdued.[6] But Portugal's war machine had not been prepared, and much work lay ahead if it were to defeat the nationalists and regain the confidence and loyalty of its population. The immediate and obvious lesson that the Portuguese Army learned in this initial action was that its conventional force was ill-suited to wage a counterinsurgency. It lacked almost every quality that was necessary in this type of conflict. Britain had entered Malaya, Kenya, and Cyprus unprepared, France had done the same in Algeria, and Portugal now found itself in similar circumstances.[7] Portugal set about the task of building an army tailored for combat against an unconventional enemy in a forbidding environment far from home.

CAMPAIGN ORGANIZATION FOR COUNTERINSURGENCY

The first serious events in Angola prompted a remodeling of the command structure in the territories in which the duties of the Commander of the Military Region for each theater, who was part of the territorial organization, and the Commander-in-Chief of each theater were separated. The Commander-in-Chief assumed additional duties as the local Provincial Governor, bringing him closer to the people and their needs. This development came with a deeper recognition that the conflict was as much a struggle to gain the loyalty of the population through socioeconomic activity as it was a military effort. The Commander of the Military Region was dependent through the administrative chain of command on the Chief of Staff of the Army, the Ministry of the Army, and the Chief of the General Staff of the Armed Forces for support in effecting the preparation, mobilization, administration, and discipline of elements under his command.[8] Somewhat later this same structure was implemented in Guiné (1963) and Mozambique (1964), as the conflict developed.

With the passage of time the Commanders-in-Chief played an increasing role in operational matters, until ultimately toward 1969 the Commanders of the Military Regions were withdrawn from this responsibility and assumed a support role for both military and civil efforts. The Commanders-in-Chief thus became responsible for intelligence and operations in an operational chain of command to the Chief of the General Staff, while the Commander of the Military Region continued to be responsible for administration, logistics, and instruction, and reported to the Chief of Staff of the Army.[9] Below these levels were the Territorial Commanders and Intervention Zone Commanders. The Territorial Commanders were largely administrative, presided over a low-threat environment, and consequently reported through the Commander of the Military Region. Intervention Zone Commanders were largely operational, faced a combat situation, depended on the Commander of the Military Region for administrative and logistical support, and reported to the Commander-in-Chief. These adjustments reflect the assumption of an increasing pacification role by the military and were an attempt to respond to combat conditions as they evolved in the *ultramar*.

The Territorial Commanders and their organization represented the original, prewar structure responsible for the security of Portugal and its colonies. It was also a key element of the military organization and formed part of the Army's organizational structure at the campaign and tactical levels. It oversaw the recruitment, formation, mobilization, and logistic and administrative support of military contingents needed for the wars. While the territorial organization had a long history and tradition, the modern organization was a reflection of the experience gained in the 1895 Campaigns of Africa as well as the country's more recent participation in World War II and in NATO.

In the *ultramar* at the beginning of the Campaigns, the territorial commands were subordinated to the general headquarters of their respective military region and were the purview of the Commander of the Military Region. Each of these commands was subdivided into zones. Each zone was further subdivided into sectors. Sectors were again divided into zones of operation (*zona de acção*) and assigned to a battalion commander and his companies. The battalion commander normally directed the activities within a *zona de acção*.[10]

This *quadrillage* concept had been modified from the French Army strategy of pacification in Algeria and introduced into Angola by General Carlos Miguel Lopes da Silva Freire. The system entailed full cooperation between the military, the police, and the civil administration at all levels. The accent was traditionally on the prominent force in the area. In cities it was the police. In the rural areas it was the army. Each supposedly helped the other, and the entire effort was linked to a civil development program and the protection of the population from insurgent intimidation.

During the period of transition in the status and duties of the Commander of the Military Region as dictated by the course of the wars, there was a division of responsibility according to enemy activity. In areas of little or no enemy activity, battalion operations would be coordinated through the Territorial Commander or at the regimental field command level. In a high-threat environment, a special sector would be created to address the problem, and the senior battalion commander appointed as the sector commander (*comando de sector*) to oversee and coordinate battalion activity.[11] Often a battalion was the only one in a special sector, and its commander was also the *comando de sector*. In this case, he would report to the Commander-in-Chief, Commander of the Military Region, or Zone Commander, as assigned.[12]

From time to time, particularly in the early years of the campaigns, when insurgent activity was comparatively widespread, several sectors would be combined in a zone of intervention (*zona de intervenção*). When the conflict began in Mozambique in September 1964, it was necessary to establish a zone there that extended north from the Zambezi River to the Tanzanian border on the Ruvuma River.[13] Its commander was located in Nampula in a forward command post (*posto de comando avançado*), as the general headquarters of the military region was distant in Lourenço Marques. Similarly, in anticipation of insurgent activity that developed in the east of Angola in 1966 with the Chipenda faction of the MPLA, a comparable zone (*Zona de Intervenção Leste*) previously established in 1961 with its commander strategically relocated to Luso was augmented from battalion strength to command by a brigadier in 1966. Because of the nature of the war in Mozambique and its concentration along the

Tanzanian border, the general headquarters of the military region and of the Commander-in-Chief was moved to Nampula in November 1969, and the term "intervention zone" was changed to "operational zone" (*zona operacional*) in 1971 as a matter of the Commander-in-Chief's style.

Each of the changes described represented an effort to protect the population as much as to destroy the enemy by using a mutually supporting zone system. The British Army in Malaya (1948–1960) used a tactical organization known as framework deployment, which was similar to the Portuguese arrangement. Malaya was divided into districts that were normally the responsibility of an infantry battalion. These districts would have corresponded to the Portuguese zones of operation (*zona de acção*) or, later in the war, special sectors. The battalion's companies each occupied an assigned sector of the district. From time to time it was possible to retain one company as a reserve for unforeseen circumstances, but normally the districts were so large that such reserves could be maintained only at the higher levels of command. Each company knew its assigned sector intimately and was thus able to hunt there effectively. Maintaining a fixed assignment for a company proved to be very important, as the troops would become familiar with the terrain and the habits of the local guerrillas (Chinese terrorists or CTs), and this acclimatization would give them a proficiency that otherwise efficient units introduced to a strange sector could not duplicate. These infantry companies permanently assigned to a sector were able to act immediately on intelligence with devastating results.[14]

The French in Algeria (1954–1962) addressed the concentration of guerrilla forces inside the country by covering it with a checkerboard of outposts. This *quadrillage* depended on the thorough knowledge of local conditions that the troops in each post possessed. The duties of these troops included routine security and police work, collecting intelligence, various construction projects, and limited military operations. Whenever possible the troops were permanently assigned to these posts to maintain the continuity of their relationship with the local citizens and knowledge of area operation conditions. These local garrisons were reinforced by mobile units that helped to foil guerrilla contact with the population. Larger offensive operations were performed by an intervention force, the *Reserve Générale*, composed of elite troops. In the latter stages of the war about 300,000 troops were committed to the *quadrillage* system and an additional 10 percent or 30,000, to the *Reserve Générale*.[15] This system worked well against a widely dispersed guerrilla force, and was adopted and modified by the Portuguese Army for certain situations in its Campaigns.

The Portuguese had failures as well in limiting guerrilla access to their people. The fact that they were not always successful, however, does not negate the effort. One such example occurred between 1968 and 1969, when the Portuguese stationed a company of infantry in the *posto* of Madina do Boé in the eastern expanse of Guiné next to its southern border with the Republic of Guinea. The area was isolated, remote, and sparsely inhabited. Sent there to administer to and defend the civil population and to interdict the PAIGC incursions from Guinea, the troops found the situation impossible. There were very few people who needed help, no structures of any importance to preserve, and dozens of kilometers of permeable frontier. Other than protecting the odd bridge and the occasional *tabanca* (very small local settlement), its main job was that of defending itself.[16] There was a reluctance to withdraw the company from its untenable and overextended position, as the PAIGC would then declare the region "liberated." A similar situation had developed earlier in the more eastern zone of Beli, and upon Portuguese troop withdrawal the PAIGC had declared the area to be a "liberated zone." Eventually the same situation developed with the withdrawal of the company at Madina in 1969, and the PAIGC proceeded to entertain foreign journalists on Portuguese soil with the consequent unwanted publicity. The area was of no economic value, the sparse population was not strategically important to either side, and the Portuguese troops were better utilized in other duties. In hindsight it is apparent that the civil and military resources in this case were not part of a joint plan thoroughly coordinated. Then, too, the jungles and swamps of Guiné provided protective cover for the guerrillas that the *bled* of Algeria lacked. The French more easily dispersed and destroyed guerrillas in these areas and were able to protect their outposts more effectively than did the Portuguese at Madina do Boé.

While the Portuguese command structure was described in laws and regulations, their interpretation and the actual solutions differed from one theater to another. These differences depended on various factors, such as the expanse of the theater, the tempo of the conflict, the personalities of the Commanders-in-Chief, and their relations with Lisbon. Because of these factors each structure had evolved somewhat differently over the course of the Campaigns. Nevertheless, they represented the command and control solution to the problems of each theater and were effective in maintaining pressure on the enemy. Each is the result of a continuing reassessment in the midst of war and represents a willingness to learn and adapt.[17]

The Portuguese constantly sought to rethink and refine their command and force structure to address the execution of their counterinsurgency plan, which sought to maintain the initiative through the long-term patrolling of small areas, operating extensively at night, acting on intelligence about the insurgents' infrastructure, and maintaining contact with the population. While mistakes were made, solutions were sought within their resources, and they never lost sight of the fact that the purpose of their armed forces was to cement this all-important relationship with the people.[18] To this end the gradual and ponderous changes in the campaign command structure supported the implementation of established counterinsurgency principles adapted to the *ultramar*.

ORGANIZATION FOR CIVIL-MILITARY COORDINATION

The Portuguese knew that this struggle was a war that the military could not win on its own. The intricate web of civil administration, police, and military had to be woven into a cohesive whole, capable of functioning as a war machine. The Portuguese honored the concept explained by Sir Gerald Templer soon after being appointed High Commissioner for Malaya in 1951: "I should like it to be clearly understood that in Malaya we are conducting the campaign against communism on all fronts. We are fighting not only on the military front, but on the political, social, and economic fronts as well."[19] The Portuguese were no less emphatic in the definition of their own intent, as described by Lieutenant Colonel Oliveira of the General Staff of the Army: "National mobilization must not rely exclusively on the armed forces, but absolutely on a country's every resource."[20]

The Portuguese wrestled with the proper method of integrating the military and civil structures in the most efficient way. During the wars they considered and used three:

- Parallel civil and military structures
- A single military structure
- A mixed structure with a combination of civil and military organizations.[21]

They saw advantages and drawbacks to each of these systems. The first was employed in normal circumstances when the colonies were at peace and included the initial period of subversion in which preventive measures were being taken. The daily lives of the population remained largely unaffected. Because the two systems were separate, it was not easy to coordinate between the two structures at all levels, and there was always the possibility of conflicting objectives and a duplication of effort.

The second was used when the civil government had lost control of the situation and was unable to function in the face of insurgent activity. Military intervention became necessary and a military government was established to coordinate the civil and military functions. Military functions were substituted for civil ones, or civil functions were integrated into the military hierarchy. This system ensured a convergence of civil and military objectives, a unity of enforcement, and a close coordination at every level. The drawback was the suspension of certain civil liberties and the consequent inconvenience and disruption of the normal routine of the population.

The third was initiated once the situation had stabilized and was envisioned as the proper vehicle for pacification operations. There was considerable debate over just how to establish the mixed structure, having one side dominate or having the civil and military work together, with each dominating certain sectors of government. In Guiné, the system was unipolar with a single person responsible for both the civil and military functions. This system adhered to the principle of unity of command and was ideal for countersubversion. In Angola and Mozambique the bipolar system was used. This system diluted the principle of unity of command but was adopted for political or psychological reasons or as a concession to the civil government, and depended on a clear understanding and perfected coordination between the two authorities. This coordination was achieved through the Provincial Defense Councils, which represented an integration of the duties of the Governors-General and Commanders-in-Chief. While in the unipolar system these two offices were embodied in one person and thus functioned as an executive organization, the bipolar system was in comparison labor-intensive, in that it was a committee organization in which many people needed to coordinate at each level. The decision-making process was slow and cumbersome because of the diverse nature and interests of these participants; nevertheless, all sought to overcome the inherent weaknesses of the bipolar system and to make it work.

Probably the largest impediment to coordination in either system between civil and military authorities was the structural rigidity in each. The armed forces struggled internally in coordinating operations of the three services under a theater Commander-in-Chief. Often the in-theater service chiefs were senior to the theater Commander-in-Chief and resented assigning operational control to a junior. If the armed forces suffered from organizational arteriosclerosis, then the civil departments were even more affected.[22] Health, education, public works, veterinary, agronomy, and the other departments were part of a rigid structure with a strong inbred resistance to change to cope with the war needs. This inflexibility manifested itself in conflict between the civil governor and the Commander-in-Chief in a bipolar system, and success came only when the posts were combined. In Guiné the system worked relatively well, as General António de Spínola held both offices. However, it was never easy to make the civilian departments understand that civil and military doctors could work side by side in civilian hospitals or that sergeants could teach alongside the civilian staff of the education departments.[23] The military tended to encounter civil problems more broadly because of its size and mobility and consequent increased contact with the population. The civilian departments tended to be office-bound, and because of their limited budgets, to be reduced in presence and authority. For instance, the Chief of the Health Department in Guiné had four doctors in the field while the Army Medical Corps had forty.[24] The Chief of Public Works and Communications had two engineers able to repair two miles of road per day, while the Army Engineering Corps had twenty engineers and a workforce adequate to rebuild twenty miles of road a day, including the repair of bridges.[25]

Notwithstanding the problems stemming from the differences in resources, structurally the military and civil systems were parallel. In the case of both the single and the bipolar system, the military commands equated to the political subdivisions in the continuing effort to coordinate activities and obtain a unity of effort, as shown below:

- *Província* (Province) = Military Region or Territorial Command
- *Distrito* (District) = Territorial Command or Military Command
- *Concelho* or *Circunscrição* = Military Command or battalion-size Unit
- *Postos, Freguesias* (Parish), or *Aldeias* (Settlement) = Units or Detachments.[26]

In Mozambique, for example, in 1963 there were three Territorial Commands having limits coinciding with the boundaries of districts:

Northern Territorial Command (CTN): All districts north of the Zambezi River: Niassa, Cabo Delgado, Moçambique, and Zambezia.
Central Territorial Command (CTC): All districts between the Zambezi and Save Rivers: Tete and Manica e Sofala.
Southern Territorial Command (CTS): All districts south of the Save River: Inhambane, Gaza, and Lourenço Marques.[27]

At the end of 1964 CTN was redesignated the Northern Intervention Zone (ZIN) and subdivided into three sectors corresponding to the three districts:

Sector A—District of Niassa
Sector B—District of Cabo Delgado
Sector C—District of Moçambique.[28]

As an example of the coordination required, it is helpful to examine the countersubversion organization at the provincial level for Angola as it existed in 1971. There were four levels of organization:

- Provincial Council for Countersubversion (province level), which included the Governor-General, who acted as its president, the Commander-in-Chief, the Secretary-General, the Provincial Secretaries, and the local commanders of the three military services
- Countersubversion and Inspection Groups (there were three: Silva Porto, Luanda, and Nova Lisboa)
- District Councils for Countersubversion (district level)
- Local Commissions for Countersubversion (*concelho* and/or *posto* level).

Each of these bodies had both civil and military members and addressed diverse problems at their respective levels. Often the Catholic Church, traditional local authorities, chiefs of militia, or agency heads for education or health were represented at their meetings to develop solutions and to provide insight into problems. In addressing such problems, each council or commission always made a supreme effort to find a solution at the local level rather than seeing the issue elevated to a higher one, where its importance was diluted in a crowded and less personal agenda. Those closest to the problem were invariably best fitted to craft a solution. The work of coordinating these bodies with the different orientations of their members was tedious and time-consuming, and required a prodigious effort in all the participants. It was, however, a proven way to address an insurgency.[29]

This Portuguese system for civil-military coòrdination was similar in many ways to the British apparatus established in 1950 by Lieutenant General Sir Harold Briggs, Director of Operations in Malaya. While the Portuguese system was a combination of committees and agency liaison, the British one was an elaborate committee system that was closely associated with the scheme for relocating the population. The committees were established at the district, state, and federation levels and provided liaison with all involved in counterinsurgency operations. The District War Executive Committee was the basic building block of the system. Chaired by the civilian District Officer, it included representatives of military and civilian authorities. The next level was the State War Executive Committee, one for each of the nine Malay states and one for two of the three British colonies. The Federation Executive Council was the ultimate authority and chaired by the High Commissioner.[30] This three-tier system compares closely with the four-tier hierarchy in Angola in 1971, which was indicative of other Portuguese theaters as well. The Portuguese included the Catholic Church and traditional local authorities as a concession to their counterinsurgency environment. The British tended to keep membership to civil and military officials. Both were reflective of the counterinsurgency environment and government structure.

The Portuguese approach represented a blend of the British and French approaches. As *guerre révolutionnaire* was almost wholly military in character, its application in Algeria to civil-military integration was met by extending the responsibility of the armed forces. The role of civilians in counterinsurgency remained largely unexplored in Algeria, and without this dimension a counterinsurgency cannot fully respond.[31] The Portuguese authorities likewise used their military to perform a bulk of civil duties simply because military manpower for such applications was readily available. The Portuguese were quite aware that an extension of civil authority was more appropriate than military in the case of counterinsurgency because the social, political, and economic dimensions dominated; however, Portugal was forced to use its available resources to respond. Its counterinsurgency organization sought and integrated civilians into its decision-making process even though the military predominated, and this solution was indicative of the improvisation and compromise the Portuguese found necessary throughout the Campaigns to find the affordable means to achieve the desired ends.

SHIFTING TO SMALL UNITS OF LIGHT INFANTRY

The Portuguese armed forces were well versed in the principles of counterinsurgency, were aware that the troops were not fighting a classic conventional war, and knew that the forces needed to be modified and adapted to the job at hand. There was substantial concern throughout the armed forces, and the Army in particular, in undertaking such a wholesale and radical change, as not only would it affect all aspects of tactics, techniques, and psychology, but it would also disturb professional career paths. Portugal thus compromised between the creation of an entirely new army uniquely tailored to counterinsurgency and adapting its present army to the new type of struggle.[32]

From 1961 onward the names of Portuguese Army units did not necessarily indicate their duties. This situation reflects the counterinsurgency requirement that the majority of forces be trained as light infantry. Light infantry companies are the most effective counterguerrilla force in a modern army, as they can "seek out and destroy the enemy on his terrain, using initiative, stealth and surprise."[33] Thus, infantry companies, artillery batteries, and cavalry squadrons, as such, did not necessarily lend themselves to countersubversive war. In order to fulfill the counterinsurgency requirement, almost all units, whatever their original designation and purpose, were effectively made light infantry companies and functioned as such. While these units were organized into infantry companies (*companhias de caçadores*), they often retained their old designations and were subdivided into "combat groups" instead of infantry platoons. The fact that they still retained their artillery or cavalry designations, for instance, meant that unit members did not necessarily forsake their traditions, and intimated that when the war was concluded, they would resume the career path in their chosen field of warfare. These designations were particularly important, as unit esprit de corps was very closely tied to a unit's original function and consequently had a large influence on the type of individuals that it attracted. It should also be noted that cavalry squadrons and artillery batteries in some cases did not shift to the infantry function. The cavalry exception and its unique role in Portuguese counterinsurgency will be addressed in a forthcoming chapter.

A battalion of infantry and its companies of combat groups was reorganized as follows:

- Battalion Commander
- Command and Service Company, with
    —Battalion Formation
    —Reconnaissance and Intelligence Platoon/Combat Group
    —Signals (Communications) Platoon/Combat Group
    —Sapper Platoon/Combat Group
    —Maintenance Platoon/Combat Group
- Three Infantry Companies, each with a
    —Commander
    —Staff/Administrative Platoon/Combat Group
    —Three Infantry Platoons/Combat Groups

Each infantry company of about 120 men was comprised of three platoons of infantry and a support platoon, providing four identical elements or combat groups of 30 men each. This structure allowed one platoon or combat group in reserve, one for immediate support to the company, and two always ready for mounting a patrol. In the event of high-tempo operations, the command and service company would supply security and reserve platoons or combat groups for the other infantry companies to the extent of its resources. This flexible organization represented a departure begun in 1953 from the former French pattern of three platoons per company (*Tipo Português* or *"TP"*) to the U.S. pattern with four to five platoons per company (*Tipo Americano* or *"TA"*). This more powerful structure provided the local commander with additional options in addressing a guerrilla threat.[34]

These units would need augmentation in both manpower and special skills from time to time. This reinforcement would come from reserve forces comprised of normal units or of special forces (*comandos, fuzileiros especiais, tropas pára-quedistas, etc.*), depending on the skills needed. These reserve forces were called intervention forces (*força de intervenção*) and were used as the Commander-in-Chief saw fit to adjust for deficiencies in a particular sector or zone.

The creation of elite, special-purpose forces that operated in small units with the attendant flexibility proved particularly valuable. This augmentation was embraced by all three services with the formation of the Army *comandos* (commandos), Air Force *tropas pára-quedistas* (paratroops), and the reestablishment of the Navy *fuzileiros especiais* (special marines). The Portuguese Army began training *caçadores especiais* (special hunters) in 1960 at its new CIOE and deployed four companies to Angola that same year. The training was subsequently modified and extended to all units after 1961 with the *caçadores especiais* name no longer applying. *Comandos* (commandos) were formed in Angola beginning in 1962 on the recommendation of the Chief of Staff of the Military Region, Colonel Bethencourt Rodrigues.[35] In 1963 the first of these new troops were deployed in small numbers, and in September 1964 the *1.ª Companhia de Comandos* (1st Company of Commandos) began operations from Belo Horizonte, Angola. Subsequently *comando* units and training centers were established in Guiné and Mozambique, which produced *Comandos Africanos*.

The *tropas pára-quedistas* were established on 14 August 1955 through the sponsorship of General Arriaga when he was Subsecretary of State for Aeronautics. First offered to the Army, which did not appreciate the need for such exotically trained troops, the *pára-quedistas* were then assigned to the new Air Force and trained as a quick-reaction force that could be rapidly applied to a security problem.

The Portuguese *fuzileiros* have a long history dating from 1618 and are the most ancient of Portuguese infantry troops. Disbanded in 1890 and activated for a short period from 1924 to 1926, the *fuzileiros* were reactivated in 1961 for naval contingencies in the *ultramar*. Admiral Armando Reboredo, Chief of the General Staff of the Navy at the time, sponsored the reactivation, believing that patrol craft and small ships with infantry detachments would be indispensable in counterinsurgency. Initial training was conducted in the United Kingdom through the Royal Marines while the *Escola de Fuzileiros* (School for Marines) was established at Vale do Zebro. Subsequent experience enabled the Portuguese to modify the training there to fit their specific theater and way of fighting. *Companhias de Fuzileiros* (Marine companies with a complement of about 180 men) were used in defense of naval installations, in maritime and riverine security patrols, and in supporting Army operations by water. *Fuzileiros Especiais* (Special Marines) were formed in detachments of 70–80 men and trained in special operations techniques. Each detachment had expertise in a particular geographical area and operated there. Detachment personnel were usually inserted into their operating area by rubber boats for a normal two-day operation, always traveling cross-country and avoiding roads because of mines.[36] The normal range of a patrol was about thirty kilometers because of the difficult terrain and tidal action.[37] They complemented the Army's commandos in the type of operations undertaken and were similar in capability to Royal Marine Special Boat Units and U.S. Navy SEAL teams.

These troops were used in counterinsurgency operations and were widely respected by ally and enemy alike. The paratroops and Special Marines were employed as intervention forces in areas where air mobility or water assault was appropriate and were generally operated with Army forces. Both the air and naval forces normally supported Army operations, as that service had primary responsibility for the war. Air Force support comprised primarily transportation, reconnaissance, and combat air support. Naval support involved protecting the riverine lines of communication, transporting and inserting troops by water, and waterborne fire support.

Portugal had thus changed its Army to fit the war rather than trying to change the war to fit its Army. This complete restructuring from top to bottom of a nation's armed forces to fight a counterinsurgency was uniquely Portuguese and stands in stark contrast to the U.S. force structure in Vietnam, the British force structure in Malaya, Kenya, and Greece, and the initial French force structure in Algeria, all of which began as conventional forces untrained in counterinsurgency. The United States seemed particularly insensitive to the requirements of a counterinsurgency force. Ambassador Maxwell Taylor, when he learned that the United States intended to introduce ground forces into Vietnam, made the observation in a series of cables to Washington on 22 February 1965 that the American soldier, "armed, equipped, and trained as he is, [is] not suitable as [a] guerrilla fighter for Asian forests and jungles."[38] Later, on 8 March 1965, witnessing the initial U.S. Marine Battalion Landing Team come ashore at Da Nang, Ambassador Taylor was distressed to note the accompanying tanks and self-propelled artillery that would be of little use in a counterinsurgency.

The British Army entered each of its conflicts, Malaya, Kenya, and Greece, with poorly trained and inexperienced troops. The lack of a proper command structure meant that authority was dispersed, and there was no counterinsurgency doctrine to guide the soldiers. Eventually the deployed troops were restructured and trained for counterinsurgency, but much time had been lost and the insurgencies gained momentum.[39] France in approaching the war in Algeria made the same mistakes in 1954 that had cost it Indochina. It required until 1956 to develop a collective counterinsurgency force and plan. Alistair Horne has described the initial French experience in the deployment of its ponderous, NATO-style forces that proved nearly useless. None of the commanders had any experience in guerrilla warfare nor did the troops under their command have any training in counterinsurgency.[40] The Portuguese had studied these British and French campaigns at the IAEM and had noted the errors of improper troop deployment. Acting to avoid these costly mistakes, the Portuguese Army strove to field a force properly structured, equipped, and trained early in its campaign.

EDUCATION AND TRAINING FOR COUNTERINSURGENCY

Portugal's preparation of its armed forces for counterinsurgency was constantly rethought and adjusted to reflect experience gained not only from others but also in its conflict. The Army had studied extensively and had organized its education and training based both on the theoretical approach and on its practical experience in the early days of the 1961 Angolan uprising. The British experience in Malaya held lessons that were absorbed by the Portuguese Army mission to Maresfield Park Camp in 1958-1959. The British had found that training in the art of jungle warfare against an elusive enemy was the key to success.[41]

The Portuguese approach attempted to emulate this British success and represented a stark contrast to the U.S. Army's training exercises and service school instruction, which was generally pro forma in nature. Even when the U.S. Army made serious attempts to train, the effort was more often a bastardized form of conventional operations than a reflection of counterinsurgency doctrine.[42] This misplaced training emphasis and doctrinal confusion left the U.S. Army unprepared for its entry into Vietnam in 1965. The French in Indochina (1946-1954) were similarly oriented and seemed to have forgotten their counterinsurgency principles and the teachings of Joseph Gallieni and Hubert Lyautey. They did not implement programs reflecting their heritage until much later in Algeria (1954-1962). As one historian explained: "The fall of Dien Bien Phu marked the fall of an empire in South east Asia—and the demolition of much military dogma. Here a notably backward Oriental country triumphed smashingly over one of the most technically advanced Western countries, well supplied with airpower, tanks, artillery, and graduates of the Ecole de Guerre."[43] Even as the campaign was closing, Colonel Charles Lacheroy, a veteran of Indochina, asserted, "Without delay we must examine the degree to which the War of Indochina was for us a lesson and how it has turned our doctrine and 'military practices' topsy-turvy."[44]

Portuguese education and training of troops for counterinsurgency was lifted from British experience and addressed four interrelated issues:

- The educational function of attuning men's minds to understand subversion and insurgency—the way in which force is employed to achieve political ends, and how political considerations affect the use of force
- Instruction on the integration of military and civil measures to achieve a single government aim
- Development of leadership skills in the context of counterinsurgency warfare
- Instruction in the tactics used in combat in a counterinsurgency environment.[45]

These four issues were taught on the three levels of officer, sergeant, and soldier. At each level the instruction was tailored to the duties and responsibilities of the audience. While the initial contingent of forces entering Angola in March 1961 had little such training, they fully briefed their replacements and the new troops arriving while a more formal program of instruction was being established. This situation was not uncommon in the opening phase of a counterinsurgency and is reflected in a British officer's comment on arriving in Malaya in 1954: "If I was going to have to lead jungle-patrols in what seemed a strangely hypnotising kind of half-war, then it looked as if I would have to start learning all over again, from the beginning."[46] By 1962 troops entering the war zone had the benefit of special courses in counterinsurgency warfare. By 1965 the course of instruction on all levels was refined and capable of supporting the accelerating increase in troop deployment, including the establishment of training facilities in the *ultramar* for local recruiting and, later in 1968, for acclimating new arrivals.

DEVELOPMENT OF SPECIALIZED
COUNTERINSURGENCY INSTRUCTION

There was a sequence of specialized instruction activities established early in the wars to address specific problems and situations in the *ultramar*, and these programs sought to provide an improved overall understanding of the operational requirements there. Most were administered at the CIOE; however, certain technical training was located elsewhere at other specialized centers. Their establishment and demise reflect the changes both in the course of the wars and in the seasoning of the training regimen and of the armed forces. The establishment of each was not only a reflection of the changing face of the war but of necessary adjustments to the maturation of the Portuguese Army in the conflict. Training sites were also progressively shifting from the *metrópole* to the *ultramar* both in response to the increased recruiting there and in recognition of the need to train in the combat environment. More important, this entire evolution was indicative of the principle that without sufficient counterinsurgency training for the troops engaged, the conflict will last longer and be more costly to fight.[47] These adjustments acknowledged this premise and the sustainability of the Campaigns that it implied.

Training in the *ultramar* sought to accomplish two objectives: (1) training locally recruited troops and (2) acclimatizing new arrivals from the *metrópole* in the ways of counterinsurgency in Africa.   In the first instance, basic instruction in the *ultramar* paralleled that in the *metrópole* with adjustments to accommodate the differences in the local orientation of recruits.   Reconciling local culture and language with the military requirements of a soldier presented the greatest challenges, and adjustments were necessary for both the Portuguese and the local recruits.   Local education was irregular.   As a result the Army adopted a policy of making all recruits complete the four-year equivalent of primary school, and soldiers attended the Regimental School each day after training to satisfy this requirement.   Many of the recruits spoke only rudimentary Portuguese, and consequently it was necessary to include a language course in the first phase of training.   After 1954 the introduction of relatively modern armament and equipment outstripped local language capabilities for instruction in its use.   Consequently, the Portuguese language became so important to train in technical matters that the European instructors were no longer allowed to speak the local dialects in classrooms.[48]   Portuguese lessons became mandatory for everyone not proficient in the language.   With these exceptions, training in the *ultramar* was little different than in the *metrópole*.

The training system was theoretically well conceived; however, in practice there were shortcomings.   The Portuguese troops originally assigned to a *zona de acção*, for instance, while indoctrinated in subversive war, were not specifically prepared to engage the enemy aggressively.   They tended to confine themselves to the local encampment and simply reacted to enemy attacks, thereby abdicating the initiative.[49]   With the experience gained from this initial disappointment, the military leaders shifted to a new organizational concept in 1968 based on small-unit operations at the company and platoon or "combat group" level.[50]   This shift became most apparent in Guiné following General António de Spínola's arrival in 1968 and his vigorous implementation of the reformed organization.   Not only did General Spínola implement this new concept, but he also modeled it after that of the guerrilla units in Guiné.   These PAIGC units were called *bi-grupos* (bi-groups) and were similar to a reinforced Portuguese subcompany platoon or "combat unit."

The PAIGC armed forces (FARP) had originally had a basic unit of twenty-one men divided into three groups of seven each.   The bi-group or *bi-grupo* was a subsequent development from the February 1964 Cassacá Congress in which the FARP was reorganized.   The *bi-grupo* was formed by combining two of these three groups into a single unit.[51]   The size of the unit consisted of about twenty to twenty-five men optimally aligned as follows: the leader, the political commissar, three bazooka aimers, three bazooka loaders, three light machine gun aimers, three light machine gun loaders, nine riflemen, and three snipers.[52]   Normal supporting arms were two mortars and two heavy machine guns.   The *bi-grupo* could, however, be divided, and each of the *grupos* could operate independently. This basic building block of the small commando group was maintained by the PAIGC for the duration of the war. While seldom concentrated in large numbers because of vulnerability to air attack, *bi-groupos* had flexibility in their potential to be assembled into units of 200 to 300 men. General Spínola's new emphasis in 1968 on small, aggressive units swung the initiative in Guiné to the Portuguese. The smaller units were much more mobile than a company or a battalion and were thus able to concentrate their firepower on the enemy with greater effectiveness than the larger, more cumbersome entities, given the limitations of the combat environment.

In conjunction with this emphasis on small-unit operations, General Spínola faced another problem. Despite the best efforts of the training facilities in the *metrópole*, soldiers arriving in the *ultramar* were decreasing in quality and enthusiasm from 1966 onward.[53] It consequently became obvious to the commanders in the *ultramar* that this deficiency needed to be corrected in situ. The British were faced with a similar situation in Malaya, where they created an elaborate program to acclimate arriving units to the operational environment.[54] General Spínola borrowed the concept from the CIOE, adapted the course syllabus to Guiné, and called it Operational Proficiency Instruction (*Instrução de Aperfeiçoamento Operacional*, or IAO).[55] It had been proposed earlier that IAO training be established in the *ultramar*; however, budget constraints had precluded this move.[56] IAO addressed the retraining and sensitizing of all new troops arriving from the *metrópole* and focused entirely on counterinsurgency warfare as it was fought in the operational theater. It also extended to local recruits and represented new basic instruction for them. The establishment of IAO was a recognition that soldiers familiar with the people, culture, and geography of their operational theater are indispensable to a successful counterinsurgency program. Its obvious appropriateness in response to a problem made it a permanent fixture for the duration of the wars. IAO proved extremely effective, and once the teething problems were resolved, it was adopted in Angola.[57] For unexplained reasons it was never implemented in Mozambique.[58] In both Guiné and Angola the nationalist movements became a standoff militarily by 1970 and reflected the effectiveness of these changes among other factors.[59]

This type of adaptation was a factor in the military effectiveness of troops in other counterinsurgencies. The British Army found local IAO-type training to be indispensable, and veterans of the British Emergency in Malaya endorsed its importance in training new arrivals. Lieutenant Colonel Roland Mans stressed its value from personal experience "that troops should never be introduced 'cold' to such operations. A carefully coordinated training program, preferably carried out in a comparatively safe area within the country in which they are going to fight, enables them to learn their trade in the right locale and at the same time become thoroughly acclimatized."[60] First Lieutenant Oliver Crawford, a graduate of the Far East Training Centre in southern Johore, amplified the value of its instruction: "The School drew on the accumulated experience of the whole Army. Its theory of jungle-warfare was quite possibly the most advanced in the world—particularly for Malaya, where every month of the past seven years' fighting had helped to test and refine it. "[61]

Theater indoctrination was also deemed important by the French, who in Algeria in 1956 established and ran an extensive program at the Centre d'Instruction de Pacification et Contre-Guerrilla at Arzew.[62] Conversely, this in-theater indoctrination was not treated seriously by the U.S. Army in Vietnam, where its "conduct of the war was a failure, primarily because it never realized that insurgency warfare required basic changes in Army methods to meet the exigencies of this 'new' conflict environment."[63] The Portuguese implementation of IAO largely paralleled that of the British with commensurate dividends.

ADAPTING TO COUNTERINSURGENCY

Portugal had faced a wholesale shift in the mission of its armed forces from a conventionally oriented force to one of counterinsurgency. This conventional organization had to be dismembered and reoriented to face an insurgency in Africa, and required not only a huge conceptual leap by Portugal's military leadership but also the establishment of a completely new doctrine with associated tactics and training. At the campaign and tactical levels Portugal's uniqueness in organizing itself for the African Campaigns lay in its learning from the earlier experiences of others and, as the conflict progressed, both adapting these practices and applying the lessons of its own observations to its conduct of the wars. Following the initial uprising and the use there of largely conventional troops to restore order, Portugal demonstrated that it could learn in the face of adversity and in doing so gained the initiative after some difficult homework. By 1970 the insurgents in Angola had been stalemated militarily and "reduced to little more than nuisance value by efficient Portuguese security action, geographical limitations and leadership conflicts."[64] In Guiné the military reorganization and the new operating concepts and methods of General Spínola led to the stabilizing of a deteriorating situation and negotiations for talks with the PAIGC in the closing months of 1972.[65] Mozambique was quiescent until 1970 because of internecine struggles and purges within the nationalist movements. Thereafter, the conflict became "slow-moving shadowboxing with hardly any punches landing on the opponents."[66]

The Portuguese had always been close to the British commercially and militarily, and believed the British experience with counterinsurgency to be among the richest in the world. If the British forgot about counterinsurgency between wars, they always seemed to relearn quickly. Emphasis on tactical flexibility was a centerpiece in their counterinsurgencies, and one that the Portuguese sought to embrace. As Christopher Harmon observed, "The British drew from their experience the principle of tactical flexibility. They proved willing and able to set aside their textbooks on conventional war, delve into the thin literature of the pamphlets, or the unconventional, draw extensively on personal experience and, as Clausewitz would have advised, draw on secondary experience garnered from colleagues who had been there."[67] Although the Portuguese struggled in the early years to find the proper combination in Angola and Guiné, they followed this British flexibility, and with the advent of small-unit tactics and General Spínola's reemphasis of IAO in 1968, drew the earlier efforts together in a cohesive and effective force. Their experience in learning was not unlike that of the British in Malaya, where "In the beginning, we had to improvise and gain experience, and this took time. Nevertheless, in the final event, we were able to devise methods that enabled all the varied forces involved to inflict a decisive defeat on militant Communism."[68]

French learning was prompted by their defeat in Indochina and resulted in the development of their *guerre révolutionnaire* concept as a new way of countering anticolonial insurrections.[69] This thinking became dominant in the strategy to retain Algeria and shaped overall defense policy. It was likewise a powerful influence on Portuguese thinking and was rigorously sifted for solutions to the problems in Africa. The Portuguese search also contrasted sharply with the U.S. attitude in Vietnam, where "their first mistake was a product of military arrogance, i.e. their complete rejection of any lessons that may have emerged from the French experience up to 1954."[70]

So the Portuguese, like the British, went to "small patrols of well-trained men who could penetrate rugged terrain to gather intelligence, kill guerrillas, disrupt food gathering and courier traffic, call down artillery or air strikes where appropriate, and above all, make contacts with the population."[71] This patrolling kept the initiative away from the insurgent. When the Portuguese followed these practices, as in Angola and Guiné, they were successful. When they deviated, as in Mozambique with Operation "Gordian Knot," they suffered.

The foundation of the military dimension of Portuguese counterinsurgency was not the grand operation but the mundane infantry patrol, which would be routinely performed by a combat group of thirty men and would last four to five days, although it could extend to twice that duration. The troops would generally be taken to the target area by vehicle and would patrol from there by foot, carrying everything with them. During the period they would cover from 50 to 100 kilometers, depending on the nature of the country. For food there would be the normal packed combat ration. Apocryphally their rations consisted of a bag of beans, some chickpeas and possibly a piece of dried codfish, all to be soaked in any water that could be found—probably infected with bilharzia—then cooked and eaten in the evening. Contact with the villagers was important not only to show military strength but also to gain intelligence on the insurgents.[72] On one such patrol in eastern Angola an observer reported shadowing an insurgent group for three days, guided by a local tracker. Surrounding and ambushing the group at twilight, the Portuguese quickly overcame them with surprise and firepower. Immediately afterward the Portuguese troops were offering the enemy water from their canteens, binding their wounds, and interrogating prisoners.[73]

In contrast, Operation "Nó Górdio" occurred in July 1970 in northern Mozambique, lasted 36 days, and with over 8,000 personnel involved was the largest operation undertaken in the *ultramar* during the African Campaigns (1961–1974).[74] By the end of 1969 the area around Mueda in the north of the Cabo Delgado district next to the Tanzanian border had become alarmingly infiltrated with insurgents. General Arriaga, as the Commander-in-Chief, had established a perimeter around the infected area and attempted to drive the insurgents into the waiting force with air-supported ground assaults in a modified hammer-and-anvil tactic. While many guerrilla bases were destroyed and weapons captured, the enemy melted into the 20,000-strong local population fleeing the area to avoid the fight. FRELIMO moved eastward and escaped. The operation could not be concealed because of its large scale, and other areas of Mozambique were denuded of troops to support it, leaving the population vulnerable elsewhere. It was not a counterinsurgency operation, and it predictably yielded disappointing results at great expense. Further, Sir Robert Thompson, the Secretary of Defense for Malaya, was emphatic about avoiding large-scale operations in counterinsurgency. They took much time, talent, and manpower to organize, and when launched, were no secret. The insurgent could avoid contact or choose the battlefield. The results for the government were generally disappointing. The constant pressure of small patrols was far more effective in its low-key, low-cost approach.

In addition to learning from others, the Portuguese learned by doing. While the Portuguese had observed that the small-unit tactics of the British in Malaya had worked well, it was necessary to adapt them to the African environment. Observing the PAIGC *bi-grupo* operations provided the Portuguese with an important demonstration that was to guide their force restructuring for counterinsurgency operations in Guiné and Angola. As the British in Malaya appreciated the value of in-theater training, so Portugal learned to appreciate its importance as well. Development and implementation of its IAO proved a sound solution to irregular troop quality and fighting apathy in Africa.

The Portuguese Army had intensely studied the British and French methods for structuring and training a counterinsurgency force and sought to adapt the successful practices of these two to its situation in Africa. While the Army strove to shorten the period of adjustment necessary to train and deploy effective troops in reaction to the insurgencies, it still required an inordinately long time to field the proper force. Like the British, the French, and the Americans, the Portuguese had to overcome hidebound views on insurgency at the highest command levels to achieve the proper formula. Portugal seemed inordinately slow in this process and required about seven years to implement a fully coordinated approach. The French in Indochina and the Americans in Vietnam never accomplished this feat. The French, following the lessons of Indochina, required two years in Algeria to implement the *guerre révolutionnaire* concept. The British experience varied from about four years in Malaya to two years in

Kenya to make the needed adjustments.[75] Given that the reorganization of the Portuguese armed forces for modern conventional war had required from 1937 to 1960, the seven-year span for counterinsurgency by comparison appears brief.[76] The delay, however, was unnecessarily costly in time, treasure, and manpower, and one of its important manifestations was the 1968 recruiting crisis, which compounded the difficulties of managing the war. This problem of implementing the doctrinal principles for counterinsurgency was acknowledged at the time and later described by the Army's Commission for the Study of the African Campaigns (1961–1974):

However, the great problem surfaced much more in the implementation of doctrine rather than in its definition, which was understood. Its fulfillment faced a natural inertia and difficulty in rapidly adapting to the actual requirements demanded in an anti-subversive war, so different in doctrine, organization, and training, which until then had been solely oriented to conventional warfare. Such adaptation went as far as to demand a mental predisposition toward acceptance which is normally slow.[77]

Nevertheless, the Portuguese Army solved these problems by 1968 and by 1970 had gained control of the conflict in all three theaters. It could then claim that it had the correctly structured force, properly trained and led, that it was successfully applying proven counterinsurgency concepts adapted to its situation in Africa, and that the insurgencies were under relative control. These achievements were no small accomplishment. The goal of attaining a subdued, low-tempo conflict had been realized alongside an apparent indefinite sustainability. Forthcoming chapters will examine the specific components of recruiting, operations, and logistics in this accomplishment.

NOTES

1. Estado-Maior do Exército, *Resenha Histórico-Militar das Campanhas de África (1961–1974)* [Historical-Military Report of the African Campaigns (1961–1974)] (Lisbon: Estado-Maior do Exército, 1988), Vol. I, 426; Colonel Luís Alberto Santiago Inocentes, interview by the author, 18 March 1994, London. "*TP*" or *Tipo Português* was the earlier, pre-1953 method modeled largely on the French army, and "*TA*" or *Tipo Americano* reflected the U.S. Army organization developed in World War II.

2. Kaúlza de Arriaga, "Portuguese National Defense during the Last 40 Years and in the Future," lecture delivered on 20 October 1966, Lisbon, 14, 44. The reorganization and integration of the armies into a single structure was completed only in 1960. The Air Force was created as a separate service in 1952, and its extension to the *ultramar* completed in 1957. The Navy by 1958 had completed a restructuring as well to bring itself in step with NATO. General Arriaga observed that while the reorganizations had been based on very good principles, they had been applied sluggishly, with a consequent delayed effectiveness. General Arriaga had been appointed when he was a Lieutenant Colonel to assume the duties initially as the Subsecretary of State for Aeronautics and later as the Secretary of State for Aeronautics in building the Portuguese Air Force. In 1952 the air arms of the Army and Navy were combined to form the Portuguese Air

Force, and this new service was by 1957 organized and structured to be in step with its sister services and NATO, and to extend its infrastructure and operations to the *ultramar*. While the number of aircraft of all types had grown from a beginning level of 200 in 1952 to nearly 600 at the start of the African Campaigns, the truly important achievement had been the construction of the aerial infrastructure both in the *metrópole* and particularly in the *ultramar*. This joint civil-military project produced about 750 airfields, of which 65 could accommodate medium aircraft and 22, the largest ones. In Angola there were about 400 fields, 27 of which could handle medium and in some cases large aircraft. In Mozambique the numbers were 300 and 20, respectively. It was at the time considered one of the "greatest construction projects on a national scale that had ever been undertaken in Portugal." This timely development was instrumental in mobilizing Air Force support during the Angola uprisings of 1961 and in conducting the subsequent campaigns.

3. *Resenha Histórico-Militar das Campanhas de África (1961–1974)*, Vol. II, 72.

4. Ibid., Vol. I, 260–261.

5. Hélio Felgas, *Guerra em Angola* [War in Angola] (Lisbon: Livraria Clássica Editora, 1961), 109.

6. *Resenha Histórico-Militar das Campanhas de África (1961–1974)*, Vol. I, 259.

7. Bruce Hoffman and Jennifer M. Taw, *Defense Policy and Low-Intensity Conflict: The Development of Britain's "Small Wars" Doctrine During the 1950s* (Santa Monica: Rand Corporation, 1991), 1, 20; Alistair Horne, *A Savage War of Peace: Algeria 1954–1962* (Harmondsworth: Penguin Books, 1987), 100.

8. *Resenha Histórico-Militar das Campanhas de África (1961–1974)*, Vol. I, 202.

9. Ibid., Vol. I, 203.

10. Brigadeiro Hélio A. Esteves Felgas, interview by the author, 22 November 1994, Lisbon.

11. Ibid.

12. *Resenha Histórico-Militar das Campanhas de África (1961–1974)*, Vol. I, 203–204.

13. Ibid., Vol. IV, 103; Estado-Maior do Exército, *Subsídios para o Estudo da Doutrina Aplicada nas Campanhas de África (1961-1974)* [Aid for the Study of Doctrine Applicable in the Campaigns of Africa (1961–1974)] (Lisbon: Estado-Maior do Exército, 1990), 116–117. The Northern Territorial Command (*CTN* or *Comando Territorial do Norte*) was changed to the Northern Intervention Zone (*ZIN* or *Zona de Intervenção Norte*) in late 1964.

14. Lieutenant Colonel Rowland S. N. Mans, "Winning in the Jungle—Malaya," *The Guerrilla and How to Fight Him*, ed. T. N. Greene (New York: Frederick A. Praeger, 1962), 123.

15. Peter Paret, *French Revolutionary Warfare from Indochina to Algeria: The Analysis of a Political and Military Doctrine* (London: Pall Mall Press, 1964), 103.

16. Felgas interview, 22 November 1994.

17. Christopher C. Harmon, "Illustrations of 'Learning' in Counterinsurgency," *Comparative Strategy* (January–March 1992): 29.

18. General José Manuel de Bethencourt Rodrigues, interview by the author, 9 November 1994, Pedrouços (Lisbon).

19. Mans, 120.

20. Hermes de Araújo Oliveira, "Guerra Subversiva: Subsídios para uma Estratégia de Reacção" [Subversive War: Aid for a Strategy of Response], *Revista Militar* (November 1964): 672.

21. *Subsídios para o Estudo da Doutrina Aplicada nas Campanhas de África (1961–1974)*, 113.

22. Inocentes interview, 8 February 1995.

23. Ibid. This coordination was so important that every country in Africa facing difficulties with it was anxious to overcome them. In 1966–1967 the Rhodesians invited a large contingent of Portuguese officers to their headquarters for a briefing on civil-military coordination and on their solution to the problem. Not all of their solutions were applicable or transferable from the relative compactness of Rhodesia to the vastness of Angola or the thousand-kilometer length of Mozambique. Nevertheless, the Portuguese were constantly trying to improve this coordination.

24. Ibid.

25. Ibid.

26. *Subsídios para o Estudo da Doutrina Aplicada nas Campanhas de África (1961–1974)*, 115.

27. Ibid., 116.

28. Ibid., 117.

29. Ibid., 129-130; Colonel Carlos da Costa Gomes Bessa, interview by the author, 18 November 1994, Lisbon; Gomes Bessa, "Angola: A Luta Contra a Subversão e a Colaboração Civil-Militar" [Angola: The Fight Against Subversion and Civil-Military Collaboration], *Revista Militar* (August–September 1972): 421.

30. Thomas R. Mockaitis, *British Counterinsurgency, 1919-1960* (London: Macmillan, 1990), 117–118.

31. Paret, 125.

32. *Subsídios para o Estudo da Doutrina Aplicada nas Campanhas de África (1961–1974)*, 124–126.

33. Lieutenant Colonels James K. Bruton and Wayne D. Zajac, *Cultural Interaction: The Forgotten Dimension of Low-Intensity Conflict*, paper presented as a part of the syllabus for the seminar "Introduction to Special Operations" at the U.S. Air Force Special Operations Command, Hurlburt Field, Fla., March 1990, 1. The authors quote from General John Wickham's 1984 White Paper on the primary role of the U.S. Army's light infantry divisions.

34. *Subsídios para o Estudo da Doutrina Aplicada nas Campanhas de África (1961–1974)*, 131.

35. Brigadeiro Renato F. Marques Pinto, correspondence with the author, 9 August 1995, Oeiras.

36. Corpo de Fuzileiros, *Fuzileiros Especiais* (Lisbon: Ministério da Marinha, 1987), 14, unpublished history.

37. Vice Admiral Nuno Gonçalo Vieira Matias, interview by the author, 23 November 1994, Lisbon. Admiral Matias is a former detachment commander of *Fuzileiros Especiais* (Special Marines) in Guiné.

38. Andrew F. Krepinevich, Jr., *The Army and Vietnam* (Baltimore: Johns Hopkins University Press, 1986), 141.

39. Hoffman and Taw, v.

40. Horne, 100.

41. Mans, 127–128.

42. Krepinevich, 53.

43. Mans, 145.

44. Colonel Charles Lacheroy, *Action Viet-Minh et Communiste en Indochine ou une Leçon de "Guerre Révolutionnaire,"* paper given at the Conference on the War in Indochina, Institut de Défense Nationale, Paris, July 1954, 2.

45. General Sir Frank Kitson, *Low-Intensity Operations: Subversion, Insurgency and Peacekeeping* (London: Faber and Faber, 1971), 165–167.

46. Oliver Crawford, *The Door Marked Malaya* (London: Rupert Hart-Davis, 1958), 17.

47. Hoffman and Taw, 35.

48. Inocentes interview, 22 October 1994.

49. Joaquim Moreira da Silva Cunha, *O Ultramar, a Nação e o "25 de Abril"* [The Overseas Provinces, the Nation and the "25th of April"] (Coimbra: Atlântida Editora, 1977), 297–298.

50. Ibid., 299. This change was endorsed by the Minister of National Defense (General Sá Viana Rebelo), the Minister of the Army (Brigadeiro Bethencourt Rodrigues), the Subsecretary of State for the Army (Colonel João Pinheiro), the Chief of the General Staff of the Armed Forces (General Venâncio Deslandes), and the Chief of the General Staff of the Army (General Câmara Pina) in March 1968.

51. Patrick Chabal, *Amílcar Cabral: Revolutionary Leadership and People's War* (Cambridge: Cambridge University Press, 1983), 99.

52. John Biggs-Davison, *Portuguese Guinea* (London: Congo Africa Publications, 1970), 21–22.

53. Thomas H. Henriksen, "Portugal in Africa: Comparative Notes on Counterinsurgency," *Orbis* (Summer 1977): 404.

54. Mans, 128–129.

55. *Resenha Histórico-Militar das Campanhas de África (1961–1974)*, Vol. I, 331–334.

56. Marques Pinto correspondence, 9 August 1995.

57. *Resenha Histórico-Militar das Campanhas de África (1961–1974)*, Vol. I, 331–334.

58. Silva Cunha, 299.

59. Willem van der Waals, *Portugal's War in Angola 1961–1974* (Rivonia: Ashanti Publishing, 1993), 140.

60. Mans, 128.

61. Crawford, 74.

62. Alf Andrew Heggoy, *Insurgency and Counterinsurgency in Algeria* (Bloomington: Indiana University Press, 1972), 176.

63. Krepinevich, 259–260.

64. van der Waals, 140.

65. Avelino Rodrigues, Cesário Borga, and Mário Cardoso, *O Movimento dos Capitáes e o 25 de Abril* [The Movement of the Captains and the 25th of April] (Lisbon: Moraes Editores, 1974), 244; Guilherme de Alpoim Calvão, *De Conakry Ao M.D.L.P.* [From Conakry to the M.D.L.P.] (Lisbon: Editorial Intervenção, 1976), 89–90.

66. Thomas H. Henriksen, *Revolution and Counterrevolution: Mozambique's War of Independence, 1964–1974* (London: Greenwood Press, 1978), 48.

67. Harmon, 36.

68. Mans, 143.

69. Paret, 7.

70. Michael Elliott-Bateman, *Lessons from the Vietnam War*, Report of a seminar held at the Royal United Services Institute in London, 12 February 1966, 4.

71. Harmon, 36.

72. Duke of Valderano, interview by the author, 17 March 1995, London.

73. Colin M. Beer, interview by the author, 14 March 1995, London.

74. *Subsídios para o Estudo da Doutrina Aplicada nas Campanhas de África (1961–1974)*, 181–185.

75. Hoffman and Taw, 28–29.

76. Kaúlza de Arriaga, "Portuguese National Defense during the Last 40 Years and in the Future," lecture delivered on 20 October 1966, Lisbon, 12.

77. *Subsídios para o Estudo da Doutrina Aplicada nas Campanhas de África (1961–1974)*, 138.

5

PORTUGUESE AFRICANIZATION OF COUNTERINSURGENCY

One of the most significant elements in the Portuguese conduct of the Campaigns was the Africanization of its armed forces. By shifting the predominant burden of supplying manpower to run the wars from the *metrópole* to the *ultramar*, Portugal gained in four ways. First, it broadened the source of military manpower through an inclusion of the colonial population. Second, it reduced the cost of fielding troops through a reduction in transportation and training costs. Third, it gained a large measure of almost indefinite sustainability through the first two aspects. Last, it kept the conflict subdued and low-tempo by moving a large portion of the conscription and casualties away from the *metrópole*. This chapter will review the origins of Portugal's recruiting problems and its experience in using local African troops, and examine the application of local recruiting in the theaters, analyzing its implementation and comparing it with contemporary experiences in counterinsurgency.

ORIGINS OF THE MANPOWER SHORTAGE

After crafting its counterinsurgency doctrine and redesigning its armed forces for the Campaigns, Portugal faced the severe constraint of raising an army and maintaining it at the necessary levels. The *metrópole* presented a limited and fragile source of manpower to conduct the Campaigns. While there was an element of chauvinism in the initial years, by 1966 this patriotism had worn thin, and by 1968 Portugal faced a problem of identifying manpower sources simply to run the wars.[1] Portugal proper with a population of just under 9 million was conducting a counterinsurgency campaign in three colonies whose populations aggregated about 12 million. This distribution would seem to dictate that proportionately about 60 percent of the manpower should be supplied by the colonies. In 1966, 30 percent of the Army's manpower came from the *ultramar.* In 1968 it had drifted upward to 32 percent. Subsequently, this trendcontinued: 1969, 38,118 or 31 percent; 1970, 39,406 or 32 percent; 1971, 54,451 or 40 percent; 1972, 55,448 or 40 percent; and 1973, 61,816 or 42 percent.[2]

European recruiting was displaced by colonial recruiting beginning in 1966 and increasing until 1971. During the 1971–1974 period in Angola local recruitment in the armed forces had stabilized at 42 percent. In Mozambique it exceeded 50 percent during the same period. In Guiné, where there was only a limited population from which to draw, local recruitment never exceeded 21 percent. It should also be noted that the Portuguese recruited African troops according to the same laws in effect in the *metrópole*, a code that required all able-bodied men (*efectivos*) between the ages of twenty and forty-five to serve two years. In 1968 the two years were extended to four, two of which had to be served in Africa.[3] The law was loosely enforced in Africa until the manpower requirement became acute in the 1966–1967 period.[4]

These figures are for the Army alone. The Navy and Air Force numbers were modest by comparison, and if aggregated with the Army, would not significantly change the percentages above.[5] But these numbers do not tell the whole story. The militarization of the population in the form of self-defense units, police, and other paramilitary forces that were not integrated into the primary organization of the armed forces had the effect of increasing the foregoing percentages constructively to 50 percent.[6] In the case of Mozambique, locally recruited troops in all categories reached 54 percent of the total force.[7] In Angola it increased to about 50 percent.[8]

The problem began in 1961, when the Portuguese knew that the war would last longer than simply a few months to stabilize the situation in Angola. Just how much longer was uncertain; however, the process would be measured in years and not months. With this prospect in mind, the government turned to the population of the country to satisfy its military personnel needs. The official census by the Portuguese government conducted on 15 December 1960, just before the beginning of the campaigns, showed the following broad population distribution:[9]

Metrópole	8,889,392
Angola	4,830,283
Guiné	525,437
Mozambique	6,603,653

From these figures and additional census data the number of able-bodied males between the ages of twenty and twenty-four in the four recruiting areas was 816,781, distributed as shown in Table 5.1.[10] From the age profile contained in the census it was determined that approximately 163,356 able-bodied males would reach their twentieth birthday and would thus become available annually to add to the pool of eligible candidates. These numbers were always nominally adequate to support the recruiting required to man the armed forces between 1961 and 1974, as the annual addition to the pool from all sources was never less than the replacement requirement. The difficulty came in adjusting to the increasingly high delinquency rate in the *metrópole*, which squeezed the seemingly favorable numbers and shifted a disproportionate burden to the soldiers currently serving and to recruiting in the *ultramar*.

Table 5.1
Able-Bodied Males

	Males Aged 20-24 Years in 1960	Approximate Annual Addition
Metrópole	336,672	67,334
Angola	208,853	41,771
Guiné	21,256	4,251
Mozambique	250,000	50,000
Total	816,781	163,356

Table 5.2 traces the recruiting picture in the *metrópole* during the course of the wars.[11]

Table 5.2
Recruitment in the *Metrópole*

Year	Registered	Called	Delinquent
1961	75,366	48,832 (64.8%)	8,722 (11.6%)
1962	79,357	57,073 (72.0%)	10,211 (12.8%)
1963	85,410	59,676 (69.8%)	13,328 (15.6%)
1964	86,977	61,249 (70.4%)	14,357 (16.5%)
1965	90,289	64,805 (71.7%)	16,972 (18.8%)
1966	87,506	63,342 (72.3%)	16,008 (18.4%)
1967	86,065	62,017 (72.6%)	16,512 (19.2%)
1968	95,634	70,504 (73.7%)	17,838 (18.6%)
1969			(19.6%)
1970	88,693	63,996 (71.5%)	18,554 (20.9%)
1971	91,363	65,746 (72.0%)	15,644 (20.3%)
1972	92,613	66,681 (72.0%)	18,841 (20.3%)

There are several dynamics apparent in the trend of the figures, despite the missing data for 1969. The estimated pool of able-bodied males aged twenty to twenty-four at the beginning of the wars was 336,672. To this number each year was added about 67,334, and based on the eleven years of data, on the average 62,175 were chosen. For military purposes, therefore, the pool was theoretically adequate for the entire period of the conflict.

There were, however, other elements competing for this manpower in the *metrópole* and disturbing this equation. Portugal's population has always been one of its leading exports, and the census figures do not fully reflect this drain, particularly clandestine emigration. Continental Portugal with a population at the time of nearly 9 million had an estimated expatriate population of 3 million. On top of this problem was an intense psychological campaign waged from abroad and aimed at planting doubts about the war in Portugal's recruiting-age youth, raising the spirit of the enemy, and supporting deserters, however few.[12] This campaign was centered in the universities, and while quite disruptive, was containable. Open student demonstrations began on 17 April 1968 with the inauguration ceremony dedicating a new building at Coimbra University, and student indiscipline continued at a high level until the force of the law and the academic authorities restored order later in the year.[13] This disorder was attributed to communist incitement against "the colonial war" primarily through the outlawed Portuguese Communist Party, which had clandestine operatives within the country. The entire episode had a demoralizing effect on the recruiting effort generally and on officer recruiting specifically, and the morale of the armed forces suffered accordingly.[14]

The recruiting figures do, however, show an accelerating problem in attracting personnel. The wartime manpower demands on the *metrópole* increased from 48,832 in 1961 to a height of 70,504 in 1968 and remained just below that number for the remainder of the wars. Draft registrations peaked in 1968 and declined thereafter. Certainly one cause of this decline was an extension in required service. In 1968 the normal two-year conscription period was effectively extended to four through a new charter that required two years of service in Africa.[15] In order to arrest this decline and maintain a sufficient level in the theoretical pool, it was recommended that the draft age be lowered from twenty years to eighteen years effective in 1971. The Portuguese military establishment agonized over these two decisions but could reach no other conclusions regarding recruiting in the *metrópole*.[16] The wars would have to be fought largely with the soldiers who existed in 1968, particularly if the skills acquired on the battlefield were to be preserved and not lost to wholesale personnel turnover. The *metrópole* was limited as a manpower resource under the current recruiting parameters, and new recruits in sizable numbers would have to be found in the *ultramar*.

Draft delinquencies or "no shows" were 11.6 percent in 1961, a manageable figure within Portugal's twentieth-century experience. This number increased on both an absolute and percentage basis through 1970, leveling thereafter. The delinquent rate of 20.9 percent in 1970 is unremarkable alongside a sample of other years (1900, 15.7 percent; 1912, 22.7 percent; 1922, 36.8 percent; 1933, 16.6 percent; 1940, 12.7 percent; and 1950, 9.8 percent); however, in the context of the wars, the trend is unmistakably negative.[17] Recruiting in the *metrópole*, while it always satisfied the nominal military requirements for manpower, increasingly reflected a lack of enthusiasm for the war alongside the available alternatives. The lure of a European economic boom north of Portugal as well as an expanding domestic job market became increasingly attractive in contrast to the personal inconvenience and relative danger of serving in Africa.

Emigration had always been largely from the rural areas and over time they became depleted, leaving the more developed areas as the primary centers supplying recruits.[18]

The limitations of the domestic population base threatened the war effort. From the beginning of the wars in 1961 until the conclusion in 1974, the number of personnel in the primary Army organization expanded from 49,422 to 149,090, representing an average annual rate of increase of about 11 percent.[19] Portugal's need to recruit ever increasing numbers was driven by two factors: the expansion of guerrilla activity from Angola to Guiné and finally to Mozambique, and the increasing use of the military as a manpower pool for expanding psychosocial activity.[20] In relation to the expanding guerrilla activity, the insurgents numbered about 22,000 in all theaters by 1974, giving Portuguese forces at that time a numerical superiority of about 6.8 to 1.[21] Maintaining this ratio strained Portugal's resources. Compared with other insurgencies, this ratio fell short of the British experiences in Malaya of 37.5 to 1 and in Cyprus of 25 to 1, and of the French in Algeria of 16.7 to 1, and exceeded that in Kenya of 4.6 to 1.[22] It was similar to the combined U.S. and Republic of Vietnam experience, where in 1964 the ratio was an estimated 4 to 1 and in 1968 about 8.75 to 1.[23]

The momentum of the psychosocial program would be maintained by a shift of available manpower and its orientation. Through a series of government directives in 1968, a five-point plan was implemented to address the issue: (1) intensify recruitment in the *ultramar*, where the demographics held the potential to sustain a flow of candidates; (2) expand the numbers of special forces for counterinsurgency; (3) expand the local *ultramar* paramilitary forces; (4) reduce *metrópole* forces proportionately to the expansion in forces recruited in the *ultramar*; and (5) modify the force structure to include additional small units suitably effective in counterinsurgency.[24] Thus, faced with this necessary expansion and the recruiting difficulties at home, Portugal in 1968 pragmatically shifted its focus to local recruiting in the colonies. Reinforcing this shift was also the belief that indigenous forces would strengthen the political legitimacy necessary for success against the insurgents.

RECRUITING LEADERSHIP

In addition to the search for raw manpower, the expansion of the armed forces necessitated the recruitment, training, and development of leaders in the form of officers and sergeants. The Military Academy produced adequate numbers of permanent officers for the first four years of the war, but thereafter was never able to recruit properly from the universities and fulfill the requirements. In 1966 Portugal began to draw from the Central School for Sergeants to fill this need for permanent officers and did so until 1972. The dynamics of this problem are reflected in Table 5.3.[25]

Table 5.3
Military Academy Permanent Officer Commissioning

Academic Year	Vacancies	Contestants	Admitted	Unfilled Vacancies	Commissioned Sergeants	Net Deficit
1961–1962	265	559	257	8	—	8
1962–1963	266	444	266	0	—	0
1963–1964	200	392	180	20	—	20
1964–1965	262	307	137	125	—	125
1965–1966	350	283	129	221	42	179
1966–1967	377	199	90	287	118	169
1967–1968	410	175	90	320	236	84
1968–1969	430	149	58	372	261	110
1969–1970	460	112	33	427	226	201
1970–1971	400	151	62	338	287	51
1971–1972	550	169	103	447	200	247
1972–1973	495	154	72	423	—	423
1973–1974	243	155	88	155	—	155

Contestants for vacancies at the Military Academy exceeded openings until the 1965-1966 academic year, after which the deficit became increasingly a problem. Officers from the sergeants' ranks did not wholly satisfy the need, but produced adequate numbers of leaders in the form of permanent officers to run the war until 1972. To supplement the corps of permanent officers, reserve officers (*milicianos*, literally "militia") were recruited to flesh out the junior officer ranks. At the end of their contract these officers had the option of extending it, or later of applying to continue as permanent officers, or of resigning.

The recruiting difficulties in the *metrópole* adversely affected the ability of the armed forces to attract and retain the key leadership skills embodied in the officer and sergeant ranks. The normal *miliciano* contract was two years in duration, and means were constantly explored to grant these officers and sergeants special privileges if they would extend their military obligation.[26] Also the idea of giving *miliciano* officers with good records the option of accepting a regular commission was regularly studied. This retention mechanism had long been popular with Western military services and provided an opportunity for entry into a military career through several avenues outside the Military Academies. This practice would have been implemented long ago, according to Douglas Porch, "had its effects on the rather archaic promotion system in the Portuguese army not proved so disruptive. Most armed forces attempt to strike a balance between seniority and ability in the promotion stakes, giving preference perhaps to top Military Academy graduates. But Portuguese promotion was based almost exclusively on seniority."[27] It would be fair to say, however, that with the advent of the wars, seniority was less of a determining factor in promotion.[28]

The specter of having the *milicianos* be given credit for all of their former service by establishing their seniority in a system where seniority was everything was too much of an obstacle. Despite the fact that Dr. Caetano personally became interested in changing the system and all of the Commanders-in-Chief who came to Lisbon from the operational theaters supported the plan, the resistance of the regular officer corps to this move was just too strong.[29] The initial solution to the problem was borrowed from one adopted following the Great War in which a special category of officer (*quadro especial de oficiais*, or QEO) was created. The QEO provided for the granting of regular commissions to limited numbers of *miliciano* officers of good standing but confined their advancement to the rank of lieutenant colonel.[30] The first small contingent of ninety officers was added to the regular officer corps through this mechanism in 1970, thus temporarily solving the problem.

The problem only worsened, however. By 1973 the QEO allotment had been exhausted, and the retention difficulties had again reached crisis proportions. Thus the situation was reexamined by the new Minister of National Defense, General Sá Viana Rebelo. This review resulted in the Council of Ministers approving Decree Law No. 353/73 in July 1973, which under certain conditions gave the *miliciano* officers regular commissions with seniority based on their length of service as a reserve officer.[31] Although fewer than 200 *miliciano* officers were eligible and would affect the force of over 2,800 regular junior officers, these "Rebelo decrees," because of their implications, were immediately and strongly unpopular with the officer corps and particularly within the captain ranks of the armed forces. This fissure was also heightened and exploited by the communists to undermine service morale.[32] Dr. Caetano's experience was indicative of approaching problems, as he later observed: "It was not many days later that my military adjutant...informed me that the decree law did not sit well with much of the Army because of the changes in relative seniority caused by the ex-*miliciano* officers.... And he reminded me of the enormous importance that a soldier attaches to his seniority on the ladder: 'seniority means a promotion.' "[33]

While the Rebelo decrees solved the retention problem for the *miliciano* officers, the bitterness caused by the implementation of this long overdue reform sowed the seeds of junior officer revolt that contributed to the revolution on 25 April 1974.[34] It was likewise in this context that Portugal sought to expand its sergeant and officer ranks through local recruiting in the war theaters.

PRECEDENT FOR AFRICANIZATION

Portugal increasingly turned to its colonies to fill its wartime manpower need, as it had done in the past, although never on the scale of the Campaigns. African troops represent a tradition of having served or cooperated with Portugal in times of need since the earliest days of the colonies. In almost every year between 1575 and 1930 there was a colonial campaign somewhere in Portuguese Africa, and the African auxiliary and irregular forces proved indispensable. Called the *guerra preta* ("black war") from the campaigns of 1681 until this century, they had a history of loyalty and could be raised on short notice.[35] This flexibility meant that Portugal did not have to mobilize large numbers of its continental troops and transport them to Africa in times of colonial crisis. While these earlier campaigns were pacification operations and were not in the same genre as modern insurgencies with their political theme, they nevertheless set a precedent for Portugal's extensive Africanization of the late Campaigns.

A typical example is represented by the 1888 campaign in the Zambezi Valley, in which more than 90 percent of the soldiers in the Portuguese pacification force were Africans. During this period Portuguese influence in the Zambezi Valley beyond its coastal regions was on a negotiated basis with the leaders of a series of small kingdoms or *prazo* states, and half of these troops were furnished by the co-opted leaders of these fiefs. These leaders kept private armies of warrior slaves or *achikunda* as a secondary force for protection of their *prazo* holdings, and thus the typical Portuguese force was comprised largely of these *achikunda* and a contingent of African militia. Leadership and direction were provided by Portuguese officers and the friendly leaders of the secondary states. Allen Isaacman provides a valuable assessment of the use of locally recruited troops in this 1870–1902 campaign for control of the Zambezi Valley: "Lisbon's ability to recruit a large African force provided crucial support for its success. Less than three per cent of the total army of twenty thousand were of Portuguese descent...."[36]

In the twentieth century the *guerra preta* continued to be used both in pacification operations until their conclusion in 1930 and in the Great War of 1914–1918, and endured as a formidable force for defense of the colonies.[37] General Norton de Matos had recommended in 1924 that indigenous troop levels be maintained in Angola at 15,000 regulars supported by a system that could mobilize an additional 45,000 reservists in time of war.[38] The continuing reliance on colonial troops as a source of manpower was established defense policy, and in 1924 it was estimated that from all sources 460,000 men in 28 divisions could be fielded in a national crisis.[39] In this calculation Angola and Mozambique were to supply 71 percent or 20 divisions totaling 325,000 men.

Mozambique had also been a fertile recruiting ground for troop requirements in other colonies beginning in the early twentieth century. One to two companies were formed each year and deployed for two-year tours between 1906 and 1932.[40] These deployments included virtually every colony: Angola, Guiné, Timor, Macao, São Tomé, and India. Consequently, the reputation of Mozambican troops was well established by 1961.

During the Great War, Portugal fought in France, in the south of Angola, and in the north of Mozambique. The largest campaign conducted was the defense of Mozambique against the German incursion. Portugal sent 32,000 troops from the *metrópole* and hurriedly recruited another 25,000 locally.[41] The composition of this force was 44 percent African. Portugal had had an urgent manpower requirement on its border between Mozambique and German East Africa and had had no choice but to rely on local troops.[42] Many companies of indigenous personnel were formed and trained under the most difficult of conditions, and acquitted themselves admirably in this campaign. At the conclusion of hostilities, a Portuguese major who had led troops there acknowledged their vital role in this conflict: "During the four years of struggle our native African infantry always fought with courageous determination, when well supported and led.... Many citations acknowledged this dedication which was characterized by natural bravery and valor. But of this most important contribution to the cause for which we fought, the majority of the Portuguese people remained unaware."[43] Before the beginning of the African Campaigns (1961–1974), the history of locally recruited African troops and their exploits was not widely appreciated, particularly in the *metrópole*. Just why their contribution remained so obscure is a mystery, despite the fact that it was the most venerable of any of the African colonial powers.

DEVELOPMENT OF AFRICANIZATION

Africanization within the primary organization of the Army went largely according to the plan developed in 1968, which was to level recruiting efforts in the *metrópole* and expand the force to the desired levels through increased recruiting in the *ultramar*. Africans serving in first-line units of the Army represented 30 percent of the force in 1966 and by 1971 had increased by a third to 40 percent, where it remained throughout the wars. This expansion represented an increase in local troops in all theaters from about 30,000 to 54,500, or nearly 25,000 new troops. There were, however, more than this first tier of troops in the Africanization process.

Prior to the Campaigns and to this augmentation, local troops were raised not only by the armed forces but also by the comparable civil authorities, and employed as "second line units" with the functions of guides, civil militia, auxiliary forces, self-defense groups for villages, and other specialized roles.[44] The self-defense units were simply armed civilians who had been organized and trained to act in defense of their village, if surprised by guerrillas. This organization provided a degree of confidence to local communities through a rudimentary ability to defend its members. Supposedly these paramilitary forces coordinated their activities with local Army operations; however, this cooperation was not always present.[45] Army units consequently might to their surprise find themselves patrolling the same area concurrently with another friendly force.

This sanctioned activity continued during the Campaigns, and in the three theaters these irregular troops fought well and provided an invaluable service. In Angola the various police forces and "third line units" of the *Organização Provincial de Voluntários e Defesa Civil* (Provincial Organization of Volunteers and Civil Defense, or OPVDC) were organized as a single body.[46] The OPVDC was composed of contracted individuals whose original duty was to protect the rural areas in the north of Angola. The organization began as a vehicle for mobilizing the white settler population but became increasingly multi-racial toward 1970.[47] Later these duties were expanded to include the guarding of road construction equipment in areas of aggressive guerrilla activity.

This centralized organization was not always the case. Initially in Angola, for instance, Portuguese mobilization was fragmented. There were:

- *Milícias Tradicionais de Regedoria* (Traditional Local Jurisdiction Militia)
- *Forças de Contra-Guerrilha* (Counter-Guerrilla Forces), which were created according to diverse criteria for various duties and with neither a structure nor a mission that was well defined. Originally in this grouping there were
    Tropas Especiais (TE)
    Forçes Especiais (FE)
    Grupo Sonda in the *Zona Militar Leste* (ZML)
    Pseudo Terrorists (PT) in Nambuangongo
    Milícias Armadas de Malanje.[48]

In addition to the regional militias, the OPVDC, also known as the *Corpo de Voluntários* (Volunteer Corps), was created, as described earlier, and gathered momentum only in Angola. From about August 1967 there was a move to consolidate and gain control of these local paramilitary forces and to direct their efforts more effectively. The *Grupos Especiais* (GE), TEs, and OPVDC were the primary vehicles for this tighter organization, although during the course of the wars this task was constantly challenged by the surfacing of additional bodies. The following paragraphs will address the more unusual aspects of Portuguese Africanization, some of which began outside of the conventional recruiting, force structure, and normal soldiering duties. Ultimately many of these were officially incorporated into the Portuguese armed forces and account for the recorded increase in numbers of locally recruited troops. Others remained part of the paramilitary Africanization until 1974.

Tropas Especiais (Special Troops)

Called *Tropas Especiais* (TE) because of the special nature of their recruitment, this force had its origin in the 1965 defection of Alexandre Taty, the Minister of Armaments of the UPA/FNLA/GRAE and a prominent Cabindan. Taty, who had studied to be a priest and forsaken the cloth for a job in the post office, had a strong affinity for women and drink. He stole from his employer to support these interests, and when discovered, fled to the Belgian Congo and ultimately joined Holden Roberto's organizations. He next attempted and failed to replace Roberto, and subsequently through Portuguese agents of the PIDE negotiated the forgiveness of his postal robbery and his return to Angola. With him he brought about 1,200 loyal troops, half of whom remained in the Congo to gather intelligence.[49] Taty was instrumental in helping the Portuguese control Cabinda and the adjacent northern border of Angola.

Cross-border operations were routine for the TEs, who were composed entirely of black troops and carried no Portuguese identity cards.   Their missions were thoroughly planned, and they prepared for them by practicing on full-scale model replicas of the targets at their camps in northern Angola.   They wore insurgent uniforms and carried Soviet bloc weapons and equipment on their numerous raids.   The Portuguese authorities were never sure if these missions were fully accomplished, and while skeptical, felt that this activity kept the insurgents occupied defensively and off balance.   Initially the troops were irregularly trained and were organized in groups of thirty-one men consisting of a leader and three sections of ten men each.   Later they were expanded through Taty's recruiting efforts and organized on the Portuguese pattern into four battalions of sixteen combat groups of thirty-one men each.   This force of sixty-four groups operated from Cabinda and the districts of Zaire and Uíge in northwest Angola.   When the ZML became active in 1966, a battalion was sent there.   Portugal paid and fed the troops and ran the operation with a low profile to avoid criticism of harboring and using former insurgents.[50]   In 1972 they numbered about 2,000 and were incorporated into the regular forces.[51]

Grupos Especiais (Special Groups)

In 1968 a series of similar groups appeared in the east of Angola.   These were formed from captured insurgents or those who presented themselves, and were organized with the designation *Grupos Especiais* (GE).   As time went by, they were used throughout Angola, but particularly in the eastern sector (ZML). There were ninety-nine groups of GEs, and these were likewise incorporated into the regular forces in 1972.   By 1974 these ninety-nine groups with an average compliment of thirty-one men per group totalled 3,069 troops.[52]

In Mozambique, GEs were also organized in 1970 and they paralleled the structure, training, and duties of those in Angola.   The first organization consisted of six groups aggregating 550 men.   They were originally constituted as small units in the mold of a typical light platoon or combat group, and eventually numbered about 7,700 men in eighty-four such groups.   At first they were led by European officers and sergeants; however, as cadres matured, Europeans were replaced by black officers and sergeants.   Later in 1971 GE training was extended to include an initiation of parachute qualification. Twelve units from this program were established as *Grupos Especiais Pára-quedistas* (Special Groups Parachutists, or GEP) and attached to the Air Force as an adjunct to the normal *tropas pára-quedistas*.   Each of the twelve units had a lieutenant as its commander, a sergeant specialist in psychological operations, four sergeants as subgroup commanders, sixteen corporals, and forty-eight soldiers, or a total of seventy men.   All totaled the GEPs numbered about 840 troops.   Other than the qualification jumps, the units were rarely used in this fashion and were deployed by helicopter similarly to the normal paratroop units. One might conclude that their special training was a manifestation of General Kaúlza de Arriaga's earlier interest and sponsorship of the Portuguese paratroops. Much later there was also a small number of *Grupos Especiais de Pisteiros de Combate* (Special Groups of Combat Trackers, or GEPC) who were quite specialized and simply incidental to "first line units." In all the GEs, GEPs, and GEPCs in Mozambique totaled about 8,500 troops. While originally trained as a counterinsurgency force, their chief duties evolved as protective cadres for the population in the *aldeamentos* (resettlement villages), which will be addressed in a forthcoming chapter.[53]

Milícias (Militia)

In Guiné units similar to the TEs and GEs were formed in 1964 as paramilitary forces, taking the designation of *Milícias* (Militia). They came to be called *Milícias Normais* (Normal Militia) and *Milícias Especiais* (Special Militia), depending on the duties of the units. The Normal Militia assumed a defensive role in protecting the population from attack, lived in or near their villages, and fell under the operational control of the local military commander. The Special Militia conducted offensive counterinsurgency operations away from the local defenses. In 1971 a new *Corpo de Milícias* was formed to integrate all of the *Milícias* and *Tropas de 2.ª Linha* (Second Line Troops) into the regular Army. The *Corpo* was organized by companies of combat groups and aggregated some forty companies with more than 8,000 men. They were armed primarily with the Portuguese G-3 assault rifle and bazookas. There was also a *Comando Geral de Milícias* (Militia General Command) that oversaw their administration and training. Their training was conducted at three centers, and the course of instruction lasted three months. The Militias were quite effective in protecting the villages and in the consequent freeing of regular troops for other operations. Toward the latter stages of the Campaigns the Militias were accounting for 50 percent of insurgent contact.[54] By the end of the Campaigns these Militia totaled forty-five companies of Normal Militia (about 9,000 men) and twenty-three groups of Special Militia (about 713 men).[55]

Katanganese *Fiéis* (Faithful)

After the granting of independence to the Congo by Belgium in 1960, there was an enormous political upheaval centered in the *Force Publique*, the new nation's army. This spread of disorder prompted Moise Tshombe to declare the Province of Katanga an independent state, expel the mutinous elements of the *Force Publique*, and raise his own force of gendarmerie. Eventually the United Nations intervened and returned Katanga to the control of the central government in January 1963, at which point Tshombe went into exile in Spain. During this period Portugal had openly encouraged the Tshombe government and from eastern Angola supported it against the U.N. forces. In June 1964 the United Nations withdrew, and Tshombe was unexpectedly invited to return as Prime Minister in a government of reconciliation. Unfortunately Tshombe could not bring harmony to the situation, and it degenerated into a civil war. Faced with a weak and demoralized Congolese National Army, he took the controversial step in September 1964 of hiring white mercenary troops to assist his army in regaining order. General Joseph-Désiré Mobutu, the army commander, along with selected army units and mercenaries quelled the rebellion. The Portuguese again established strong ties with Tshombe, and this relationship dampened insurgent activity through 1965. In the autumn of 1965 General Mobutu overthrew Tshombe in a coup, and again he left for Spain. With the Tshombe exit the MPLA was given access to eastern Angola. In 1967 General Mobutu suspended the new constitution and the National Assembly and prevented Tshombe from returning to the Congo. At this point the old gendarmerie, loyal to Tshombe, crossed into eastern Angola at Teixeira de Sousa to fight for the Portuguese.

These *Fiéis* or "faithful ones" numbered about 4,600 with women and children. The Portuguese initially screened and selected some 2,300 men, whom they organized into three battalions of fifteen companies. Each of these battalions was based at one of three camps: Chimbila, on the border between the districts of Lunda and Moxico; Camissombo (near Verissimo Sarmento), in Lunda; and Gafaria (the old leper colony near Cazombo), in Moxico. The *Fiéis* retained their command structure with their own officers and sergeants, and were under the general command of "Brigadier" N'Bumba Nathaniel; however, in performing missions they were placed under the operational command of the local military commander. Their primary duty was to protect the crews building roads in eastern Angola. These black troops were "fearless soldiers who fought like tigers"; by 1972 they had sustained thirty-one killed in action, thirty-four killed in accidents, and thirty-six seriously wounded. By 1974 they numbered about 3,000 troops and posed a continuing threat to General Mobutu.[56] The Portuguese exploited this situation to maintain their influence over him and the insurgent activities that he influenced from the Congo sanctuary.

Commandos

Comandos and *Comandos Africanos* (African Commandos) had their more modern origin in the lessons that the Portuguese learned from their own colonial pacification operations earlier in this century and additionally from observing the French experience in Algeria, which was "the paradigm of subversive war and the laboratory for counterguerrilla techniques."[57] The Portuguese, having identified the need for a small specialized force, established in 1959 a series of "quick reaction units" to be used in the special operations of internal security, countersubversion, and counterguerrilla activities. Three of these *Companhias de Caçadores Especiais* (Companies of Special Hunters, or CCE) completed training in April 1960 and were sent to Angola in June. Others followed to Mozambique and Guiné, as each theater commander realized that he needed a cadre of special troops to conduct counterinsurgency operations.[58] The CCEs were not produced after 1961, as their training was extended to all Army units. The need for a specialized force remained, and in 1962 it was recommended by Lieutenant Colonel Bethencourt Rodrigues, the Chief of Staff of the Military Region of Angola, that *comandos* be formed.[59] Centers were established for their expansion through local recruitment and training in each of the three theaters, beginning with Angola, and later in 1970, Mozambique and Guiné. In Guiné locally recruited Commandos were known as African Commandos.[60]

In directing the establishment of the 1st Company of African Commandos on 11 February 1969, General António de Spínola set the tone for its formation and use in keeping with the tenets of Africanization established in Lisbon in 1968: "Our African Military Force has been established at a growing rate and now includes the elite unit, 1st Company of African Commandos, formed exclusively from the native sons of Guiné.... Your ascension to the position of Commando in the Portuguese Army marks a significant stage in the course of progress for all Guineans."[61]

In Angola there were five companies operating by the end of the war. Each company had a complement of about 125 men for a total of 625 Commandos. The units were mixed rather than largely European or locally recruited. Thus it is difficult to give a close assessment of Africans serving in this capacity. In Guiné there were three companies of African Commandos in the Commando Battalion at the conclusion of the war. With about 125 men in a company the total of locally recruited Commandos was about 375 men. In Mozambique by the end of the war there was a battalion of Commandos with eight companies of about 125 men each.[62] Half of the companies or about 500 men were recruited locally.

Fuzileiros (Marines)

The Portuguese *Fuzileiros* had their origin in the formation of the Royal Naval Regiment of Portugal in 1618. Deactivated in 1890, they remained so until 1961 except for a brief period from 1924 to 1926. Responsible for maritime and riverine security, the *Fuzileiros* played key and varying roles in all of the theaters. Almost exclusively recruited and trained in the *metrópole*, the *Companhias de Fuzileiros* (Companies of Marines, or CF) were responsible for coastal security and river support. Special operations were conducted by the *Destacamentos de Fuzileiros Especiais* (Detachments of Special Marines, or DFE), the first naval forces to be used in the Campaigns with the deployment of DFE 1 to Angola on 10 November 1961.[63] Subsequently deployments reached a height in 1971–1972 with eleven DFEs and eight CFs in the three theaters. Locally recruited units were restricted to Guiné, where in February 1970 two *Destacamentos de Fuzileiros Especiais Africanos* (Detachments of Special African Marines) were formed at the *Centro de Preparação de Fuzileiros Africanos* (Training Center for Special African Marines) at Bolama.[64] These units, DFE 21 and 22, served throughout the Campaigns, and while not a large portion of the Navy's overall complement, were very important. As the normal DFE held a complement of 80 men, the two units totaled only 160. This level represents about 9 percent Africanization.[65]

Flechas (Arrows)

Last, the most controversial African force was the *Flechas*. The Portuguese intelligence apparatus required specialized augmentation in Africa, and PIDE was designated to perform these counterinsurgency duties.[66] PIDE and its successor, the *Direcção Geral de Segurança* (DGS) normally performed the various police and security duties that would typically fall to the British MI-6, Special Operations Executive, Scotland Yard's Special Branch Officers, or the U.S. Federal Bureau of Investigation and Central Intelligence Agency. When the Campaigns began, the new requirements in Africa attracted the best talent in PIDE for this purpose. PIDE faced initial problems in adjusting to the new environment and to gathering intelligence on the insurgents' movements in Angola. The population continued to be terrorized, the local situation remained confused, and there was a consequent pressing need for a long-term solution. PIDE continued to experiment with this uncertain situation in its search for the key. One obstacle to its efforts was the proliferation of languages spoken, as there were perhaps fifteen different dialects. By about 1967, in an attempt to make its reconnaissance missions more effective, it had begun to use local auxiliaries with their knowledge of the immediate terrain, familiarity with the population, and unique language skills. This initiative proved partially successful, and about 600 agents were eventually employed to address both the vastness of Angola and the large number of languages. This original number was expanded to about 1,000 by 1974.[67]

This use of auxiliaries began around the city of Luso in eastern Angola, and employed people who had been born and raised there to go into the familiar bush and discover what was happening. These locals could travel easily through the country for extended periods, blending with the population and maintaining a low profile. Initially these agents were simply supposed to observe and collect information on insurgents; however, PIDE found that they were being captured and tortured, so it began to arm them for their own defense and train them properly. It found that the Bushmen were the best for this purpose. These people inhabited the vast remote area of the Cuando-Cubango district in southeastern Angola, which was also aptly named *"Terras do Fim do Mundo"* (Lands of the End of the Earth). It is here that the Bushmen lived and were largely employed, and it is here that the *Flechas* began.[68]

PIDE had to make a number of concessions in employing the Bushmen for reconnaissance work. They were small in stature and could not carry heavy weapons. And indeed, the Portuguese G-3 9mm assault rifle was too heavy and unmanageable for them. Thus they continued to carry their bows and arrows armed with poison tips. The insurgents were allegedly terrified of this weapon, and because of the awe that it evoked, the men who wielded it were named for it—*flechas* or arrows. Before eventually settling on the Soviet AK-47, they tried many weapons. By 1974 standardization had begun on the lightweight U.S. M-16 assault rifle.[69]

PIDE began with the most primitive people in the sense of civilization and not of intelligence. These Bushmen were initially motivated by their hatred and mistrust of the blacks, as historically the blacks had treated them as chattels and sold them as slaves. PIDE exploited this animosity and compensated the *Flechas* through booty. Later blacks were employed to work primarily in western Angola and adjustments were made to dampen the ill feeling. Pay methods were changed but had to be handled carefully. While the value of the compensation was the same as that of Europeans, they could not be paid in quite the same way. As many would immediately spend their earnings on drink and have little left to support their several wives and numerous children, multiple disbursements were made to families to accommodate this propensity.[70]

The Army had great respect for the *Flechas* and operated with them frequently either in small reconnaissance groups or in larger contingents as part of an Army operation. These reconnaissance missions were wide-ranging, deep-penetration patrols in known or suspected enemy areas and were spartan and low profile. When *Flechas* operated with the Army, they reported to the local Army commander and were used to guide the normal troops. The Army relied on the *Flechas* to maintain the continuity of local operating knowledge in an area, as the overall experience level of a typical unit tended to degrade with the constant rotation of its troops.[71]

Flechas were organized into combat groups along the same lines as the Army and received their training from the Portuguese Commandos. Often training was extensively modified, as *Flechas* always seemed to have a unique African way of solving problems. Their groups never exceeded thirty men, and they invariably operated in areas where they were familiar with the language and terrain. The primary centers for their operations were Carmona (Uíge), Caxito (Luanda), Gago Coutinho (Moxico), and Serpa Pinto (Cuando-Cubango). Gago Coutinho was the site of the first turned guerrillas in late 1968, and this recruiting avenue yielded about 200 former insurgents scattered throughout the *Flecha* ranks. In the beginning there were eight *Flechas*, and by 1974 there were about 1,000. The concept was also implemented in Mozambique late in the war, and several hundred *Flechas* were established there.[72]

It is thus apparent that the range and degree of formal militarization varied greatly. In addition to the specialized units described above, there were thousands of men recruited locally both in and out of the armed forces. Those who were members of the armed forces served generally as infantry soldiers or in other non- or low-technical duties. Those in civil support jobs, such as drivers, also were performing a low-technology service.[73] Soldiers from the *metrópole* generally performed the more technical tasks because of their higher education level. The count for those formally employed as soldiers is included in published figures. Conversely, civilian employment data are so irregular as to be only gross estimates.[74]

The lack of delinquency figures on African recruiting would indicate either that the census was inaccurate and data could not be calculated, or that there was no real delinquency problem. The answer is most likely the absence of an accurate count, although if *efectivos* were not recruited by the Portuguese in some capacity, then the likely alternative was serving one of the nationalist movements. The Portuguese were always able to recruit at a higher rate than the insurgents for a number of reasons. While life was spartan for the Portuguese soldier, it was even more difficult for the guerrilla.[75]

The best estimates of nationalist strength show a peak of about 22,000 guerrillas by 1974 against 61,816 locally recruited troops in the formal Army organization.[76] If one adds the paramilitary forces, the ratio of African against African would easily exceed 3 to 1. This experience is similar to that of the French in Algeria, where "At no time from 1954 to 1962 did the numbers of Algerians fighting with the F.L.N. for independence match the number of Algerians fighting on the French side."[77] There were about 200,000 Algerians serving France, of whom about 171,000 were auxiliary troops, against the 35,000-man FLN army in 1961 or about a 6 to 1 ratio.[78]

This Portuguese Africanization compares favorably with the efforts of the French in the *jaunissement* or yellowing of their Indochina War (1946–1954) and their use of locally recruited troops in Algeria (1954–1962). It was also far more extensive than the U.S. Vietnamization between 1963 and 1973. At the height of the Indochina War in 1954 the French Expeditionary Corps numbered 235,721, to which about 54,000 Vietnamese were added, for a *jaunissement* of 19 percent.[79] In Algeria French troop strength leveled at about 600,000 in 1961, of which about 200,000 were Algerians, for an "Arabization" of about 33 percent.[80] In Vietnam the U.S. and Republic of Vietnam forces totaled in 1968 about 700,000, of which 200,000 or 29 percent were Vietnamese.[81] Thus while the use of indigenous forces in counterinsurgency was not a new concept, in none of the foregoing cases were locally raised troops used to the relative extent that the Portuguese employed them, and few reached the absolute numbers.

MOTIVATIONS

In a war of national liberation in the modern era, the question inevitably arises as to why such a large percentage of the Portuguese Army was local, and why these locally recruited troops fought the nationalists with such determination. There are several explanations for this development. The two general motivational factors that prevailed in all three theaters were (1) the opportunity of relatively well-paid employment as a soldier with the security of medical care and other benefits, and (2) the belief that Africans would benefit more now under a government by the Portuguese than potentially under a victorious nationalist movement.[82]   These two factors were paramount, and other elements, such as ethnic differences, were never as compelling.

Certainly the local populations were very poor. From 1962 onward the Portuguese government established a policy in which locally recruited troops would receive the same pay as European troops. This overture made voluntary enlistment overwhelming, and there were always more volunteers than openings to fill.[83]   As to the other factor, the Africans tended to believe that the Portuguese would win.[84]   They were benefiting with new schools, medical care, and prosperity and did not perceive the nationalists as being able to defeat the Portuguese and deliver on their promises.

Portuguese use of locally recruited troops reflected a further dimension. These troops were fully integrated into the Portuguese armed forces in a complete "miscegenation" of units. This practice contrasted with that of the French in Algeria, where the Algerians serving in a military capacity were not integrated into French units. Algerian career officers were particularly sensitive to this discrimination and were never treated as the equals of their European peers. This inequity was highlighted in their classification at various times as "autochthonous," "native," "Franco-Muslim of native statute," and "Muslim officers." There was many a *crise de conscience* for an Algerian officer and few served in Algeria after 1954.[85]   In Malaya the British also had separate British and Malayan units in the Commonwealth Forces, segregating them.[86] This practice held for Kenya as well.[87]   The European Portuguese felt quite comfortable working alongside African Portuguese, and this relationship allegedly helped to maintain a strong solidarity with the population.

SENSITIVITY TO CASUALTIES

Casualties in any war represent a policy dilemma in that they erode public support at home for continuing to fight.   The greater the casualties are proportionately, the greater the potential is for waning public support.   Portugal in its Africanization of the wars was accused of letting Africans die in the place of its European soldiers.   The implications of this accusation are that by replacing potential *metrópole* casualties with African ones, public support at home could be maintained. The counter to this concept is that the Africans were also Portuguese citizens fighting for their way of life, and they, too, would not fight long if they felt that they were dying simply for a European colonial cause. Consequently, did the African troops shoulder a disproportionate burden in the fighting in the attempt to retain the colonies and consequently suffer unequally? The total number of deaths from all causes in the three theaters for the entire war was 8,290, of which 5,797 were recruited from the *metrópole* and 2,493 were recruited from the colonies.[88]   Not only was the gross figure for *ultramar*-recruited troops lower, but the death rates were likewise lower. Given that on average between 1961 and 1974 about 71,067 troops were deployed from the *metrópole* and 36,025 were locally recruited, death rates were 0.63 per thousand for European troops and 0.53 per thousand for African troops. This statistical data refutes the nationalist claims that Africans were fighting and dying disproportionately for a European colonial cause and shows that, indeed, the black Portuguese troops fought and died at nearly an equal rate with their white counterparts.

When only combat deaths are considered, the figures are even more emphatic, as depicted in the following table.

Table 5.4
Army Combat Deaths by Recruitment Source

	Local	Metrópole	Total
Angola	208	1,098	1,306
Guiné	255	985	1,240
Mozambique	454	1,027	1,481
Total	917	3,110	4,027

Combat deaths in the three theaters over the thirteen-year Campaign were 4,027, of which 917 or 23 percent were locally recruited and 3,110 or 77 percent were European troops.[89]   Clearly the African troops were not disproportionately at risk in the thick of combat.

SUCCESS AND CONTROVERSY

Portugal in shifting its recruiting efforts to the *ultramar* to support the war achieved a number of important gains. First, the recruiting pressure on the *metrópole* was relieved with the consequent benefits in public sentiment. In this shift Portugal was not only following its tradition of using African troops to fight African wars but was also relieving a domestic impediment to continued fighting. With this change in policy, pressure on mobilization in the *metrópole* was alleviated, and manpower requirements and casualties would increasingly be assumed by local recruits in the theaters.   There would thus be fewer emotional reminders returning from Africa, and domestic public dissatisfaction would remain subdued, indeed even quiescent.

Second, Portuguese Africans who had the greatest interest in the outcome of the wars, and thus the highest motivation for a successful conclusion, would now seemingly be doing their portion of the fighting. Engaging the African in his own defense was also seen as one of the best forms of political mobilization.

Third, this policy introduced efficiencies in the allocation of manpower, as the European recruits with their higher technical skills and education were directed toward the more complicated tasks, while their African counterparts with their irregular education and general lack of technical skills were employed in the more labor-intensive tasks, and wars are labor-intensive.

Fourth, employing African troops reduced overall manpower costs in that it was far less expensive to recruit and train a soldier in the local theater of operations than it was to do so in Portugal with the added cost of transporting him to Africa. While initially the African soldier was paid less than his European counterpart, this inequity was corrected early and played little, if any, part in the cost differential. The primary savings occurred in transportation, as the African recruit was generally trained and employed near his home.

Portugal had been forced to mobilize about 1 percent of its population to fight in Africa and simply could not sustain this domestic manpower drain. On a percentage basis it had more men under arms than any other nation outside of Israel.[90] Portugal's mobilization would have been the equivalent of the United States putting 2.5 million men in Vietnam instead of 500,000. The Africanization of the conflict was thus a pragmatic decision in that Portugal had no other choice but to follow this route if it wished to continue. Portugal was indeed fortunate in that it had a loyal population in Africa willing to shoulder the burden of fighting the nationalists. Unlike the French experience in Algeria, where there were mass defections of Muslim bands, the Portuguese allegedly experienced not one incident of rebellion or of mass desertion.[91] Africanization from the Portuguese perspective was thus a sound response to a manpower shortage. It added sustainability to the conflict and helped Portugal counter the long-range guerrilla strategy of attrition. And finally, by moving the recruiting away from the *metrópole* to the *ultramar*, Portugal was able to realize its goal of maintaining a subdued, low-tempo, affordable war.

NOTES

1. Estado-Maior do Exército, 1.ª Repartição, *Estudo sobre Problemas de Recrutamento 1968* [Study on the Problems of Recruitment 1968] (Lisbon: Estado-Maior do Exército, 1968).

2. Estado-Maior do Exército, *Resenha Histórico-Militar das Campanhas de África (1961–1974)* [Historical-Military Report of the African Campaigns (1961–1974)] (Lisbon: Estado-Maior do Exército, 1988), Vol. I, 259–260.

3. Ibid.

4. Douglas L. Wheeler, "African Elements in Portugal's Armies in Africa (1961–1974)," *Armed Forces and Society*, 2, no. 2 (February 1976): 240.

5. *Resenha Histórico-Militar das Campanhas de África (1961–1974)*, Vol. I, 251. The Army total of 216,195 at the conclusion of the wars on 25 April 1974 was augmented by approximately 2,500 Navy and 6,000 Air Force personnel, including *tropas pára-quedistas* (paratroops).

6. Joaquim Moreira da Silva Cunha, *Ultramar, a Nação e o "25 De Abril"* [The Overseas Provinces, the Nation and the "25 of April"] (Coimbra: Atlântida Editora, 1977), 297.

7. *Resenha Histórico-Militar das Campanhas de África (1961–1974)*, Vol. I, 259–260.

8. General Joaquim da Luz Cunha, et al., *África: A Vitória Traída* [Africa: Betrayed Victory] (Lisbon: Editorial Intervenção, 1977), 159.

9. *Resenha Histórico-Militar das Campanhas de África (1961–1974)*, Vol. I, 213–214. The figures cited in the 1960 census were to be the most accurate for the foreseeable future in the colonies. The 1970 census numbers for Portuguese Africa were suspect because of the war disruption and its attendant refugee migration, and no census of either Angola or Mozambique has been taken since.

10. *Resenha Histórico-Militar das Campanhas de África (1961–1974)*, Vol. I, 214.

11. Ibid., Vol. I, 258; *Estudo Sobre Problemas de Recrutamento 1968*, 17.

12. Américo Simões Gaspar, *Emigração em Portugal* [Emigration in Portugal] (Lisbon: Instituto de Altos Estudos Militares, 1974), 36–38.

13. Marcello Caetano, *Depoimento* [Deposition] (Rio de Janeiro: Distribuidora Record, 1974), 55–56.

14. Silva Cunha, 290.

15. *Resenha Histórico-Militar das Campanhas de África (1961–1974)*, Vol. I, 233.

16. *Estudo sobre Problemas de Recrutamento 1968*, 3–4. These two options had been proposed in this 1968 study.

17. *Resenha Histórico-Militar das Campanhas de África (1961–1974)*, Vol. I, 268; and *Estudo sobre Problemas de Recrutamento 1968*, 17. These relatively large delinquency percentages are also due in part to the Portuguese system of conscription, in which several notices were sent asking that an individual report for induction. If he failed to report on the initial notice, then he was delinquent. Because of the largely rural nature of Portugal, the fact that the inductee might have been working in a Renault factory outside of Paris, or other similar impediments, many reported late as a matter of routine. The Portuguese authorities were aware of these problems, and disciplinary measures were taken only after reasonable induction efforts had failed.

18. *Estudo sobre Problemas de Recrutamento 1968*, 18.

19. *Resenha Histórico-Militar das Campanhas de África (1961–1974)*, Vol. I, 259.

20. Silva Cunha, 295.

21. Wheeler, 277. There were 6,000 guerrillas for the PAIGC, 10,000 for FRELIMO, and 4,500 for the MPLA. UNITA and the FNLA combined had fewer than 1,500 full-time guerrillas in Angola.

22. Bruce Hoffman and Jennifer M. Taw, *Defense Policy and Low-Intensity Conflict: The Development of Britain's "Small Wars" Doctrine During the 1950s* (Santa Monica: Rand Corporation, 1991), 38; Colonel Virgil Ney, "Guerrilla Warfare and Modern Strategy," in *Modern Guerrilla Warfare*, ed. Franklin Mark Osanka (New York: The Free Press of Glencoe, 1962), 36.

23. Frank N. Trager, "Military Requirements for U.S. Victory in Vietnam," in *Viet Nam: History, Documents, and Opinions on a Major World Crisis*, ed. Marvin E. Gettleman (Greenwich, Conn.: Fawcett, 1965), 347.

24. Silva Cunha, 295.

25. Estado-Maior do Exército, 6.ª Repartição, Notice No. 17/IE, 18 March 1982.

26. Silva Cunha, 295.

27. Douglas Porch, *The Portuguese Armed Forces and Revolution* (Stanford: Hoover Institution Press, 1977), 65.

28. Colonel Luís Alberto Santiago Inocentes, interview by the author, 5 September 1994, London.

29. Caetano, 184–185.

30. *Resenha Histórico-Militar das Campanhas de África (1961–1974)*, Vol. I, 236–237. Decree Law No. 49 324 of 27 October 1969 created the QEO and limited it to the following officer numbers: lieutenant colonel, 20; major, 40; captain, 120; and subaltern, 180.

31. Caetano, 185.

32. Inocentes interview, 5 September 1994.

33. Caetano, 185.

34. Silva Cunha, 305.

35. C. R. Boxer, *Race Relations in the Portuguese Colonial Empire 1415–1825* (Oxford: Oxford University Press, 1963), 32. They were also known as *empacasseiros* from a word meaning "buffalo hunters."

36. Allen F. Isaacman, *The Tradition of Resistance in Mozambique* (London: Heinemann Educational Books, 1976), 65.

37. Gastão Sousa Dias, "A Defesa de Angola" [The Defense of Angola], *Revistar Militar* (July–August 1932): 611–619.

38. José Mendes Ribeiro Norton de Matos, "O Exército em Angola" [The Army in Angola], *Revista Militar* (March 1924): 85.

39. Gaspar do Couto Ribeiro Villas, *As Tropas Coloniais na Vida Internacional* [Colonial Troops in International Affairs] (Lisbon: Sociedade de Geografia, 1924), 72.

40. E. A. Azambuja Martins, *O Soldado Africano de Moçambique* [The African Soldier of Mozambique] (Lisbon: Agência Geral do Colónias, Ministério das Colónias, 1936), 34.

41. Luz Cunha, 73; Carlos Selvagem, *Tropa d'África* [African Troops] (Pôrto: Renascença Portuguesa, 1919), 410, 416.

42. German East Africa, 1885–1920; subsequently Tanganyika Territory as a British Mandate, 1920–1961; Tanganyika, 1961–1964; and Tanzania, 1964–present.

43. Francisco Aragão, *Tropas Negras* [Negro Troops] (Lisbon: Seara Nova, 1926), 22, 23.

44. *Resenha Histórico-Militar das Campanhas de África (1961–1974)*, Vol. I, 242.

45. Inocentes interview, 5 September 1994.

46. Silva Cunha, 297.

47. Peter Abbott and Manuel Ribeiro Rodrigues, *Modern African Wars (2): Angola and Moçambique 1961–1974* (London: Osprey, 1988), 41.

48. *Resenha Histórico-Militar das Campanhas de África (1961–1974)*, Vol. I, 243–244, and Vol. II, 154.

49. General Joaquim Miguel Mattos Fernandes Duarte Silva, interview by the author, 3 April 1995, Lisbon. When he was a Major, General Duarte Silva was the Portuguese Army liaison officer to the TE operation under the code name *Lourenço* between 28 January 1966 and 14 July 1967.

50. Ibid.

51. *Resenha Histórico-Militar das Campanhas de África (1961-1974)*, Vol. I, 243-244, and Vol. II, 347.

52. Ibid., Vol. I, 243-244, and Vol. II, 173, 347.

53. Ibid., Vol. I, 243-244, and Vol. IV, 156, 347.

54. Colonel Carlos Fabião, interview by the author, 31 March 1995, Lisbon.

55. *Resenha Histórico-Militar das Campanhas de África (1961-1974)*, Vol. III, 110.

56. Colonel Dionísio de Almeida Santos, interview by the author, 30 March 1995, Porto. Colonel Almeida Santos was Portuguese liaison to the *Fiéis*.

57. Colonel Rio Carvalho, "As Companhias de Caçadores Especiais" [The Companies of Special Hunters], *Jornal do Exército* (April 1994): 26.

58. Colonel António Dias Machado Correia Dinis, *Subsídios para a História dos Comandos Portuguese* [Supplementary Information on the History of the Portuguese Commandos] (Lisbon: Associação de Comandos, 1981), Vol. III *Guiné-1963*, 14.

59. Brigadeiro Renato F. Marques Pinto, correspondence with the author, 9 August 1995, Oeiras.

60. Joaquim Lopes Cavalhairo, *Forças Especiais na Guiné: O Batalhão de Comandos 1971-1973* [Special Forces in Guiné: The Battalion of Commandos 1971-1973] (Lisbon: Instituto de Altos Estudos Militares, 1979), 1-2.

61. General António de Spínola, address given on 11 February 1969 establishing the 1st Company of African Commandos, Bissau, Guiné, as quoted in Ibid., 1.

62. *Resenha Histórico-Militar das Campanhas de África (1961-1974)*, Vol. I, 243-244, and Vol. IV, 167, 170, 184.

63. Corpo de Fuzileiros, *Fuzileiros Especiais* (Lisbon: Ministério da Marinha, unpublished history written in 1987), Schedule of Deployments (Angola).

64. Vice Admiral Nuno Gonçalo Vieira Matias, interview by the author, 23 November 1994, Lisbon; Corpo de Fuzileiros, 15.

65. Corpo de Fuzileiros, 17. There were 11 DFEs at 80 men each and 8 CFs at 120 men each, for a total of 1,840. Africanization at 160 men represented 9 percent of this figure.

66. Marques Pinto correspondence, 9 August 1995. The Portuguese Army, although it did not have an intelligence service of professionals, had a system of intelligence with divisions or sections at all headquarters commands. These cells were manned by officers with a subspecialty and schooling in intelligence. There was thus a system functioning at all levels of command, and it was supported by the Air Force with visual and photo reconnaissance and by radio monitoring attachments. The PIDE was responsible externally for intelligence collecting and internally for counterintelligence and in this case countersubversion. In Angola and Mozambique the entire intelligence picture was coordinated through the *Serviços de Centralização e Coordenação de Informações* (Service of Centralization and Coordination of Intelligence, or SCCI), which analyzed the raw information and produced intelligence reports.

67. Óscar Cardoso, interview by the author, 1 April 1995, Azaruja, Portugal. Sr. Cardoso is a former Inspector with the PIDE/DGS and was instrumental in founding the *Flechas*.

68. Ibid.

69. Ibid.

70. Ibid.

71. Ibid.

72. Ibid.

73. Inocentes interview, 22 October 1994, London.

74. General Pedro Cardoso, interview by the author, 17 November 1994, Lisbon.

75. Edgar O'Ballance, "To Turn His Coat—or Not?" *Royal United Services Institute Journal for Defense Studies* (March 1973): 85–87.

76. Wheeler, 277.

77. Alistair Horne, *A Savage War of Peace: Algeria 1954–1962* (Harmondsworth: Penguin Books, 1987), 255.   F.L.N. is the abbreviation for Front de Libération Nationale.

78. Ibid., 255, 476; Alf Andrew Heggoy, *Insurgency and Counterinsurgency in Algeria* (Bloomington: Indiana University Press, 1972), 179, 261.

79. Douglas Porch, *The French Foreign Legion: A Complete History of the Legendary Fighting Force* (New York: HarperCollins, 1991), 531, 550.

80. Horne, 235, 506; Heggoy, 179.

81. Trager, 338; Andrew F. Krepinevich, Jr., *The Army and Vietnam* (Baltimore: Johns Hopkins University Press, 1986), 192.

82. Inocentes interview, 5 September 1994; and Major Luís Alberto Santiago Inocentes, interview by Al J. Venter in *Portugal's Guerrilla War: The Campaign for Africa* (Cape Town: John Malherbe, 1973), 134.   Colonel Inocentes expanded in the more recent interview on the motivational characteristics of the local troops that he had described to Mr. Venter in 1971.

83. Brigadeiro Hélio A. Esteves Felgas, interview by the author, 22 November 1994, Lisbon.

84. Pedro Cardoso interview.

85. Heggoy, 262–263.

86. Henry Miller, *Jungle War in Malaya: The Campaign Against Communism 1948–60* (London: Arthur Barker, 1972), 25.

87. Hoffman and Taw, Appendix A.

88. *Resenha Histórico-Militar das Campanhas de África (1961–1974)*, Vol. I, 264–266.

89. Ibid.

90. Thomas H. Henriksen, "Portugal in Africa: Comparative Notes on Counter-insurgency," *Orbis* (Summer 1977): 404.

91. Peter Paret, *French Revolutionary Warfare from Indochina to Algeria* (London: Pall Mall Press, 1964), 39.

6

PORTUGUESE INTELLIGENCE NETWORK IN COUNTERINSURGENCY

Locating and destroying insurgents after they had infiltrated the three colonies required "a good intelligence network and a lot of foot-slogging."[1] Gaining intelligence on the guerrillas was vital, if the Portuguese were to keep them separated from the population, to deny them shelter, food, and intelligence on military operations, and to destroy them. Information was needed on their political leaders, their military command, their forces in the field, their sources of support both within the colonies and externally, and their operational plans and intentions.[2] This information was obtained through reports of infantry patrols, air reconnaissance, interrogation of captured or surrendered guerrillas, captured documents, and paid informers and agents.[3] The Portuguese Army realized this critical need for effective intelligence and proceeded to build a productive network that helped its forces exploit weaknesses in the enemy. This chapter describes the organization and development of Portugal's systematic intelligence effort and shows its effective link in a relentless effort to rob the insurgents of their initiative. It addresses the problems encountered with these operations in the field in selected areas and follows the solutions adopted, comparing and contrasting them to the experiences of other countries with contemporaneous counterinsurgency operations. This intelligence effort was adapted not only to counterinsurgency but to the particular campaign in each theater. These several adaptations were uniquely Portuguese and in keeping with the subdued and cost-conscious strategy.

INTELLIGENCE ORGANIZATION

In the Portuguese Army there was an intelligence system at the beginning of the Campaigns that, while not being a professional service as in the British Army, operated similarly. The officers and men serving in the *2ª Repartição* or *2ª Secção* (Second Division, or on a lower echelon, Second Section, which was responsible for the intelligence function) of the General Staff of the Army and its replications down to the battalion level were personnel with diverse warfare specialties (infantry, cavalry, artillery, and so forth) who were assigned to an intelligence section. The rationale for this policy was that officers "self-specialized" themselves, following a natural interest and developing a proclivity for the intelligence craft.[4] When an intelligence service was established, these officers gravitated to it. As early as 1958 the General Secretary of National Defense attempted to draw the various services together in an intelligence-sharing effort and began training a cadre for this purpose at the Intelligence Center of the British Army, Maresfield Park Camp, United Kingdom.[5]

This effort was overcome by the events of 1961. As early as January of that year there had been a working group in Lisbon composed of representatives from the military commands, PIDE, the General Command of the Portuguese Legion, the Director General of the Political and Civil Administration, the Customs Police, and other government arms.[6] The working group recommended the creation of a local service that would draw together intelligence from all sources and disseminate it in a timely fashion to relevant users. This body would be known as the Intelligence Service of the Government General (*Serviço de Informações do Governo-Geral* or SIGG) and would be responsible for a host of duties in this vein, including psychological operations, intelligence, counterintelligence, electronic surveillance, prisoner interrogation, et cetera.[7] This path was followed in both Angola and later Mozambique, where the bodies were known respectively as SIGGA and SIGGM.

Following the March 1961 attacks in the north of Angola and the appointment of General Venâncio Deslandes as the Governor-General and Commander-in-Chief of the Armed Forces of Angola, he created a true Service of Centralization and Coordination of Intelligence (*Serviço de Centralização e Coordenação de Informações* or SCCI) on 29 June. It included not only local intelligence gathering and dissemination but was also the beneficiary of intelligence gathered through the Ministry of Foreign Affairs, the Ministry of the Overseas Provinces, and other national sources. These diverse avenues provided access to both tactical and strategic intelligence. Later an SCCI was created in Mozambique, in Guiné, and in the other colonies as and when it was deemed appropriate. Oversight of the SCCI was the responsibility of the Province's Intelligence Commission (*Comissão de Informações*), which set policy on intelligence operations, military security, counterintelligence, and the like. It was also responsible for the creation of the district, regional, and local Intelligence Commissions that held responsibility for the district, regional, and local sections of the SCCI. As with most undertakings of this magnitude, the SCCI required tuning to make it function properly across the various military and civil bodies. By February 1963 General Deslandes affirmed the progress and its importance by acknowledging that each passing day continued to reinforce the need of moving quickly to coordinate and analyze raw intelligence, to organize its procurement, and to learn not only what the enemy wanted but especially what interested the Portuguese.[8]

It was never an easy task for the SCCI to reconcile the diverse viewpoints of the various civil agencies, the police, and the military commands in the interest of an accurate, overall intelligence picture. Professional rivalries between intelligence agencies are a service tradition virtually everywhere, and Portugal was no exception. The most notable difficulty arose with PIDE, normally considered a superior and effective intelligence service, disagreeing with the Army. PIDE in a number of these instances withheld information and acted on it through the offensive operations of its own *Flechas*. For the most part, however, PIDE did not feel threatened by the military intelligence sections and worked well with the Army. Its conflict was usually with its fellow civil intelligence agencies.[9] Notwithstanding these difficulties, cooperation was viewed as essential and was pursued by the leadership. It improved considerably when the Governors-General were also Commanders-in-Chief.[10] The consequent wisdom of this concept under which the Portuguese operated was reinforced by Sir Claude Fenner, Inspector-General of the Malaysian Police, 1963–1966, who spoke from his experience in this capacity: "Intelligence is one of the most important factors affecting the conduct of the war and a multiplicity of intelligence collecting agencies entails grave hazards both to collectors and sources of intelligence alike. The ideal is to have a single, unified intelligence service...."[11] This unified effort by the Portuguese armed forces contrasted sharply with the U.S. position in Vietnam, as observed by Sir Robert Thompson, head of the British Advisory Mission there between 1961 and 1965: "Nor was there any concentration of intelligence organization—in fact rather the opposite. When I added up the intelligence organizations which were operating in Saigon in 1966 against the Vietcong there were seventeen, both American and South Vietnamese, and none of them were talking to each other!"[12]

The Portuguese sought to avoid this pitfall. In each theater Portuguese intelligence coordination was theoretically done at every level. Militarily it was effected from the smallest patrols using and gathering intelligence to the headquarters of the Commander-in-Chief. On the civil side it ran from the local *posto*'s contact with the population to the Governor-General. At every stage intelligence gathering, analysis, and dissemination coordination was sought between military and civil arms. The mechanism for this joint process was the SCCI, which existed at the province, district, regional, and local levels.[13] Contact with the population was considered paramount. Interpreters and translators were used extensively. Agents infiltrated the enemy's infrastructure. Troops moved freely and regularly among the population, and trackers accompanied the patrols to interpret the signs of the forests and jungles and locate the enemy. Special militias were also formed for the self-defense of the population and, it was hoped, reported on enemy contact. All of these activities formed a network or system of intelligence gathering that was coordinated, documented, and shared throughout the civil and military arms. Operations were planned and executed to exploit this information flow on a regular basis.[14] This system was similar to the British innovation in Malaya, where the government established district, province, and national intelligence centers run by the police with representatives of the military and civil authorities, and regularly planned and executed operations to capitalize on the intelligence produced by this network.

INTELLIGENCE OPERATIONS

The desired response to an insurgent's ability to move secretly, strike suddenly, and then disappear is "an intelligence apparatus that will pierce the screen of secrecy."[15] It is the military's responsibility to build this apparatus to support its operations against the enemy. While the requirements for intelligence vary according to the scale of command, they always center on developing a sound understanding of the environment and of the enemy. This was a difficult task in that throughout the theaters there was a lack of guerrilla organization and communication. Guerrilla thrusts were only generally organized with a vague operational plan. Consequently, it was difficult to understand precisely what they were doing until contact was made. Effecting contact was difficult, so gaining intelligence and countering incursions were almost as imprecise as the insurgent plans themselves.[16] The insurgents used no radios, so signals intelligence (SIGINT) was denied. This situation was due to three factors: (1) radios were unavailable; (2) the proliferation of languages made communication difficult; and (3) the low educational level of the insurgents made it very difficult to operate and maintain higher-technology equipment. When they began to use radios later, however, the Portuguese did listen.[17] Thus in its counterinsurgency campaign the Portuguese were forced to develop this picture piecemeal through the following sources and methods. Each of these made an important contribution in solving the intelligence puzzle, and because of this guerrilla operational vagueness, it was important that information from one reinforce that from the others to produce an accurate picture.

Ground Reconnaissance

Ground reconnaissance was the most basic method of finding and fixing the enemy in the difficult terrain of Guiné or the vast expanses of Angola and Mozambique and was a difficult job. To address this problem at the field level, each battalion had a staff that included an Operations and Intelligence Section (*2ª Secção*). This section was comprised of two officers, two sergeants, and two enlisted men. Supporting this staff was a reconnaissance platoon of twenty-nine men commanded by an officer with three sergeants and twenty-five enlisted men. It was equipped with jeeps and radios to give it added mobility. In some instances, depending on availability, helicopters might be used; however, this practice was the exception rather than the rule. Thus, there were thirty-five officers and men, or about 5 percent of battalion strength, devoted to intelligence duties, a somewhat greater proportion than is normally found in a force structured for conventional warfare.[18]

Patrols by both reconnaissance platoons seeking information on the enemy and normal combat groups obtaining intelligence in the course of performing other missions proved among the most valuable and productive sources.[19] Both types of units were constantly attempting to make contact with the enemy and maintain the initiative, and thus all operations to one degree or another embodied a reconnaissance role. Experienced troops were able to deduce information through the simple skills of knowledgeable observation, for example, the length of time an insurgent encampment had been abandoned and the number of men in the enemy force. One of the clues in this reasoning process was the state of the latrines at the campsite. Also the type, condition, and origin of any captured weapons fingerprinted insurgents reliably, as it was known who sponsored which nationalist movement with what armament.[20] This fingerprinting also indicated the capability and mission of the insurgents and their logistic needs, and this knowledge was valuable to a tactical commander in enabling him to maneuver against the enemy. These several examples of ground reconnaissance and its contribution to the puzzle illustrate the importance of "foot slogging." Attempts were always made to verify this type of information through contact with the population.

The population represented a key source of information, and indeed it was the primary battlefield, or in Clausewitzian terms, "the center of gravity" of an insurgency. The Portuguese soldier was indoctrinated in this principle and instructed by his doctrine that in his relations with the population he was always to seek intelligence on the time of sighting, nature of armament, and numbers of guerrilla forces.[21] Not only must he be alert to intelligence on the enemy, but he must also protect its primary source from guerrilla intimidation. Indeed, it was found that the higher the confidence level of the population in the Portuguese soldier's ability to protect it, the greater the information it would provide. Guerrilla intimidation could easily build a *muro do silêncio* ("wall of silence") between the population and the soldiers, and it required enormous patience, time, and goodwill to penetrate this "wall."[22] The rewards of doing so, however, were great. This well-established principle was explained by Second Lieutenant Oliver Crawford from his experiences in Malaya in 1955:

But we could not bring our military machine to bear without information, and we could not get information without the support of the population, and we would not get the support of the population unless they were free from terrorism, and we could not free them from terrorism until we had sent men to kill the terrorists. So it went round and round—a most complicated combination of vicious circles. The key to breaking these vicious circles remained one thing: information.[23]

And so the breaking of this "wall of silence" paid dividends for the Portuguese as well.

An illustration of the typical result of this type of work occurred around the village of Bissássema, Guiné, in November 1970. It was here that Portuguese patrols began to acquire information through their contacts with the population that the PAIGC were planning to attack their camp with four *bi-grupos* or about 150 men. The Portuguese consequently laid a trap in which the insurgents would attack into a cross fire between the camp and a bivouacked patrol hidden in the jungle. The only escape route was through a booby-trapped minefield. When the PAIGC force attacked, it was destroyed as a result of the skillful use of this intelligence.[24]   Of course this source was a two-edged sword. Portuguese combat groups generally patrolled by day and established ambushes at night to maintain a steady pressure on the PAIGC. The PAIGC, however, was able to detect ambushes through its contact with the population. Thus, in order to remain effective, the Portuguese were forced to move the ambush sites constantly.[25]

Aerial Reconnaissance

Aerial reconnaissance was the complementary method to ground reconnaissance and was very important in locating guerrilla activity in the difficult and vast expanses of the theaters. It was difficult to do well because of the cover provided by the forests and jungles and the deep reservoir of experience and skill required by an observer to identify the clues to insurgent presence from the air. An observer needed to know the area well, so that he could easily detect changes. He acquired this familiarity by flying over his assigned patrol area routinely in a Dornier DO-27 observation aircraft at the relatively low altitude of 200 meters for many hours. Consequently he was able to discern the typical clues to insurgent presence: a new footbridge, a new trail, new and heavy use of an old trail, boats concealed alongside a stream, shelters built at the edge of the forest rather than in the open, and a lack of crops or domestic animals around huts.[26] In observing a suspicious site, the pilot would continue to fly the aircraft on a straight course as if nothing curious had been noted. It was hoped that this routine would not flush the guerrillas. Altering course and losing altitude for a closer look could cause them to move their camp quickly. In the case of a bridge, a boat, a trail, or another object of transit for guerrilla use, however, a close look at no less than 50 meters was generally warranted.[27]

Photographs of these sightings were a useful tool, and their analysis was helpful in revealing the presence or absence of insurgents. Details not easily visible to the naked eye could be identified more readily in pictures. For instance, the construction of normal huts included a door and windows. Insurgent huts had two or three large doors, no windows, and were larger than the normal hut. These subtleties might elude the naked eye in flight but could be discerned easily from postflight photography analysis. Other clues were detectable in the use of burned-over areas, fishing structures along the rivers, suspension bridges, float bridges, trails, rafts, dugout canoes, caves, and so forth. Also, a series of photographs taken over a month could show changes in the use of these facilities. Information from aerial reconnaissance was fed to the Army on a continuous basis, as an enemy beaten in one place today would tomorrow establish new camps at another with extraordinary speed. The enemy's tactics were also in a constant state of flux, and it was vital to detect these changes promptly and to modify operations accordingly.[28]

The bulk of intelligence came from these Army patrols and aerial reconnaissance missions, and their effectiveness cannot be understated. In the north of Angola during the reaction to the 1961 incursions from the Congo, aerial reconnaissance was indispensable in locating guerrillas in the tall elephant grass and in directing the ground forces to engagement. This particular operation by the T-6 Harvard and Auster aircraft from the new military airport of Negage, named *Aeródromo-Base No. 3* (AB3), occurred in April 1961. It was centered around the village of Mucaba and its reoccupation by units of the 21st Battalion of Paratroops.[29]

The sense of urgency in reacting to the results of air reconnaissance depended on many factors: the activity of the guerrillas, their proximity to or remoteness from the population, and the availability of local troops. Normally guerrillas did not concentrate in large numbers, so locating them required quartering the large expanses of Angola and Mozambique in search of their telltale signs. Visual reconnaissance was necessarily done in daylight, and the guerrillas worked at night, so with this limitation deductions had to be made from these signs. Once the guerrillas were located, the Portuguese intelligence network began to develop a picture of their intentions. As the guerrillas moved on foot, their progress was normally slow and gave the Portuguese time to prepare a trap. The guerrillas were easily spooked, and great care had to be taken in planning any operation. They had been hunted so relentlessly that at any hint of danger they quickly melted away. The intelligence picture would then have to be redeveloped. These procedures were in step with maintaining a subdued, cost-conscious war, as the small aircraft were unsophisticated and relatively inexpensive to maintain, and were quiet and unobtrusive in the vastness of the colonies. The results of these low-profile flight operations were extremely satisfactory in light of the modest investment.[30]

Captured Guerrillas

Captured enemy personnel potentially represented the best source of information and thus "a terrorist captured alive is much more valuable for intelligence purposes than a dead one."[31] Reconnaissance patrols were often assigned the secondary mission of capturing a prisoner, and this mission required careful preparation and special training. Upon capture an insurgent was immediately interrogated to obtain current information about the local area, the presence of other insurgents, their camps and staging points, their equipment, their lines of advance and withdrawal, and so forth. This highly perishable information was generally tested for soundness and verified immediately, at least to the extent possible under field conditions.

The Portuguese were always concerned about mines and booby traps, and thus captured insurgents were also asked to unmask these devices for destruction. Some were cooperative and others less so, depending on their fear and the proximity of their guerrilla compatriots. In these cases the prisoner was asked to lead the way to the devices, for as one Portuguese veteran commented, "After all, they laid them and they knew where they were."[32]

A second interrogation would occur at battalion or sector headquarters to obtain more detailed information on the insurgent himself, his training, background, companions, and instructors. While most of these interrogations were performed by Portuguese specialists, there were exceptions. In Zala, for instance, there was an insurgent captured in 1965 who was named Alfredo and who now worked for the Portuguese. He had developed a talent for interrogation, as he knew the language of the guerrillas who habitually infiltrated into the area and had formerly served an insurgent commander in interrogating captured Portuguese. Captain Ricardo Alcada from the garrison post at Nambuangongo, Angola, explained that Alfredo "usually spent an hour or two with a man in a room. By the time he came out he knew the man's history, who his grandmother was, whether she was a communist, what the man was doing in the area, what his unit was, what he was going to do—in fact everything the Portuguese could wish to know."[33]

An assessment would then be made as to whether the man was wholeheartedly with the nationalist movement or whether he had been coerced into joining by fear, promises, or both. In these cases the prisoner was shown troops in training and demonstrations of firepower. An attempt was made to convince him that the Portuguese would prevail in the struggle. The prisoner was also exposed to the new villages and the social work that was being done for the population, including the *apresentados*. These latter individuals were Africans living in the bush due to fear either of the insurgents or of the Portuguese troops and who had presented themselves to the authorities for resettlement in the new villages. They could also be civilians working for the insurgents as porters, cooks, and the like, and had simply run from the camp. With this exposure to an environment of law and order, organized administration, and medical care, the prisoner was supposed to conclude that life under a Portuguese administration would be infinitely preferable to the hard and dangerous existence of an insurgent in the bush.[34]

Treatment of Africans by the insurgents also contrasted sharply with that of the Portuguese. Anything from a minor mistake, such as the loss of a weapon or kit, to a rational questioning of authority could draw a severe penalty from the insurgent leadership. It was thus very rare for a captured insurgent, *apresentado*, or deserter to rejoin the insurgents, although he had the opportunity to do so.[35] The alternative was one of the prisoner of war camps. These facilities were isolated, and all were similar to São Nicolau on the southern coast of Angola, which was bounded by shark-infested sea on one side and desert on the other. With the opportunity to flee foreclosed by natural obstacles, the atmosphere was relaxed. Frequently the former insurgents would take a new wife and with Portuguese help build a new life.[36]

This benign approach was not necessarily the norm, however, and all depended on circumstances at the time of capture. If the capturing patrol was on an operation and believed that it was in immediate danger, then treatment would acquire a sense of urgency. In late 1970 during operations in Guiné around the confluence of the Geba and the Corubal rivers, a PAIGC infiltration group crossed the border from Kandiafara with the mission of cutting and mining the Bafata road. The unit had attacked Bambadinca one evening and withdrawn to await rendezvous with two *bi-grupos* for further assaults. The following day a Portuguese patrol from Artillery Battalion 2917 captured a PAIGC scouting party intact without firing a shot. Included in the group was a senior PAIGC officer. He was flown to Bambadinca by helicopter and given a choice of revealing all or dying. General Spínola was allegedly privy to the entire battle plan within a few hours.[37]

Lieutenant Colonel João Barros e Cunha, garrison commander at Nambuangongo in 1968 described another aspect of the rehabilitation program: "We offer the hand of friendship to these people—partly because we feel we have to, from a Christian point of view, and partly because we know they can help us win the war."[38] In exchange for their lives the terrorists were required to disclose all from beginning to end: "names, places, codes, signals, dates of training, future and past programs and explain any documents and plans that may have been found in their possession."[39] Finally, in a moment of truth, the prisoner was required to lead the Portuguese to his former headquarters and provide a tour of his operational area.

Torture was formally prohibited by directives of the Commanders-in-Chief. It was never sanctioned, in contrast with the French in Algeria, and was entirely contrary to Portugal's policy of winning the allegiance of the population, including captured insurgents. It was further seen as alienating both domestic and foreign allies. Both of these reactions would seriously undermine the overall war effort, and certainly the French experience in Algeria was an object lesson. The French malfeasance in the use of torture in intelligence operations, among other factors, made ties to France ever less desirable and tenable for the Algerians.[40] Even military success for France could not overcome this adverse political factor. While it would be manifestly untrue to state that torture was never used by the Portuguese, information received through its use was always suspect, and its practice appears to have been limited.[41]

Under normal conditions prisoners seemingly were treated well. Most had been indoctrinated with the myth that, if captured, they would be subjected to a slow and painful execution. When they were actually captured and were treated decently, the revelation became a major factor in developing sound intelligence. Lieutenant Colonel Barros e Cunha described the rehabilitation of Alberto Imbu, a former guerrilla who had received his training at Tclemen in Algeria and had been badly wounded on 18 March 1967 in an operation near Nambuangongo. After recovering under Portuguese medical care, he had led a patrol in an ambush on his old camp, where many of his former comrades were killed.[42] This behavior was not uncommon in guerrillas from other conflicts and cultures. In Vietnam, for instance, the U.S. Marine Corps found that once wounded Viet Cong had received hospital care, and their fear and pain had been replaced with relief, they would routinely be very cooperative.[43] The British experienced the same prisoner reaction in directing the counterinsurgency campaign in the Sultanate of Oman in the early 1970s. Professors Blaufarb and Tanham explain the procedure there: "In the early phases of the program, captured insurgents were interrogated in the normal businesslike fashion. This proved unproductive. It was then decided to try handling them according to the rules pertaining in that desert society for welcoming guests. They were greeted politely, offered coffee, and chatted up before being asked questions of interest. This approach worked well and was followed for the rest of the war."[44]

When the Portuguese followed these tested principles of treating prisoners, they generally acquired sound, reliable intelligence. When they did not, the process resulted in inaccurate information, it discouraged the disaffected enemy from surrendering, and it degraded the Army's standing in the eyes of the people. Certainly this situation was the case in the Tete district of Mozambique in 1968 when FRELIMO opened an offensive there from its new sanctuary in neighboring Zambia. In mid-1971 General Kaúlza de Arriaga, the Commander-in-Chief of the Armed Forces of Mozambique, installed a brutal military governor in Tete, Colonel Armindo Videira. Once the extent of this officer's systematically applied terror became apparent and culminated in the tragedy of Wiriyamu on 16 December 1972, he was dismissed.[45] The damage had been done, however, and Portugal never fully recovered the confidence of the population there.

Captured Documents and Equipment

Captured documents and equipment represented an important facet of the intelligence collection effort and were carefully handled and preserved. Normally documents were written in Portuguese, as it was often the only common language available to the insurgents.[46] For the most part the local languages of Portuguese Africa are spoken only. When a prisoner of any importance was captured, documents were usually found on him or with his equipment. These documents were used to verify his story during interrogation and provided a valuable index to his credibility. In many cases the circumstances of capture proved to be as important as the document itself. For example, any document listing guerrilla units was particularly important if connected with the precise time and place of capture. Battlefield searches also often uncovered official papers. Particularly important was a search of the dead insurgents, as they often carried documents that revealed their intentions and were of immediate tactical value. These were always processed as rapidly as possible through channels, as such information was invariably perishable.[47]

In one instance captured documents provided the Portuguese with confirmation that their operations were effective in denying the PAIGC permanent camps in Guiné. A field message captured in July 1971 near Gadamael on the southern frontier was written in Portuguese and reiterated a decree to the effect that no PAIGC unit was to remain in a local area for more than two days. It also reminded *bi-grupo* leaders and commissars of the consequences of disobeying this order both from the PAIGC command and from the Portuguese Air Force once the unit had been located.[48] They would be punished by both.

Captured equipment provided the Portuguese with an indication on the type and degree of support that the guerrillas were receiving from external sources. The taking of such equipment confirmed or complemented the strategic intelligence provided by Lisbon. The Portuguese published booklets describing the equipment and its capabilities, cataloging all types of armament used by the enemy and their location of capture. By these means the troops knew the enemy's order of battle and what to expect in combat. The information on mines and booby traps was particularly helpful.[49]

Agents and Informers

For the Portuguese the use of agents and informers was a normal process in obtaining information. In some cases within the theaters such agents worked with the military directly, and in others they sought the police, depending on which authority was present in the area. It was for this reason that a close liaison between the two was so vital and competition and jealousy in intelligence gathering were so counterproductive. More often than not, the police were in closer contact with the population than the Army and possessed better facilities for centralizing this activity.[50]

In penetrating the sanctuary countries where the nationalist movements resided, border agents were generally handled through the Army and agents on missions further afield were handled by PIDE.[51] Competition between the various factions within the movements provided a fissure that bred informers and fostered agents. Disaffected members of all the movements proved a fertile source of recruits and an opportunity for PIDE to sow the seeds of dissention.[52] In Guiné, the PAIGC "suffered from internal frictions between the mulatto Cape Verdean leadership and the African Guineans; and this was naturally exploited by the Portuguese."[53]

In Mozambique the main nationalist movement, FRELIMO, was in open competition with rival nationalist forces until 1972 not only for external sponsorship but also for nationalist movement dominance. Additionally, within FRELIMO there was a split between those committed to revolutionary socialism and the conservatives. The conservatives found themselves isolated and followed their leader, Lazaro Kavandame, in joining the Portuguese. Shortly thereafter, in February 1969, FRELIMO's leader, Eduardo Mondlane, was assassinated by a parcel bomb. Earlier he had recognized the factionalism and its opportunities for exploitation, particularly by PIDE:

Another difficulty, particularly acute in the early stages of development, when many of the movement's members know little about one another, is the danger of infiltration by Portuguese agents. And this is connected with the problem of splinter groups, since these may use a member of the main organization to try to spread dissent, so as to bring over a section of the membership. The complexity of motives behind divisive conduct makes it the more difficult to guard against: individual neuroses, personal ambitions, real ideological differences are muddled up with the tactics of the enemy secret service.[54]

The Angolan nationalist movements spent most of their time fighting among themselves and thus had little united war effort. The Portuguese were so successful in exploiting these differences and causing defections that it prompted René Pélissier to comment in 1971 that "the PIDE networks and Portuguese informants in Congo-Kinshasa are equal in effect to a division of parachutists on the ground."[55]

It is likely that the Portuguese in their missions to Algeria learned something from the French experience there. Here the French had proved very adept in their use of agents, as Alistair Horne's description of events in August 1957 indicated that "the French were resorting to new and subtler techniques of penetration.... [S]elected turncoats clad inconspicuously in workers' dungarees, or *bleus de chauffe*, were unleashed in the Casbah to mingle with their former terrorist associates and lead...intelligence operatives to the bosses' lairs. The technique was to achieve such success that the expression *la bleuite*, or "the blues," later assumed a particularly sinister connotation in the war as whole."[56] It would also be a gross dereliction for a country fighting an insurgency not to exploit the personal weaknesses of a movement's leaders and its organizational deficiencies, as explained by Michael Elliott-Bateman:

It is a mistake to start off by imagining the enemy are a solid block of communists on one side of the fence and we are a solid block of anti-communists on the other. If one starts off with that attitude one misses half the game, and will fail to note the incredible strains and stresses in any revolutionary movement. For a start, great struggles for leadership and power are going on within the enemy structure which can be exploited. If there is one lesson or one technique that should be developed in counter-insurgency, it is the ability to infiltrate within the structure of the enemy's organization so as to splinter and debase it.[57]

The Portuguese consistently sought to undermine the organizational structure of the nationalist movements during the Campaigns. The existence of many and varied ethnolinguistic groups throughout the theaters made the task of maintaining constituency order far more difficult for the insurgents than for the Portuguese. Any action, normally brutal, against the population by either side was an unpardonable offense and an unbearable transgression against a group, particularly if it were inflicted by insurgents of a different group. An undercurrent of vendettas was a continuing condition of the Campaigns[58]

Guides and Translators

The Portuguese routinely used guides and translators to identify and track insurgents and to communicate with the population. Normally such guides were simple, unsophisticated people whose confidence and cooperation were vital to Portuguese success.[59] In Angola, for instance, the best trackers were Bushmen from the Kalahari Desert in the southeast, who were also initially employed as PIDE agents. The Bushmen were intelligent and gifted people who had lost none of their age-old talent for tracking in the bush.

With the plethora of local languages in each of the theaters, translators were attached to every unit to accommodate those who might be encountered in its operating area. In Guiné, for example, each company had between twenty and twenty-three translators attached, as there were some twenty different languages that they might use in the course of their operations. These translators also provided a bridge between the population and the soldiers in the field and took great pride in their responsibilities for the simple reward of appreciation and the satisfaction of their physical needs.[60] Their pay, while normally equal in value to that of a Portuguese soldier, was a mixture of kind and cash, and often payment was divided and made not only to the translator but to his wife or wives.[61]

The importance of being able to communicate with both the population and the captured enemy cannot be overemphasized in the political atmosphere of an insurgency. This requirement was not unique to the theaters in Portuguese Africa. Colonel Robert O'Neill, Commanding Officer of the 5th Battalion, Royal Australian Regiment, deployed to Vietnam 1966–1967, explained the difficulties of cross-cultural communication and his use of native interpreters not only because he did not speak Vietnamese, "but because the interpreter formed a social bridge between myself and the person with whom I was talking.... This consideration was important not only for interrogation, but for general contact with Vietnamese officials and civilians, for a good interpreter knew the social form, he knew the local area, he could effect the right sort of introduction at the commencement of a conversation, he knew what humour to use...."[62]

In contrast, the U.S. Army in Vietnam lacked the attuned approach of the Portuguese and its "intelligence operations were hampered by a lack of familiarity with the language and culture of the people with whom they were working as well as by the absence of any Army procedures for the procurement of such intelligence."[63] The Portuguese soldiers recruited in Africa knew one or more local tongues and seemed to have a facility for acquiring them.[64] After all, "you cannot fight a political war if you cannot communicate with the people for whom and with whom you are fighting."[65]

THE KEY TO COUNTERINSURGENCY

The Portuguese clearly understood that the centralized flow of intelligence was the key to counterinsurgency and that this flow would come primarily from the population. They consequently designed their intelligence-collecting machinery to work in this special environment. It was here again that their entire effort was reoriented from conventional war with its focus on the enemy as the primary source of information to counterinsurgency, in which the operating area and the civil population there were primary. The understanding of this principle was well articulated by a Portuguese junior officer writing in a military journal of the time: "The primary objective of the terrorists is to destroy the population's confidence in the guarantees of protection that can be provided by local government. With this objective achieved, the local population is reluctant to provide intelligence to the authorities for fear of reprisals. Only with well conducted operations will it be possible to reestablish this loss of confidence. And these depend upon the timely utilization of reliable intelligence...."[66] The search for information was the key to success in counterinsurgency, and the killing, or preferably capturing, of insurgents who had infiltrated into the three theaters was Portugal's military aim.

As intelligence networks operate largely in secret, the details of their organization and operations are not often visible to outsiders. The litmus test for the effectiveness of an intelligence apparatus is the frequency with which it is taken by surprise. In the Campaigns the Portuguese were seldom caught unawares, but when they were, the results were severe. The initial events in Angola in 1961 represented more a failure to act on intelligence than poor intelligence itself. Thereafter, the system in all three theaters appeared to work relatively well, and it was more often the insurgents who were taken by surprise in operations that were planned and executed regularly to exploit information. The contribution of a good intelligence network was one of the decisive factors in Portugal's ability to sustain the conflict for thirteen years and to employ its limited resources in effectively controlling the guerrilla threat. It was able to anticipate the guerrilla well and largely defeat him over this prolonged period through consistently thorough intelligence work. The most notable exception lay in the Tete district of Mozambique, where FRELIMO in 1969 shifted from attacks on the massive Cabora Bassa dam project to politicizing the population. FRELIMO began systematically eliminating tribal chiefs north of the Zambezi, and the security situation deteriorated rapidly, catching the Portuguese largely unawares. It became readily apparent that the intelligence network in Tete had either failed or been disregarded. The failure in the north of Angola in 1961 may have been understandable. The failure of the intelligence apparatus in Tete in 1969 represented a serious void in that Portuguese complacency about FRELIMO's capabilities allowed a rapid subversion of the district. Notwithstanding this setback, information was the cornerstone of Portuguese counterinsurgency, and no operation proceeded without substantial intelligence. This strength sustained an otherwise fragile military presence stretched across the three theaters and was indicative of Portugal's use of leverage in pursuing a relatively inexpensive advantage over its opponents.

NOTES

1. Lieutenant General Janie J. Geldenhuys, Chief of the South African Army, "Rural Insurgency and Counter-Measures," in *Revolutionary Warfare and Counter-Insurgency*, ed. M. Hough (Pretoria: University of Pretoria, Institute for Strategic Studies, 1984), 41.

2. Edward E. Rice, *Wars of the Third Kind: Conflict in Undeveloped Countries* (Berkeley: University of California Press, 1988), 103.

3. D. S. Blaufarb and George K. Tanham, *Who Will Win?: A Key to the Puzzle of Revolutionary War* (London: Crane Russak, 1989), 26.

4. Colonel Luís Alberto Santiago Inocentes, interview by the author, 5 June 1995, London.

5. Pedro Alexandre Gomes Cardoso, *As Informações em Portugal* [Intelligence in Portugal] (Lisbon: Instituto da Defesa Nacional, 1980), 106.

6. Estado-Maior do Exército, *Resenha Histórico-Militar das Campanhas de África (1961–1974)* [Historical-Military Report of the African Campaigns (1961–1974)] (Lisbon: Estado-Maior do Exército, 1988), Vol. I, 360–363.

7. Cardoso, 107–108.

8. Ibid., 109–118.

9. Brigadeiro Renato F. Marques Pinto, interview by the author, 30 March 1995, Oeiras. Marques Pinto was Chief of Military Intelligence in Angola 1963–1965, and Director of the SCCIA 1965–1968.

10. Inocentes interview, 5 June 1995.

11. Sir Claude Fenner, *Lessons from the Vietnam War*, Report of a seminar held at the Royal United Services Institute in London, 12 February 1966, 6.

12. Sir Robert Thompson, *Lessons from the Vietnam War*, Report of a seminar held at the Royal United Services Institute in London, 12 February 1966, 2.

13. *Resenha Histórico-Militar das Campanhas de África (1961–1974)*, Vol. I, 368–370.

14. Estado-Maior do Exército, *Subsídios para o Estudo da Doutrina Aplicada nas Campanhas de África (1961–1974)* [Information for the Study of Doctrine Applicable in the Campaigns of Africa (1961–1974)] (Lisbon: Estado-Maior do Exército, 1990), 159–160.

15. Blaufarb and Tanham, 26–27.

16. Marques Pinto interview, 7 November 1994.

17. Inocentes interview, 14 April 1994.

18. Duke of Valderano, interview by the author, 17 March 1995, London; Marques Pinto, correspondence with the author, 18 July 1995, Oeiras.

19. José Emídio Pereira da Costa, "Informação e Contra-Informação Militar em Ambiente de Guerra Subversiva" [Military Intelligence and Counterintelligence in the Environment of Subversive War], *Revista de Artilharia* (September–October 1961): 149.

20. Ibid., 149.

21. Estado-Maior do Exército, *O Exército na Guerra Subversiva* [The Army in Subversive War] (Lisbon: Estado-Maior do Exército, 1963), Vol. II, Pt. 1, Chap. V, p. 2.

22. *Subsídios para o Estudo da Doutrina Aplicada nas Campanhas de África (1961-1974)*, 157.

23. Oliver Crawford, *The Door Marked Malaya* (London: Rupert Hart-Davis, 1958), 180–181.

24. *Resenha Histórico-Militar das Campanhas de África (1961-1974)*, Vol. III, 168; Lieutenant Colonel Baptista Lopes, interview by Al J. Venter in *Portugal's War in Guine-Bissau* (Pasadena: California Institute of Technology, 1973), 90–91.

25. Inocentes interview, 9 April 1994.

26. Joaquim Vito Corte-Real Negrão, "Subsídios para o Reconhecimento Aéreo Visual" [Aid to Visual Air Reconnaissance], *Boletim do Estado-Maior da Força Aerea* (December 1962): 34.

27. Ibid., 42.

28. Ibid., 34–43.

29. Augusto Cândido Soares de Moura, "Testemunho Norte de Angola (1961/1962)" [Witness of the North of Angola (1961/1962)], *Mais Alto* (1981–1989 period): 51.

30. Negrão, 43.

31. Pereira da Costa, 150.

32. Inocentes interview, 14 April 1994.

33. Captain Ricardo Alcada, interview by Al J. Venter in *The Terror Fighters: A Profile of Guerrilla Warfare in Southern Africa* (Cape Town: Purnell and Sons, 1969), 72.

34. Valderano interview, 17 March 1995.

35. Inocentes correspondence, 5 June 1995, London.

36. Marques Pinto interview, 30 March 1995.

37. *Resenha Histórico-Militar das Campanhas de África (1961-1974)*, Vol. III, 167; Lieutenant Colonel João Monteiro, interview by Al J. Venter in *Portugal's War in Guine-Bissau* (Pasadena: California Institute of Technology, 1973), 151.

38. Lieutenant Colonel João Barros e Cunha, interview by Al J. Venter in *The Terror Fighters: A Profile of Guerrilla Warfare in Southern Africa* (Cape Town: Purnell and Sons, 1969), 55.

39. Ibid.

40. Christopher C. Harmon, "Illustrations of 'Learning' in Counterinsurgency, *Comparative Strategy* (January–March 1992), 33.

41. Valderano interview, 17 March 1995.

42. Barros e Cunha interview.

43. U.S. Marine Corps, *Professional Knowledge Gained from Operational Experience in Vietnam, 1967* (Washington: Headquarters, United States Marine Corps, 1969), 136–137.

44. Blaufarb and Tanham, 27.

45. Thomas H. Henriksen, *Revolution and Counterrevolution: Mozambique's War of Independence, 1964–1974* (London: Greenwood Press, 1978), 130.

46. Marques Pinto interview, 30 March 1995.

47. Pereira da Costa, 149.

48. Lieutenant Colonel Lemos Pires, interview by Al J. Venter in *Portugal's War in Guiné-Bissau* (Pasadena: California Institute of Technology, 1973), 45.

49. Marques Pinto correspondence, 26 June 1995, Lagos.

50. Pereira da Costa, 148–149.

51. Marques Pinto correspondence, 26 June 1995, Oeiras.

52. James Eliot Cross, *Conflict in the Shadows: The Nature and Politics of Guerrilla War* (London: Constable & Co., 1964), 34. The author argues that "first-rate counterespionage or counterintelligence is critical for all guerrilla and counterguerrilla operations. Treason, or even the fear or danger of it, can stop an insurrectionist movement dead in its tracks. There is no defense against it, for any important information that reaches the authorities gives them the very advantage they need to trap and destroy the militarily weaker guerrilla." The late President Magsaysay of the Philippines once told the author that one of the most effective counterinsurgency measures was judiciously applied bribery.

53. Peter Janke, "Southern Africa: End of an Empire," *Conflict Studies*, no. 52 (December 1974): 3.

54. Eduardo Mondlane, *The Struggle for Mozambique* (London: Zed Press, 1969), 132.

55. Douglas L. Wheeler and René Pélissier, *Angola* (London: Pall Mall Press, 1971), 216.

56. Alistair Horne, *A Savage War of Peace: Algeria 1954–1962* (Harmondsworth: Penguin Books, 1987), 212.

57. Michael Elliott-Bateman, *Lessons from the Vietnam War*, Report of a seminar held at the Royal United Services Institute in London, 12 February 1966, 4–5.

58. Inocentes correspondence, 5 June 1995.

59. Pereira da Costa, 149.

60. Ibid.

61. Óscar Cardoso, interview by the author, 1 April 1995, Azaruja, Portugal. Sr. Cardoso is a former Inspector with the PIDE/DGS and was instrumental in founding the *Flechas*.

62. Robert J. O'Neill, *Vietnam Task* (Melbourne: Cassell Australia, 1968), 75–76.

63. Andrew F. Krepinevich, Jr., *The Army in Vietnam* (Baltimore: Johns Hopkins University Press, 1986), 230.

64. Marques Pinto interview, 30 March 1995.

65. Philip Goodhart, *Lessons from the Vietnam War*, Report of a seminar held at the Royal United Services Institute in London, 12 February 1966, 16.

66. Pereira da Costa, 147.

7

PORTUGUESE APPROACH TO MOBILITY IN COUNTERINSURGENCY

"Foot slogging" by infantrymen was the most important and fundamental way to address an insurgency; however, there were limitations to their mobility. To increase their versatility, the Portuguese introduced two contrasting means, the helicopter and the horse. While there were other, more conventional solutions to the mobility problem, such as trucks, jeeps, and light armored cars, these vehicles required at least crude roads, had other terrain limitations, and were vulnerable to land mines. The helicopter had no such limitations, and the horse was ideal transportation in the rugged areas of central and eastern Angola and central Mozambique. These two methods were by no means panaceas for Portugal's ground force mobility requirements; however, they are considered here because they bear the distinctive imprint of Portuguese counterinsurgency. This chapter describes the organization and development of these two responses and examines their strengths and limitations in hunting insurgents and maintaining the initiative. It also compares and contrasts their employment with that in other contemporary counterinsurgencies.

INITIAL HELICOPTER OPERATIONS

The advent of the helicopter and its application in counterinsurgency began with the British in Malaya on 1 April 1950, with the formation of the Far East Casualty Air Evacuation Flight at Seletar with a strength of three Westland S-51 Dragonfly helicopters. During the Malayan Emergency the British used their helicopters primarily for casualty evacuation and later for airlifting troops. Their helicopters suffered from severe maintenance problems, and availability was consequently low. Helicopters at that time were relatively new, and there were many teething problems associated with their employment, especially in the tropical environment. At the height of helicopter operations in 1956, there were only seventeen medium and fourteen light helicopters, a total of thirty-one, and these numbers were always inadequate. Operations were exclusively transport, and while there were troop insertions and extractions beginning in 1952, there was nothing as advanced as a gunship with its associated tactics.[1]

The French began the war in Algeria in October 1954 with one Bell helicopter rented from a commercial firm and six months later acquired eight Sikorsky helicopters from the U.S. Air Force in Germany.[2] With this modest beginning the French Air Force proceeded to develop, refine, and expand helicopter employment, and experimented with lightly armed helicopters and airborne command posts. From 1957 onward, about three years after the beginning of the conflict, helicopter operations had become a mainstay of counterinsurgency in Algeria.[3]

The Portuguese Air Force was heavily influenced by these French developments and not only adapted them to its African theaters but also purchased French equipment in the Sud Aviation series of helicopters. The Portuguese were slower than either the French or the British to embrace the helicopter as a counterinsurgency tool, and it was five years from the beginning of the wars in 1961 until the initial combat operations occurred in Angola in 1966.

Except for the individual Portuguese soldier, the most useful all-purpose item in the theaters was the helicopter. Because of its versatility there were always missions to be flown, and consequently its use was continually rationed. The helicopter was the one vehicle that could provide the proper mobility in the difficult terrain, and illustratively, a one-minute flight in a helicopter equaled about one hour on foot in the jungle. Applying this formula in Guiné, for instance, meant that the lack of a helicopter to bring the typical patrol out of the jungle following operations resulted in a return walk of two days and a night for its men.[4] The geographical configuration of Guiné made the helicopter the most efficient method of moving forces there, as the British had earlier found to be true in Malaya. Illustratively, in February 1952, Flight Lieutenant J. R. Dowling made a number of sorties to lift seventeen men and a captured terrorist "from a swamp in the Ulu Bernam area north-west of Selangor (Malaya), when rising water threatened to cut them off. The soldiers were all suffering badly from fatigue and sickness after spending twenty-nine days in swamp country, and it would have taken a fortnight for help to reach them by surface transport."[5]

In counterinsurgency warfare there was a constant challenge to make contact with the enemy. When contact was made, complete reconnaissance was often impossible or the opportunity for engagement would be lost. Consequently, the security forces required speed, mobility, and flexibility to capitalize on these infrequent opportunities and to establish tactical success. The helicopter was the answer to responding promptly and profiting from enemy contact. The Portuguese became quite proficient in helicopter operations and followed the methods developed in Borneo, as explained by Lieutenant General Sir Walter

Walker: "We used our helicopters...to achieve a silent approach, and to achieve surprise by setting down troops unseen and unheard neatly in depth to outflank and outwit the enemy."[6] This type of capability did not come easily, and the Portuguese worked hard to mold and train a composite force of aviators and ground troops based on helicopter capabilities and their adaptation to the African environment.

PORTUGUESE ADAPTATION

The first helicopter operations were begun in 1966 near Madureira and Zala in Angola against UPA attacks on convoys. Initially ten rotorcraft were deployed in the Dembos region and would deposit a picked body of Commandos behind an ambushing insurgent force, thereby blocking its escape and catching it in a cross fire.[7] This procedure was the simplest and most obvious use of heliborne troops and had been employed by the British and French since the early years of Malaya and Algeria.[8] Thereafter operations became quite refined.

In Angola the Portuguese formed flights of five helicopters together capable of putting twenty men on the ground quickly and judiciously to take advantage of insurgent contact. The order of battle of the normal flight comprised five helicopters to accommodate the five sections of a combat group of Commandos, although the actual size depended on the number of troops to be transported. If the flight was expected to encounter resistance, then a *heli-canhão* or helicopter gunship with a 20mm cannon covered the insertion and recovery and provided support as required.[9]

The key to its successful operation was the lead pilot in the flight. He was invariably an aviator qualified in both helicopters and fixed-wing aircraft, and would spend the initial phase of his training flying many hours low over the his assigned operational area in a small Dornier DO-27 observation aircraft. In addition to familiarizing himself with the terrain, he would mark a map with suitable helicopter landing sites that might be used in future operations. In designating the landing sites, he would also mark approach routes to each. These routes were chosen for their natural terrain features that would mask a flight's arrival and potentially provide as near total surprise as possible. In conjunction with the area familiarization for the pilots, the Commandos and other troops rehearsed operations until the members were proficient as a team.[10]

Once prepared, the team was kept on alert at a primary base, such as Luanda or Luso, until an operation was imminent. At that point the group would relocate to a major airfield in the area of anticipated operations, where there might be a wait of several days before an opportunity occurred. The entire success or failure of the mission depended on the factor of surprise, and considerable pains were taken to achieve it. Reconnaissance of the target was kept to an absolute minimum to avoid flushing the guerrillas prematurely.

Discussion of the mission was forbidden outside the secure briefing area.[11] Once called, the team would quickly be given its final briefing and then launched, taking the most direct preselected route to the target area and its prescribed landing zone (LZ), and flying a nap of the earth profile en route.[12] The helicopter gunship would circle the LZ, covering the area with its cannon and providing suppressing fire, if required, while the other helicopters were most vulnerable in debarking the assault force. The 20mm cannon was much feared by the guerrillas and was an improvement over the less accurate French use of rockets and lighter machine guns. There might also be a Dornier DO-27 with two nine-rocket canisters, one under each wing.[13] These 37mm rockets were used for marking with smoke or attacking guerrilla sites. They had been developed by the French and were very reliable. The force would immediately move to engage the enemy under the covering fire of the gunship.

At the conclusion of the action, the helicopters would land at the nearest suitable site and load the assault team and, it was hoped, a highly valued prisoner. The entire action would last about ten minutes, and the team would then prepare to assault another objective. The team would normally remain in the field, pursuing the insurgents and coordinating operations with ground forces, throughout the day. At the conclusion of daylight operations, it would rendezvous with a preselected, specially equipped ground unit with whom to bivouac for the evening. As only certain units were equipped with the necessary field support in fuel, ammunition, and maintenance capability to host an air assault team, this choice required some considerable planning and coordination. During the evening the helicopters would be fueled and rearmed, and the men rested for further operations the following day. This process continued for three to four days before they returned to the original base.[14]

Upon occasion two air assault teams would be employed together, thereby doubling the force on the ground from twenty to forty troops. Unless the team was part of a larger operation and formed one of the closing forces in a "hammer and anvil" tactic or a similar maneuver, such a small body could be overrun by a larger insurgent force. Thus care had to be exercised not to insert a team into an untenable situation.

In Guiné, where there was only one squadron of twelve helicopters, the loss of a single machine was considered a catastrophe.[15] With this very limited number a team was restricted to a normal three and occasionally four helicopters. This situation was such a constraint that General Spínola was reluctant to authorize an assault just on the initiation of enemy contact. As the helicopters were relatively slow and there was little natural terrain to shield their approach, surprise was far more difficult to achieve than in Angola. When the PAIGC commanders heard helicopters approaching, they disengaged and disappeared into the jungle. Consequently, helicopters would generally not be used in the beginning of an operation, when intelligence on the insurgents was not fully defined. General Spínola's policy was to hold the helicopters in reserve while the ground commanders determined the likely intentions, strength, and withdrawal routes of PAIGC forces. It was at this point that the helicopter assault troops would be deposited behind the enemy as a blocking force, in an attempt to foreclose their withdrawal. This tactic was not always successful in terrain where an insurgent could "creep in between the lianas or a mangrove root and you won't see him even if you pass within touching distance of him."[16] Nevertheless, the surprise attacks that were conducted by the ground forces in Guiné and that were so successful between 1963 and 1966 had become ineffective. By 1968 it was impossible to surprise an enemy camp because of the sentries and defensive mining and booby traps surrounding it, oftentimes out to a distance of several kilometers. The helicopter had been the only solution to regaining the initiative.

HELICOPTER LIMITATIONS

While the helicopter was seen as a high-technology tool essential to modern counterinsurgency operations and represented a major advance in this field, it also had a number of important disadvantages. Helicopters were relatively expensive, and their addition to a campaign increased costs significantly. Because of this constraint the British in Malaya at the height of their campaign in 1956 could only muster thirty-one helicopters. The Portuguese by 1974 had accumulated a precious inventory of ninety-three helicopters and always wanted more.[17] These desires were frustrated when twelve newly delivered machines, a combination of Sud Aviation Alouette IIIs and SA-330 Pumas, were destroyed in a night sabotage raid by the Maoist underground opposition *Acção Revolucionária Armada* (ARA) at the Tancos airbase in early 1971.[18]

Added to the initial cost of a helicopter were the extraordinarily high maintenance and operating expenses, particularly in a tropical environment. Helicopters require a great number of very specialized men to service and fly them, and their expense would have been a substantial and continuing burden, particularly as helicopter usage rose. Portuguese aircraft usage was always high, as the number of available craft was severely limited. Further, the Portuguese machines were old before the strains of combat, for the inventory was largely secondhand.[19] This situation required a high standard of maintenance to ensure aircraft availability. If planes did not fly, it was generally for a lack of cash to buy spare parts. Because Portugal had difficulty affording additional helicopters, preserving its current inventory was the best answer to the shortage. Because of these limited resources Portugal never fell into the trap of having its troops carried in helicopters so frequently that they lost contact with the population and lived in a different world from the enemy. Moreover, the use of armed helicopters was carefully controlled, so damage and casualties in the population were avoided through any indiscriminate use of firepower. Helicopter assault operations were executed away from populated areas.

There was much to be said about the advantages of helicopters; however, their intelligent deployment was not always in direct proportion to their numbers. In fact, just the opposite might be said, and this principle worked in Portugal's favor. While the desire for additional helicopters was always present, the very limited number available forced Portugal to use the aircraft as effectively as possible. And indeed, search-and-destroy operations in the theaters would not have been possible without them. Nevertheless, when there was a vast quantity of helicopters, as with the United States in Vietnam, there was constant pressure to keep them fully employed. Such pressures fostered a misuse, and Sir Robert Thompson noted such a loss of purpose in his criticism of the U.S. use of helicopters in Vietnam: "I have seen hundreds of helicopters and it is a fantastic sight. It is a constant stream of helicopters and, when you get to that stage, you are not on a collision course with the enemy."[20] The U.S. Army had constantly sought methods to improve its troop mobility and saw helicopters as a quantum improvement over leg power and ground vehicles. This position was reinforced by Chief Warrant Officer Robert Mason, a U.S. Army helicopter pilot in Vietnam, who described the following conversation with a squadron mate in September 1965 at laager area Lima, two miles east of An Khe pass on Route 19: "I talked to Wendall...about the French. He had read *Street Without Joy*, by Bernard Fall. His descriptions of how the French were destroyed around here by the same people we were going against got me depressed. The major reason our leaders felt we could win where the French hadn't was our helicopters. We were the official test, he said."[21] The development of the U.S. Army's air mobile concept centered on firepower and air mobility to the exclusion of pacification and securing a population. In Vietnam after 1964 the air mobile forces busied themselves searching for main force guerrilla units and allowed the individual guerrilla to work his purpose—the infiltration of villages and subverting the rural population.[22] The entire U.S. focus was the operation of the air assault division in mid-intensity conflict.

The Portuguese had adapted their helicopter assault operations to their environment. They outflanked and out-maneuvered the enemy when contact was made, just as the British had done in Borneo, where "a combination of the judicious use of helicopters and good intelligence...enabled us to anticipate the enemy's intentions, cut him off, seal him off and destroy him before he could retreat to the safe sanctuary of his side of the frontier."[23] The helicopter and its effective utilization was without question the biggest difference in military capability between that of Portuguese forces and of the enemy.

HORSE CAVALRY

Because helicopters were in such short supply and had operational limitations, other methods had to be found to augment their capabilities and provide the necessary mobility for certain battlefields in the theaters. Helicopters were indispensable for mobility in the tidal deltas of Guiné and the Dembos jungle forests of Angola, but they could be spread only so far. There were other areas that were less difficult but still in their own way presented severe challenges in terrain and provided the insurgents with a fertile medium for operations. It was in these areas of large open savanna plains in central Angola and the highlands of Mozambique that an imaginative supplement to the helicopter was required. They were too expansive to patrol on foot, particularly with Portugal's manpower limitations, and unsuited for wheeled vehicles with the tall elephant grass and frequent rivers. While the helicopter was considered the answer, there were too few of them, and their unique requirements often were needed more imperatively elsewhere. The helicopter also had the disadvantage in its operational tendency to fly over the populations of these areas where communication with the people and securing their loyalty were vital.

In 1966 the MPLA opened its eastern front, and thereafter insurgent activity became an increasing problem in the area between Luso and Serpa Pinto. UNITA had also begun its military activity nearby in December 1966 with an attack on the Portuguese post of Cassamba. Consequently, eastern Angola became a priority, and an effective solution had to be found to address this new extension of the conflict. The first lay in developing the proper security force, one that would combine mobility over rough terrain with ability to engage insurgents and maintain strong links with the population. The second lay in isolating the guerrilla in these vast tracts of wilderness.

Dr. Jonas Savimbi, who headed UNITA and believed that a nationalist movement should operate from bases inside Angola, was soon isolated and by 1969 counted fewer than 1,500 followers. In order to survive in defeat, he and his force came to an accommodation with the Portuguese, and between 1971 and 1973 UNITA and its activities were restricted to a prescribed zone.[24] In return UNITA would cease operations against the Portuguese. As part of this understanding, UNITA also received arms and medical support. This development left primarily the MPLA to address.

The partial solution to the shape of a proper force was found in history. Horse cavalry had been used in Angola since 1571 and had participated in the early battles of Cambambe (1583) and of Rio Lucala (1590).[25] These and subsequent experiences through the 1850s had taught several lessons on the use of cavalry here:

- Mounted troops were historically superior against the much more numerous indigenous forces on foot.
- An armed rider firing from a charging horse presented an intimidating appearance to a man on foot.
- African horses were unsuitable for cavalry use because they lacked stamina as a result of a poor local diet and susceptibility to disease. This shortcoming had historically required the importation of animals from Brazil and Argentina, where they were accustomed to a similar climate and were bred with a physique and temperament more suitable for combat patrols.
- The enemy had no tradition in the use of mounted troops. Thus no opponent was

likely to employ an opposing cavalry force. This situation existed because of the restriction, which was lifted in 1796, on importing mares to Angola so that horses could not be bred and used by indigenous forces against the Portuguese.[26]

It was thought that horse cavalry might be the solution to the problem of establishing a presence on the ground in certain parts of Angola where the cooler, tsetse-free climate, varied terrain, grassy vegetation, and sparse population lent themselves to a mounted force. That the horse would present a large target and be vulnerable in a firefight, and that it represented yet another mouth to feed and animal to train, were valid concerns of the skeptics. In tests it was found that horses were a confusing target and difficult to hit when charging head-on. Experience was to support this thesis, and the normal loss rate of a cavalry squadron of 130 to 150 mounted troops was one horse per month.[27] These observations confirmed the consistent durability of horses in combat over the years, as earlier explained by Captain L. E. Nolan of the 15th Hussars in 1864: "Saddles will be emptied, horses killed and wounded, but no horse, unless he is shot through the brain, or has his legs broken, will fall; though stricken to the death, he will struggle through the charge."[28] Moreover, the cost of one Berliet truck roughly equaled that of the horses required to mount a platoon.[29]

The required logistic and veterinary support and the necessary specialized training also proved less troublesome than anticipated. Obtaining water in the central plains of Angola was normally not a problem on operations; however, it was important to be careful during the dry season, as the usual sources could be surprisingly empty. In one instance during an operation in the region of Fort Cameia, south of Lumeje, it was necessary to lead the horses for two days, resting in the shade during daylight and traveling at night, until the squadron arrived at the Luena River for watering. Health problems were fairly conventional, and both horse and man were vaccinated against the known diseases. Vitamins and dietary supplements also played a key role in maintaining the health of the horses so that they were not susceptible to sickness. Through research and experience feeding was reduced to a formula of 4.5 kilograms of ground corn and oats per day. As the normal patrol was four to five days, 18 to 22.5 kilograms of feed packed in individual plastic ration sacks were carried by each horse. This ration was also supplemented, as noted, and horses were able to eat local fodder as well. Extra rations were packed in the infrequent event that a horse became so sick that he could not move.[30]

In further experiments it was found that a patrol could go anywhere from eight to twenty-seven days without difficulty.[31] The horses had a hard, durable hoof, so shoes and farrier services were not required, and the terrain had few stones. Based on this experience it was found that the normal patrol could be extended into a long-range one of twenty to twenty-five days with resupply by helicopter or truck about every five days. A patrol of eight days would typically cover about 250 kilometers and would extend further with increased duration.[32]

The normal speed of advance was eight to thirteen kilometers per hour or about fifty kilometers per day when patrolling, which was many times that of a man on foot. Quite often the horses were transported in trucks or by railcar to their patrol area, as also was done for infantry troops, to make more efficient use of this resource.[33]

Both training and organization followed the historically tested and traditional route and were similar to those employed a century earlier by such North American figures as Lieutenant General James Ewell Brown Stuart, CSA, and Colonel John Singleton Mosby, CSA, in the 1860–1865 period, as well as by the Portuguese in the Angolan campaigns of the 1850s.[34]   A Center of Instruction for horse cavalry was established in Angola in 1970, and over 300 mounted troops were trained there in the basics of equitation and cavalry tactics during the Campaigns.   In the initial phase of the program 225 horses were imported from Argentina, and subsequently the Republic of South Africa supplied the sturdy *Boerperde* at a rate of about twenty to thirty mounts every three months for squadron replacement and expansion.[35]

Also beginning in 1970, local recruitment was sought for the cavalry squadrons.   Because there were few horses in Angola, it was very difficult for many of the early recruits to adapt to an animal that they had never seen before. Consequently, the recruiting effort gravitated toward certain peoples in southwestern Angola, the *cuanhamas* and the *cuamatos*, who were very fierce and had a history of cattle raising.   As these people were familiar with cattle, they adapted quickly to the horse and proved to be excellent riders.   While it is difficult to say precisely what percentage of the recruits were indigenous, the cavalry squadrons were for the most part comprised of local troops except for the officers and sergeants.   In one squadron all of the subalterns were *cuanhamas* and *cuamatos* with the exception of one white, two *mestiços*, and a black.[36]

The basic cavalry organization was the platoon, which consisted of three sections of ten mounted troops each, plus a support section of one machine gunner and three rifle grenadiers, an orderly, a bugler, and a farrier.   Three platoons comprised a squadron, and three squadrons equaled a group.   The typical cavalry patrol was performed by a platoon advancing in a double echelon or inverted "V" formation that was between 200 and 500 meters wide. Alternatively, the "V" could be changed to a single echelon, or to a line abreast or rank formation, depending on the terrain and visibility. The mounted troops could see over the vegetation and undergrowth and identify insurgents readily from this vantage.   It was very difficult for the insurgents to ambush a patrol, as they were on foot and unable to see the horsemen well enough through the tall elephant grass for surprise.   Should an ambush be attempted, the formation would execute a wheeling movement toward the attack and surround the insurgents.   With the advantage of speed and height, the cavalry prevented the normal "shoot and scoot" tactics of the guerrilla, and enemy encirclement and capture or destruction in such instances was almost certain.[37]   Consequently ambushes of cavalry became rare, as the insurgents could not counter it successfully.

DRAGOON OPERATIONS

Initial exploratory operations had begun in 1966 with a reconnaissance platoon based in Silva Porto. In 1968 this unit was expanded to form the three-squadron *Grupo de Cavalaria No. 1* and operated variously from there and Munhango throughout the war. This combined force approached 300 mounted troops and operated in Angola between Silva Porto and the eastern border near Cazombo. The southern boundary of the operating area was the Savimbi buffer, and the northern one was the Cassai River, which ran approximately along 11° south latitude.[38] The concept was extended to Mozambique in 1971 and operated from Vila Pery in the highlands west of Beira until the end of the Campaigns.

The Portuguese *dragões* or dragoons were trained equally for cavalry or infantry service, just as their predecessors in history had been. In some instances the horses would be used for a patrol to reach its assigned area quickly over difficult terrain; then the patrol would dismount to continue on foot for an attack or reconnaissance mission based on intelligence. In these cases one rider in every six would be left at the dismounting site to care for the horses, and the remaining troopers would conduct an infantry patrol. The typical platoon of thirty would leave five men to guard the thirty horses and form a patrol of twenty-five men. Picketing the horses for long periods lightly defended, and thus exposing them to enemy attack, was not the normal practice.[39] Nor were night actions sought, as cavalry operations were predicated on a visual advantage over the insurgents. At night this advantage evaporated, particularly as horses cannot see well in the dark. Cavalry maneuvers also depended upon visual contact for signaling, and this communication was difficult under low visibility. Darkness thus put cavalry at a severe disadvantage, and this vulnerability was to be avoided. So cavalry patrols preferred to rest at night and sought secluded bivouacs where the enemy was unlikely to pinpoint the troopers and horses for an attack.[40]

Cavalry forces tended to operate in vast tracts of wilderness where there were few roads and even fewer passable ones during the rainy season. Encountering mines was thus an infrequent event. When a horse did step on a mine, it was inevitably killed, although the rider generally survived. Likewise, in firefights horses were rarely wounded, as the guerrillas were not normally prepared to stand in the face of a charging horse with its firing rider. It was not only psychologically intimidating to the guerrilla, but it was also dangerous for him. In Angola one horse was wounded on the average about every four months, and almost all recovered.[41]

The cavalry forces from the beginning of their combat operations in 1966, and particularly after augmentation in 1968, helped to neutralize MPLA operations in central and eastern Angola and presented a continuing threat to insurgent activity. Their large, sweeping patrols found the enemy in the vast plains of Angola and destroyed him. It was not spectacular work, but it was decisive in guaranteeing the security of the population and enabling the people to lead normal lives. Cavalry was particularly effective in its psychological impact on the enemy. The mobility and quickness of reaction, especially to an ambush, was intimidating. A cavalry formation charging at a gallop and surrounding an insurgent force or pursuing it was decisive and generally successful in its action. Horses moved silently through the savanna plains relative to the helicopter and were able to surprise the insurgents quite well, and thus had better success in detecting guerrillas in the bush than helicopter-borne troops. They were not only capable of moving over vast distances during a patrol, and 500 kilometers was not considered unusual, but also of negotiating the most inaccessible and remote territory. In moving against an enemy force, they exhibited flexibility with the combination of an approach by horse and the transition to attack or reconnaissance on foot.[42]

These Portuguese cavalry operations represented a partial solution to the problem of covering approximately 250,000 square kilometers of miserable terrain, normally impassable in the rainy season. With some 300 cavalry troops and a minimum of logistic strain the Portuguese were able to gather intelligence, communicate with the population, provide a presence, and conduct operations between the larger, full-scale offenses against MPLA infiltration in the east. Only in Rhodesia with the establishment of Grey's Scouts in 1976 did a modern counterinsurgency employ horse cavalry as a solution to its mobility requirements in the way that the Portuguese did.[43]

Beginning in 1977, the South African Defence Force (SADF) used cavalry and scrambler motorcycles for hot pursuit of guerrillas in its border war with SWAPO (South-West African People's Organisation), which was concluded in 1989. This SADF use was quite different from the long-range patrolling of the Portuguese in Angola. All three of these cavalry employments were successful in their own way; however, there were limitations. Under heavy fire a horse could panic and throw his rider. While there were few equine deserters, nevertheless, this risk was present. The use of horses was also restricted to tsetse-free areas, a significantly limiting condition. Horses, like humans, could become sick. This incapacity was no less serious than a mechanical failure on a vehicle, and the training, care, and feeding of the animals was no more arduous or expensive than maintaining the same vehicle. In fact, the use of motorcycles by the SADF revealed that the horse, while not as fast, was more durable. Motorcycles in the bush tended to have a short life.[44] While such mechanical devices were useful, the mounted trooper could range much farther afield over difficult terrain than most vehicles, and certainly farther than his comrade on foot, without becoming exhausted, even in hot weather. His perspective from atop a steed gave him a distinct advantage over the guerrilla. The horse moved silently through the bush and gave mounted security forces the advantage of surprise. Finally, the most compelling argument for resurrecting the archaic horse soldier lay in the unique advantage of combining troop mobility with the maintenance of contact with the population.

Portugal's resources were stretched thin in fighting the Campaigns. In the 1970 period the nineteen Alouette helicopters and the two newly acquired SA-330 Pumas represented thin resources to cover the estimated 400,000 square kilometers of Angola's eastern front.[45] The addition of the dragoons produced a winning, cost-effective, low-key combination with the helicopters and infantrymen that resulted in a neutralization of the enemy in the east.

NOTES

1. Robert Jackson, *The Malayan Emergency: The Commonwealth's Wars 1948-1966* (London: Routledge, 1991), 95-97.

2. Alistair Horne, *A Savage War of Peace: Algeria 1954-1962* (Harmondsworth: Penguin Books, 1987), 113.

3. Major Hilaire Bethouart, "Combat Helicopters in Algeria," in *The Guerrilla and How to Fight Him*, ed. T. N. Green (New York: Frederick A. Praeger, 1962), 266-267.

4. Colonel Luís Alberto Santiago Inocentes, interview by the author, 9 April 1994, London.

5. Jackson, 98-99.

6. Lieutenant General Sir Walter Walker, *Lessons from the Vietnam War*, Report of a seminar held at the Royal United Services Institute in London, 12 February 1966, 7.

7. Captain Ricardo Alcada, interview by Al J. Venter in *The Terror Fighters: A Profile of Guerrilla Warfare in Southern Africa* (Cape Town: Purnell and Sons, 1969), 71.

8. Lieutenant Colonel Roland S. N. Mans, "Victory in Malaya," in *The Guerrilla and How to Fight Him*, ed. T. N. Green (New York: Frederick A. Praeger, 1962), 126-127; Bethouart, 266.

9. Duke of Valderano, interview by the author, 17 March 1995, London.

10. Ibid.

11. Ibid.

12. General Tomás George Conceicão e Silva, interview by the author, 3 April 1995, Lisbon. General Conceicão e Silva was the Chief of Staff of the Portuguese Air Force from 1988 to 1991.

13. Ibid.

14. Valderano interview, 17 March 1995.

15. Inocentes interview, 9 April 1994.

16. Sergeant Alphonso Mateus, interview by Al J. Venter in *Portugal's War in Guiné-Bissau* (Pasadena: California Institute of Technology, 1973), 167.

17. T. N. Dupuy, John A. C. Andrews, and Grace P. Hayes, *The Almanac of World Power* (Dunn Loring, Va.: T. N. Dupuy Associates, 1974), 112. The Portuguese helicopter order of battle comprised two Sud Aviation Alouette IIs, eighty Alouette IIIs, and eleven SA-330 Pumas, a total of 93 machines.

18. Mateus, 167.

19. Mateus, 167. In 1972 Portugal was continuing to acquire aircraft on a regular basis; however, with the exception of the two Boeing B-707s described in Chapter 9, the last new aircraft was taken into service in 1954.

20. Sir Robert Thompson, *Lessons from the Vietnam War*, Report of a seminar held at the Royal United Services Institute in London, 12 February 1966, 21.

21. Robert Mason, *Chickenhawk* (London: Corgi Books, 1983), 87–88.

22. Andrew F. Krepinevich, Jr., *The Army and Vietnam* (Baltimore: Johns Hopkins University Press, 1986), 125.

23. Walker, 7.

24. Adelino Gomes, "Exército e UNITA Colaboraram antes de 74" [Army and UNITA Collaborate Before 74], *Público* (19 October 1995): 2-4.

25. António Casimiro Ferrand d'Almeida, "Recordações de um «Dragão de Angola»" [Recollections of a "Dragoon of Angola"], *Revista Militar* (October–November 1985): 690–692.

26. Ibid., 692–693.

27. Colonel César Augusto Rodrigues Mano, interview by the author, 10 November 1994, Oeiras. Colonel Mano commanded the *Grupo de Dragões de Angola* between 1973 and 1974.

28. Captain L. E. Nolan, *Cavalry: Its History and Tactics* (Columbia, S.C.: Evans and Cogswell, 1864), 173.

29. Peter Abbott and Manuel Ribeiro Rodrigues, *Modern African Wars (2): Angola and Moçambique 1961-1974* (London: Osprey, 1988), 24.

30. Ferrand d'Almeida, 695–705.

31. Colonel Luiz Barros e Cunha, "Cavalaria a cavalo no Ultramar? Algumas reflexões" [Horse Cavalry in the *Ultramar*? Some reactions], *Revista da Cavalaria* (1967 annual issue): 277.

32. J. A. (initials only), "Cavalaria a cavalo em Angola" [Horse cavalry in Angola], *Revista da Cavalaria* (1969 annual issue): 171.

33. Lieutenant Colonel Vicente da Silva, "Lances de «Calvao» no «Xadrez» Angolano" [Moves of the "Horse" on the Angolan "Chessboard"], *Jornal do Exército* (June 1972): 28.

34. Colonel J. Lucius Davis, *The Trooper's Manual: or, Tactics for Light Dragoons and Mounted Riflemen* (Richmond, Va.: A. Morris, 1862), vii–ix.

35. Mano interview, 10 November 1994.

36. Ferrand d'Almeida, 712–713.

37. Mano interview, 10 November 1994.

38. Ferrand d'Almeida, 694.

39. Mano interview, 10 November 1994.

40. Ferrand d'Almeida, 707.

41. Mano interview, 10 November 1994.

42. Ferrand d'Almeida, 715–717.

43. Patrick Ollivier, *Commandos de Brousse* [Bush Commandos] (Paris: Bernard Grasset, 1985).

44. Willem Steenkamp, *South Africa's Border War 1966-1989* (Gibraltar: Ashanti Publishing Limited, 1989), 201.

45. Willem S. van der Waals, *Portugal's War in Angola 1961–1974* (Rivonia: Ashanti Publishing, 1993), 196.

8

PORTUGUESE SOCIAL OPERATIONS AND *ALDEAMENTOS*

Meeting insurgent force with force in counterinsurgency is a key element in protecting the population; and the initiation of appropriate and efficient action to address its needs is considered the most effective means of gaining its support.[1] Since before the establishment of the Portuguese Republic in 1910, there had been a liberal feeling in Portugal that the indigenous inhabitants of the colonies should be elevated in both their standard of living and their status as citizens. While many laws had been passed to this effect in Lisbon, they had never been backed by the necessary resources and thus remained unenforced in the *ultramar*.[2] With the outbreak of war in 1961 and the arrival of the Army, there now existed an adequate vehicle to implement Lisbon's policies in Africa. Indeed, in 1961 an Army that thought it was going to Africa to fight insurgents sometimes found in protecting the population that the enemy was the white colonists who were abusing the blacks.[3] While such social progress was admittedly long overdue and prompted by commencement of hostilities, nevertheless, social problems were perceived to be the root of the insurgency, and their correction was initiated with vigor and enthusiasm.[4] Although Portugal's motives for these improvements were always transparent to the indigenous population, these simple and direct efforts were no less genuine and beneficial in their effect.[5]

This chapter describes the development and implementation of Portugal's social programs in the three theaters, the swaying of the population through carefully orchestrated psychological operations (PSYOP) to advance the social effort, and the attempt to control and protect the population through its resettlement in the protected villages or *aldeamentos*. It will address the problems encountered in these social operations and follow the solutions adopted to achieve success, comparing and contrasting them with the experiences of other countries with contemporaneous counterinsurgency operations.

BASIS FOR SOCIAL OPERATIONS

The basis of the Portuguese effort in all three areas was contained in the experiences of France and Britain, and these elements were adapted to Portugal's anticipated requirements in the theaters. Social advancement was the centerpiece; however, it alone was not the complete solution. It was necessary to promote this action through a psychological appeal and to facilitate the population's acceptance of social benefits and self-defense. The first aspect was found principally in the French concept of *guerre révolutionnaire*, and the second was drawn not only from Portugal's long-standing experience with protected villages and population regroupment but also from the modern British and French experiences in counterinsurgencies.

The Portuguese in their contact with the French and their *guerre révolutionnaire* theory in Algeria in 1959 realized that the psychological weapons which were embodied in this concept were applicable in Portuguese Africa. An essential ingredient of this theory was the unprincipled use of psychological warfare.[6]   The French theorists divided this offensive into two parts: psychological war and psychological action. The first was directed toward the enemy, and its methods were designed to undermine his will to resist. The second was directed toward the population and the security forces, and its methods sought to strengthen both the morale and allegiance of the people and the fighting will of the soldiers. Portugal saw this aspect of counterinsurgency as being critical to its success in that with the proper approach to its indigenous African populations, it could hold its colonies with minimal expense and loss of life. If it were to work, the principles of psychological action would have to be as familiar as any other weapon to its soldiers, for they would be the prime conduit of any message to the population. Portugal would also have to use these methods to rally its domestic population and inspire its willing sacrifice.

The final point in implementing any social program was separating the population from the guerrillas so that the latter were deprived of their logistic and political support. One of the most prominent solutions to this problem was regrouping the population. This move was a sound concept and was considered an important facet in maintaining internal security. Widely dispersed or refugee populations were easy prey to insurgent intimidation and extortion. Insurgents required manpower, supplies, and intelligence on government forces, and the population was the source of this sustenance. To deny the guerrilla theoretical access to the population, villages were built by the government and the population was brought together and resettled in these strategic hamlets. This concentration facilitated the government's efforts to bring medical care, education, and food to the people as well as to preserve them against insurgent contact. Villagers were organized into self-defense forces both as a counter to guerrilla attacks and as a political mobilization. This village organization provided the government with an opportunity to deliver its message to the population. Last, if the population were controlled, then the security forces could conduct unrestricted warfare outside of the villages against the guerrillas.[7]

This resettlement concept was sound in theory but so often went wrong in execution. Success depended on thorough planning, adequate finance, and knowledgeable people. These ingredients were not always present, and indeed other factors provided obstacles. Nomadic populations did not welcome the restrictions of a permanent settlement, nor would one that was improperly built and administered help the government's position. Consequently the Portuguese, like their predecessors the British and French, had both success and failure in the application of this concept.

PORTUGUESE SOCIAL OPERATIONS

In planning social operations in the *ultramar*, the Portuguese sought two goals within the population:

- Its overall support for the defense of the colonies and the concept of Portuguese sovereignty
- Its general collaboration not only with the governing authorities but also between its constituent groups.[8]

Achieving these goals was complicated by ethnolinguistic divisions. In Angola, for instance, there were nine Banto and two non-Banto groups. The nine Banto groups, speaking nine different languages, were further divided into 101 subgroups.[9] This mosaic of peoples was similar in both Guiné and Mozambique. Each group had interests that frequently were very different, and these differences produced severe antagonisms within the population. Reconciling these divergent viewpoints in numerous languages to achieve overall harmony or "national unity" was extremely difficult and represented a continuing challenge.

A further impediment was the irregular distribution of the population, particularly in Angola. Here, for instance, according to the census of 1970 more than 80 percent of the territory had less than four inhabitants per square kilometer, and more than half of the population was concentrated on 9 percent of the land. The majority were located in the districts of Huambo (25.7 percent) and Luanda (16.6 percent). About 20 percent of the population was located in twenty-five cities, with half of this figure in Luanda and its surrounds.[10] Guiné and Mozambique were similar.

The dual nature of the colonial economies was yet another consideration. In Angola and Mozambique there were areas of stagnant and slow economic activity that lay between islands of modern and vibrant enterprise. The former were characterized by small or subsistence farming and commercial activity that served an internal market. The latter were marked by large operations serving not only an internal market but export as well. This disequilibrium produced inconsistencies in prosperity that needed to be addressed.[11] In Guiné, the economy was predominately agricultural and rested on the raising of rice in the littoral zone and corn, cattle, and peanuts in the interior.[12] This situation produced its own set of problems.

The Portuguese, in addressing the development of the colonies through social operations, sought to achieve their goals, first, by an economic expansion that encompassed the traditional agricultural pursuits and integrated them into the overall economy, and second, through a comprehensive educational program for the indigenous peoples. Agricultural support had the objective of teaching advanced and profitable crop- and cattle-raising techniques to the rural subsistence farmers, and providing marketing support for their produce. Education had the objective of teaching Portuguese to everyone so that there would be a common tongue throughout the *ultramar*, and thus easier communication between the various ethnic groups, with a view to a more cohesive population.[13] The universal knowledge of Portuguese within the theaters would also make PSYOP considerably less complicated. In addition to education and economic expansion, health services, local improvements to infrastructure, communications, and the self-defense of rural localities and villages were provided. An increasingly prosperous and content population, it was believed, would tend to support the Portuguese government rather than an insurgency.

It has been estimated that during the Campaigns military operations comprised from 10 percent to 20 percent of the war effort, and political and economic programs represented over 80 percent.[14] The implication of this statement was that the political and economic aspects were proportionately large and encompassed many types of activity, all of which were nonmilitary. And yet the only agency with the resources to effect the required change was the armed forces. This situation was not unique to Portugal. In Vietnam for instance, Ambassador Robert Komer (Deputy to the Commander, Military Assistance Command Vietnam, 1966–1968) elected in May 1967 to place pacification under the aegis of the military because "if you are going to get a program going, you are only going to be able to do it by stealing from the military. They have all the trucks, they have all the planes, they have all the people, they have all the money."[15] Consequently, the lion's share of the burden fell by default on the Portuguese military, and it shouldered a substantial, if not full, responsibility in the areas of education, health, construction of local infrastructure, communications improvements, and the training of self-defense militia for the rural villages and localities.

Education and Commercial Development

Education in Portuguese Africa was not always as it seemed. While statistics were kept on the European-style education in European-style schools, this index was not necessarily the true measure of a proper and useful schooling for the indigenous population. Africans had been educating themselves in their own way long before Europeans arrived, and indeed this type of training had far more relevance for the rural citizen than did the European process.[16] However, if an individual had aspirations of leaving the rural setting and seeking a job in the urban environment or even of participating in economic advancement, then he needed the elements of a European education. With the industrialization of Angola and Mozambique, and the consequent demand for trained workers during the Campaigns, this education was increasingly sought. The key elements of literacy in the Portuguese language and an elementary knowledge of mathematics were the means not only to a higher standard of living but also to communication throughout Lusophone Africa. Portugal accordingly recognized education as a weapon to be deployed in the struggle and assumed full responsibility for and control of it, giving priority to the training of teachers and the development of primary education in the rural areas.[17]

Portugal claimed dramatic results as reflected by the increase in teachers and students in primary education between the 1961/1962 and 1969/1970 school years.

Table 8.1
Primary Education in the *Ultramar*[18]

School Year	1961/1962	1969/1970
Angola		
Students	103,781	420,410
Teachers	2,890	10,177
Guiné		
Students	13,534	26,401
Teachers	228	563
Mozambique		
Students	388,328	578,410
Teachers	4,361	8,549

The most impressive achievement was reflected in the fourfold increase in Angola during this eight-year period. The approximate doubling of teachers and students in Guiné and Mozambique during the same period likewise appeared dramatic. Progress in secondary and university education was also exceptional. Secondary school expansion in all areas more than tripled in Angola and Mozambique and increased tenfold in Guiné. The universities of Luanda and Lourenço Marques were established and by 1970 enrollment in each exceeded 2,000 students.[19] While the expansion is impressive, it began from a very low base. In 1960 it was estimated that as much as 98 percent of the population in Portuguese Africa was illiterate and that only 50 percent spoke Portuguese.[20] Nonetheless, by 1970 Portugal believed that it had exceeded its African neighbors in offering a substantial part of its population a European-style education and felt proud of its achievement in this field.[21]

The Army played an important role in this educational expansion.

Illustratively, in Guiné for the school year 1970/1971 the Army ran 127 of the 298 primary schools, or 43 percent, compared with 91 (31 percent) official schools and 79 (27 percent) missionary schools.[22]   Each category accommodated approximately 10,000 students. The reason that the Army had so many more schools to accommodate the same number of students as the government and the missionary schools was that it undertook to address the areas of the country where the population was thin. It was in these areas that Portuguese soldiers built schools, and when there were no civilian teachers available and anti-guerrilla operational activity was not necessary, university-trained soldiers spent part of their time each day teaching.[23]

Also in Guiné the teaching job at the primary level was complicated by the duality of the education requirements, the traditional African teaching and the European-style schooling. The Portuguese authorities attempted to accommodate both. Instruction at this level addressed the traditional rural life and the fundamentals of agriculture, and arrangements were made for the necessary technical support in these courses.[24] Concessions were also made to support the cultural heritage of certain sectors of the population. In Guiné, in addition to the Portuguese language, students in Islamic areas were taught to read and write in Arabic, or more exactly a corruption of Arabic called marabout.[25] These sorts of teaching complications were prevalent throughout the theaters.

When General Spínola left Guiné in 1973, approximately 30 percent of school-age children were attending classes, and because of the groundwork that he had laid, that figure allegedly reached 60 percent two years later.[26] This effort was duplicated in the other African colonies as well. For example, in the garrison of Nangade on the Tanzanian border of Mozambique, a battalion was using the skills of its soldiers to man the school. Here in November 1972, Army personnel were teaching 312 children by day and 130 adults in the evening.[27] Other government schools worked in three shifts from seven in the morning until eleven in the evening to educate an estimated 37 percent of the children of Mozambique.[28] With this sort of effort a European-style education became increasingly available to virtually the entire population.

While the economy of Guiné was difficult to expand, those of Angola and Mozambique were growing at average rates of 11 percent and 9 percent, respectively.[29] This expansion was creating jobs and employing Africans at increasing rates, and was evident particularly after 1965, when Portugal opened the *ultramar* to wholesale foreign investment. Subsequently such projects as the Cunene River Dam with its irrigation potential in Angola began to create an estimated 500,000 new jobs.[30]   With this prosperity in Angola and Mozambique, fewer citizens were inclined to pursue an insurgency.   The ultimate proof of this policy of preempting an insurgency with prosperity lay in the fact that it was "where the greatest economic and industrial growth took place that the guerrillas were in the end least successful."[31]

The Portuguese attempted to manage their educational effort in the theaters to complement the commercial development programs, so that there was an avenue of opportunity for the population rather than the frustration of a dead end. This approach contrasted with that in the Republic of Vietnam, where "the educational system set up by the French and perpetuated by the Saigon regime effectively reserved secondary and higher education and therefore the leadership positions in non-Communist society, for the urban middle and upper classes and for the former landed class of the countryside that had fled to the towns and cities. If a peasant child managed to get through the five years of elementary education, he faced a dead end."[32]

This flaw in the French system extended to Algeria as well. Muslims were neglected in favor of Europeans, and in 1954 the extent of this neglect meant that illiteracy (in French) among the Muslims was 94 percent in males and 98 percent in females.[33] During the Algerian conflict there were enormous strides in education. At the primary level enrollment increased from 650,000 in 1958 to nearly a million in 1960; however, half of all children did not attend school and technical education was limited because of a lack of skilled personnel. Only 28,000 new jobs had been created against a target of 400,000.[34] Without the proper education there would not be industrialization. The little learning that was available created an appetite for more in the Muslim community. It also threatened to create a class of the "literate unemployed," because the economy could not absorb these newly qualified entrants into the job market. This frustration fed the nationalist cause, a situation that the Portuguese sought to avoid.

Health

Throughout the theaters the problem of health was identical to that in all of tropical Africa: a need for large investments in health care, a need for medical and paramedical personnel, a low socioeconomic level within the population, and a general lack of medicine, hygiene, and proper nutrition.[35] From the beginning of the wars Portugal continued to improve health care in the *ultramar* on a limited budget. The World Health Organization (WHO) noted this progress in its 1963 visit and reported that "certain services deserve to be cited as exemplary" throughout the *ultramar*.[36] But it was clear that more had to be done.

In 1971 the WHO standards for proper health care for a country stood at

- 1 doctor per 10,000 inhabitants
- 1 nurse per 5,000 inhabitants
- 1 hospital bed per 430 inhabitants
- 1 hospital nurse per 15 dozen hospital patients
- 5 nursing auxiliaries per hospital nurse.[37]

The Portuguese authorities took these guidelines seriously and sought to implement them in Africa, and again the armed forces became the primary vehicle in achieving the health goal. In Guiné by 1971 the Army had augmented the health system to such a degree that it met or exceeded the WHO standards. The following figures show just how vital this military support was in supplying the lion's share of resources.

Table 8.2
Health Standards for Guiné and Actual Figures by Source

	1971 WHO Standards for Guiné	Health Department	Military
Doctors	48	5	49
Nurses	96	33	100
Hospital nurses	75	—	—
Nursing auxiliaries	375	89	260
Hospital beds	1,100	918	—

In Angola in 1970 there was one doctor per 10,000 inhabitants, and in Mozambique, one per 15,000. In Angola there was one nurse per 3,080 inhabitants, and in Mozambique, one per 4,080. In Angola there was one hospital bed per 400 inhabitants, and in Mozambique, one per 600.[38] In both of these cases it was the military resources that made the difference in approaching or exceeding the WHO standards. Because of this support, medical care in the *ultramar* trailed only that of the Republic of South Africa and Rhodesia during the Campaigns.[39]

The figures, however, do not tell the whole story. Portuguese medical care had established a widespread reputation that increasingly drew patients to the clinics for treatment. In Guiné for instance, patients from Senegal without documentation to cross the border came to receive this care. Senegalese maternity patients were even given follow-up appointments.[40] This traditional role of the patient coming to the clinic was not always possible because of the long distances and difficult terrain. It was necessary, in order to reach these remote people, for the Army to establish mobile clinics. The goal was a monthly visit to every village that did not have regular contact with the more developed centers. It was hoped that this important facet of social operations and the confidence that it developed would prompt the all-important flow of intelligence and cooperation. This dividend was true to a large extent in Angola and Mozambique; however, Guiné was so small a theater that the guerrillas were around every corner, and it was thus very difficult to prevent subversion of the population.[41]

This Portuguese medical outreach program was similar to those of other counterinsurgencies. The U.S. Marine Corps MEDCAP (Medical Civil Action Program) consisted simply of the Combined Action Platoon (CAP) corpsman, with the help of the other platoon members, administering a basic "sick call" for the local village on a routine basis.[42] The Marines would conduct MEDCAP patrols as often as every day, but more likely twice a week, in the local village or villages for which they were responsible, and tried to give the program a permanence through treatment of the Vietnamese and teaching them how to care for themselves.[43] It was hoped that this association would produce a positive bond between the Marines and the Vietnamese people. The French approach in Algeria was similar in that the SAS (*Section Administrative Spéciale*) teams assigned to the remote villages in the *bled* would establish clinics to be visited by traveling teams of physicians and nurses on a regular basis with the same general intents and results.[44]

Local Infrastructure and Communications

The greatest impact of social operations was achieved in the rural areas where local administration had been weak, and consequently such modest government presence had had little influence on the population. Military security coupled with social and infrastructure advances aimed to restore or strengthen government influence through a more confident and cooperative population. The strategic emphasis was the building of local aviation runways and heliports and connecting the various centers with passable roads. Local emphasis concentrated on building irrigation dams, boring wells, constructing schools and medical stations, and helping to build zinc-roofed houses.[45] In this process the military again led the way, although its efforts were augmented throughout the theaters by civilian contractors and laborers.

While many other infrastructure projects were impressive in their scope, there was none more so than the road construction program throughout the theaters. With the goals of aiding economic expansion, supporting military operations, and connecting the district capitals, the Portuguese bent to the job with a relentless will. Angola at the beginning of the wars had about 36,211 kilometers of roads; in 1974 that figure exceeded 80,000, with 12 percent asphalted, 38 percent tarred with gravel or dirt surfaces, and 50 percent rough dirt or tracks that were generally impassable in the rainy season.[46] This dramatic increase was made even more so by the difficult terrain with which the Portuguese often had to contend. Colonel Souza at the Eastern Intervention Zone headquarters in Luso described some of these difficulties in a 1968 interview: "Almost the entire region was overlaid with sand up to a depth of about 5 meters. In some areas the sand went down to more than 40 meters. It is impossible to build roads on this kind of foundation. We do, of course, have some good roads, but it's a giant task keeping them serviceable."[47]

This construction also entailed a major bridging effort. The military initially undertook the upgrading of the road system beginning in June 1960 and completed its work by mid-1964. It took ten battalions of engineers 50 months at the rate of 90,000 man-hours per 100 kilometers of road to build, repair, or maintain the system.[48] Ultimately the job was given to contractors as a more efficient use of resources, and the military provided security. These contractors with Lisbon management and local workers became quite good, and following the war moved with their skills to the Middle East. Building of new roads continued until 1974 at the rate of about 1,100 kilometers a year.

In Guiné during the Campaigns 520 kilometers of new tarred road were built, of which 241 were completed by the resident engineering battalion and the balance by contractors hired through the Public Works Department.[49] Guiné began the war with 3,102 kilometers, of which 55 were paved with asphalt and about 2,000 were open year-round. In the end there were only 3,570 total, but they had been rebuilt and upgraded with new surfaces and bridges. This work was completed despite the mines and booby traps that the guerrillas laid in advance of the road crews to disrupt their progress.[50] This modest increase in total roadway relative to the other theaters occurred because in Guiné the rivers were more important than the roads for communication. There were about 300 kilometers of navigable rivers for large vessels, and approximately 130 such craft were capable of carrying upwards of 100 tons each and moving local cargo on a regular basis.[51]

Mozambique began the war with 37,000 kilometers of roads and boasted 48,000 in 1974.[52] Here the emphasis was placed on building new north–south roads, as the primary prewar land communication routes were east–west along the rivers and from the ports to the interior. The primary north–south traffic had traditionally moved by sea along the 1,000-kilometer length of the colony, while little more than rutted tracks had served as land links. During the Campaigns the Portuguese converted these tracks to roads with a measure of paving and a major bridging effort. This expansion totaled about 11,000 kilometers of varying surfaces; however, this achievement tended to be overshadowed by the vastness of the territories.[53] Brigadier Michael Calvert, reporting on a November 1972 trip there, commented on this immense task and put it in perspective with other counterinsurgencies in the following observation: "The road programme alone which is running at a rate of 1,400 km of tar macadam highway a year for six years compared with the Americans' total of 1,400 km of high-class road in six years in Vietnam and our 140 km in 12 years in Malaya, will cost more than the whole Cabora Bassa Dam complex."[54] With something over 45,000 kilometers of new roads built throughout the theaters during the Campaigns, like the Romans, the Portuguese appeared to subscribe to the adage, "The end of subversion depends on the morale of the population and *good roads*."[55] Good roads of course served both a commercial and military need, and while they could help move troops to critical points of conflict more rapidly than the guerrillas could travel, they also produced fruitful targets for sabotage and ambush, as we shall see in Chapter 9.

While the road system stands as the most significant infrastructure accomplishment during the Campaigns, there were others that contributed more directly to the improvement of the quality of life among the people. One of the most important in this respect was the irrigation dam or dike program in Guiné. Here the population can be roughly divided by a line separating the tidal zone from the higher interior. Toward the ocean the people live on fish and rice primarily and follow animist religions. The interior people live on corn and meat and are Muslims. The lives of the coastal people are governed by the rice cycle, and indeed, they count their age by "rains" or *épocas*. This sequence begins with the three-month rainy season in mid-July, and when it is finished in mid-October, there is virtually no rain until the next year. As the rains begin in the north and move south along the African coast in this cycle, so the people begin working the soil. This labor requirement also extended to the children, and their work in the fields during the Campaigns initially disrupted their schooling but was later resolved. Critical in this process was the building of dikes throughout the river system to separate the fresh water supplied by the rains and runoff from the salt or brackish water produced by the tidal action. It was in the basins formed by the dikes that the rice was planted, grown, and harvested.[56]

The war disturbed this agricultural cycle considerably. The insurgents used the threat of cutting the dikes and stealing the seeds to subvert the population. While protection was extended as widely as possible, other means were also sought to help the people. Special rice seed that could resist salt water was developed from Philippine strains. It took four to five years to perfect this program, but it improved the rice yield significantly.[57] To expand the dike system and repair damaged dikes in concert with this program, the Army engineers undertook to build over 630 dikes between 1963 and 1974.[58]

In the Islamic interior, drinking water was very important for cattle raising as well as the population overall because of the dry season. Consequently, there was a program of well drilling and water collection throughout Guiné for these purposes. During the period 1969–1973 the number of wells was increased from 26 to 163, along with 34 wash houses, 32 watering fountains, and 56 public drinking fountains. The civilian contractor employed to supplement the battalion activity drilled 56 wells and built associated water reservoirs with a total capacity of 550,000 liters.[59] In both of the foregoing examples the Army engineers were the prime force behind their execution.

In support of expanded education and health care in Guiné, Army engineers built 196 schools and 51 health stations in the five years from 1969 to 1974.[60] This construction was associated with the expanded education and health care programs in the three theaters in which the Army played such a key role.

Last, from about 1969 in Guiné a *reordenamento rural* (rural reordering) program was implemented to regroup the population in settlements where it would have ready access to medical care, schooling, sanitary facilities, and water.[61] Each of these settlements was based on a currently existing village and its expansion was carefully planned. Rural settlement was designed to accommodate the people in its locale and to provide the proper facilities in a pleasant setting.[62] In keeping with the people's preferences, the houses were simple and constructed of local materials. For the most part they were wood covered with clay, and the only modern concession was a tin roof. The local cibe tree was harvested and split into *rachas* or long strips made with the grain. The future occupants generally furnished the labor of weaving these *rachas* into sides, covering them with mud, and constructing the house under the supervision of the Army engineers. The tin roof was important for permanence and protection in the rainy season, and was usually covered with palm leaves to reduce rain noise and the heat in the dry season.[63] Each family took great pride in its handiwork. In the five years from 1969 to 1974 the Army engineers built 8,313 of these huts in support of the program.[64] Not infrequently a family would build a traditional hut without a tin roof next to the more modern one.[65]

In these years the bulk of the wells, schools, and medical clinics built were associated with the *reordenamento* program, which entailed the construction or improvement of sixty-one towns, villages, and settlements.[66] By establishing these centers for community life, the government could foster economic expansion and provide the basic necessities for the people. The rural population of Guiné depended on the land for its livelihood, and thus it was important to support them with farming and animal husbandry techniques, selection of seeds and feed, and pest control. The *reordenamento* program was a focal point for administering this help.

While Guiné has been cited in the foregoing examples, the situations in Angola and Mozambique were similar, and the projects there were tailored to their specific problems. In these latter two theaters, the resettled villages in threatened areas were known as *aldeamentos*, and in the more benign settings as *reordenamentos*. Similarly, the armed forces played a key, if not preponderant, role in all such social operations, and led the way in supporting the war effort with the population. In this respect it most resembled the progress made by Governor General Jacques Soustelle's program in Algeria, in which the SAS corps (*Section Administrative Speciale*, essentially the social services support) was established in 1955 to extend social operations and a protective net to the remote *bled*. About 400 SAS detachments were created, each headed by a junior Army officer. Because of the remote duty, these officers were perforce experts in a broad array of administrative fields as well as being accomplished Arabists. Alistair Horne captured the effectiveness of these men in his description: "The *képis bleus*, as they were affectionately called, were a selflessly devoted and courageous band of men, who made themselves much loved by the local populace, and for that reason were often the principal targets of the F.L.N., suffering the heaviest casualties of any category of administrator."[67]

Pacification work by the Portuguese was similar to that in other counterinsurgencies but was tailored to their specific problems in each theater. The United States in Vietnam tended to address pacification the least, as it had no deep responsibility for the population. The French doctrine of *guerre révolutionnaire* was primarily military, and accordingly pacification took a back seat in Algeria. The British in their counterinsurgencies realized that both military and social fronts existed, and addressed both in a coordinated effort. The Portuguese approach most resembled the British example generally but differed in its specific application because of the differing characteristics of the various conflicts. The last of the three aspects of pacification, population resettlement, was practiced by all four major counterinsurgency participants with vastly different results from very different approaches.

Aldeamentos

The *aldeamento* program was one of the most controversial social operations of the Portuguese armed forces. Conceived in response to the insurgencies, it was intended to facilitate three functions in controlling the rural population and in keeping it separated from the guerrillas and their demands for intelligence, food, and shelter:

- Administration of the expanded social and economic programs
- Protection of the population from insurgent intimidation
- Execution of psychological operations.[68]

Not everyone, even in the military sphere, agreed on this program. The primary consideration was the willingness of the population to be relocated or protected. There was always a compromise between what the military needed for security and the people's desires. Moving people was invariably an emotional process because of their attachment to ancestral lands. Timing was also a large factor, and moving the population after it had been subverted was pointless and generally backfired.[69] Often implemented in a rush, the program experienced unnecessary teething problems that required a sizable amount of time and money to correct.

Resettlement of a population was not for the Portuguese an outgrowth of modern insurgencies. The word *aldeamento* was derived from the mid-sixteenth-century practice developed by the Jesuits of gathering the nomadic Brazilian Indians into villages, called *aldeias* (from the Arabic *aldayá*), to facilitate their religious instruction and protection under the watchful eye of the Church, to develop a local economy, and to utilize the Christian Indians as a military force against attacks by the unconverted.[70] As time passed, the Jesuit aims diverged from those of the government, and in 1758, as a result of the Marquis of Pombal's decreeing the Indians free men and granting land to them, the *aldeias* were wrested from Jesuit power.[71]

The modern *aldeamento* program was begun in 1961 in the north of Angola, and by 1964 a total of 150 had been built, each with a capacity to accommodate about 2,000 people, or a total capacity of 300,000.[72] Here the initial, violent action between the UPA insurgents and the Portuguese had created an estimated 400,000 to 500,000 refugees.[73] These people faced starvation, were the victims of attacks by both combatants, and were unable to return to their homelands and traditional way of life. For them the *aldeamentos* held the hope of safety and the potential for employment on the neighboring coffee plantations. The problem had developed so rapidly that Portuguese action, while earnest, appeared irregular in helping the displaced population and protecting their tenuous thread of economic sustenance. After the eastern front opened in Angola, the program was introduced there. By February 1973 just short of a million Angolans were living in 1,936 *aldeamentos* in the Eastern Military Zone, and by 1974 there were a further 900 *aldeamentos* in the north.[74] At the end of the war there were well over a million Angolans living in almost 3,000 such villages.

Initially there were charges that the villages were prisons and that they resembled the turn-of-the-century camps in South Africa where the Boer civilians were "concentrated" to prevent contact with Boer forces, or worse, the German camps of World War II.[75] This appearance in the early years stemmed from the urgency of the situation in alleviating the plight of the refugees, a lack of funding, and a shortage in planning. As the program matured in Angola and these flaws were addressed, the situation improved somewhat; however, it was invariably disruptive to the economic well-being of those affected.[76] By 1972 concern ran high, and sufficient resources had been allocated largely to resolve the earlier problems of human discomfort.[77] The South African Vice Consul in Luanda also reported from a military perspective that after 1972, "The *aldeamento* policy frustrated the enemy's attempts to set up consolidated base areas in the guerrilla-contaminated zones. By these means, Portugal succeeded in disrupting the prescribed revolutionary pattern of gradual expansion and regained the strategic initiative. After 1972 there were no 'liberated' or revolutionary-controlled areas within Angola. At the most there were areas of influence."[78]

In Mozambique the first *aldeamentos* were built in 1966, and by the end of the war a reported 969,396 Mozambicans had been regrouped in 953 villages.[79] Here also there were significant problems in planning, execution, and funding that led to a less than ideal result. Certainly progress on all fronts was irregular, but nevertheless, the intent and will of the Portuguese authorities to bring benefits to the population appeared sincere.[80] The urgency of insulating the population from FRELIMO meant that mistakes were made. The short notices that were often given for regroupment and the coercive measures employed, with the consequent disruption to the routine of the population, sowed the seeds of animosity. Colonel Ronald Waring, now the Duke of Valderano, provided a personal observation:

On occasions, the new villages were badly sited in quite unsuitable places, on some occasions the local Militia, formed from the indigenous population for the defense of the villages, joined FRELIMO, taking their weapons with them, but these were very rare occurrences. Sometimes there was a certain degree of cooperation between villages and guerrilla bands, and where protected villages bought off enemy attacks by handing over food and even weapons rather than fight to defend a village perimeter. There is no doubt, too, that on occasions there was hostility to the enforced relocation of a village. As elsewhere in the world, African villagers preferred to stay on their ancestral lands rather than move to the new villages, even when, thereby, they would have a much greater degree of protection.[81]

It required much patient work to rectify this ill will. In Mozambique as elsewhere, Portugal's limited resources were constantly taxed in addressing the vastness of the task of resettling the population adequately to preserve it from FRELIMO, and of providing it with the promised benefits.[82] It was always a fine line in the trade-off between the ill will of disruption and the benefits delivered to the population in executing the *aldeamento* program.

In Guiné, as earlier described, the *reordenamento rural* program was the basis for economic and social expansion and was based on improving current villages rather than any wholesale resettlement of the population in new villages. Militias were established for any threatened villages, but because the population was already relatively concentrated in settlements, an *aldeamento* program as such was not the answer to separating the population from the insurgents in this theater.

Accusations that the *aldeamento* program was not successful overlook its primary thrust. The regrouping of the population was very inconvenient for the terrorists in that their access to it was restricted. Every effort was made to preserve the local pattern of life, and the construction of huts and other habits of the population were disturbed as little as possible. Such issues as theft, rape, and other abuses were no greater or lesser in the *aldeamentos* than elsewhere.[83]

The *aldeamento* program in Mozambique was more controversial than in the other theaters, as General Arriaga attempted to do too much too quickly with inadequate resources, and this combination produced significant problems. His urgency was prompted by his belief that the population was the battleground on which the war would be won or lost.[84] While the numbers of *aldeamentos* built and people resettled to protect the General's battleground never equaled that of Angola, he oversaw 510 such settlements and had plans for a further 293.[85] Nearly always the *aldeamentos* were viewed by the local citizens in a negative light, unless they were threatened by immediate violence; however, from a military perspective there was merit. Thomas Henriksen has argued that "Despite all their failings, a measure of *aldeamento* effectiveness can be deduced from FRELIMO's reactions to them. Labelling them 'concentration camps,' the guerrilla forces mortared and rocketed the protected villages on a fairly routine basis."[86]

The *aldeamento* plan was aimed at denying the insurgents access to the population and its support and at persuading the people that their future lay with Portugal and not a losing cause. According to this definition, the system with all of its flaws held a measure of success. It is difficult to identify an ideal, similar regroupment project with which to compare Portugal's effort. The various population relocations and their degree of success in other counterinsurgencies depended in each case on the character of the enemy and the food available to the population. No group wanted to be "regrouped" in a planned village, and such action was invariably controversial.

In Malaya the communists numbered only 8,000 strong against 300,000 counterinsurgency troops, and thus could never seriously challenge the New Village program, which settled approximately 423,000 Chinese squatters in 400 New Villages.[87] These people represented only 6 percent of the population and made no contribution to the economic life of the country.[88] Completely removing them to villages away from the fighting and zone of influence was thus a feasible alternative. Malaya was also a food-deficit area, so starving the guerrillas was an effective plan.[89] These conditions were not duplicated in Portuguese Africa. Its population, while not homogeneous, was not sharply defined, as in the Chinese-Malay contrast. It was certainly far too large to be relocated on a wholesale basis and isolated from any zone of influence. Further, Portuguese Africa represented subsistence farming with a surplus in certain areas, depending on the disruption by the fighting and the vagaries of the weather. This situation likewise presented almost insurmountable problems to an insurgent operating where the only food available was that which was cultivated. Water was also scarce in such areas as remote eastern Angola. The cases are thus quite different in both scope and complexion.

The French in Indochina and the Diem regime in Vietnam each faced a 13 million population, 10 million of which lived in a food-surplus area, so starving the guerrilla into submission as in Malaya was not a viable option. Nor could the population be removed effectively from the fighting area, as the British had done. The French had 380,000 troops facing 500,000 VietMinh and could not protect a regrouped population adequately without a village self-defense initiative. While this concept was implemented with success in Cambodia in 1951–1952 through a regrouping of the Khmer peasants, it was not universal and came too late in the war to stem the tide.[90] As in the later U.S. involvement, a military solution was the preferred option.

Following the French exodus, the government of South Vietnam in 1962 attempted overambitiously to move more than 9 million people or two-thirds of the population into about 7,500 strategic hamlets.[91] The plan ultimately failed through lack of planning and resources, but not before it had achieved some success despite its flaws. It aimed to seize the initiative in the contest with the communists at the level of the enemy's attack and to reverse their progress in the countryside. The communists recognized it as a major threat and reacted accordingly, concentrating attacks on hamlets, destroying their defenses, and denouncing the mobilization of the peasantry. Had problems been addressed and resolved, it could have been devastating to the Viet Cong.[92] As it was, the plan fell prey to a deficiency in all of the three requirements for a successful social operation: detailed planning, sufficient funding, and an adequate number of trained people to administer the operation. With the program in disarray, the

United States moved to seek a military solution.

The primary touchstone of counterinsurgency practice for the Portuguese was the French experience in Algeria. Relocation of the Muslim population there, as the military element of the Challe Plan, was far more controversial than the *aldeamento* program. Two million Muslims were forced to participate in a policy of rehabilitation in which the Army engineers followed behind the troops and rapidly built roads that connected a string of newly constructed military outposts as a part of the *quadricula* system. Communities for these Muslims were established within this framework with an organized self-defense militia and the obligatory SAS detachment. These "self-defense" communities or camps had the propensity to become horror stories and often resembled "the fortified villages of the Middle Ages to the concentration camps of a more recent past. In the latter conditions were nothing short of scandalous. Hunger first, and cold secondly, were the enemies."[93] The public gaze was directed in July 1959 by an article in *Figaro* that focused on the camps. This pressure prompted a strong effort to improve living conditions. While the French appear to have resettled about the same number of people as did the Portuguese, they seem to have focused on isolating the Muslims from the insurgents without the strong emphasis on social benefits and the consequent gain in confidence and support of the population.

Alongside this inventory of modern experience, the Portuguese program reflects initial planning problems because of the sudden demands for action in the north of Angola, and a persistent lack of resources to execute relocation on the scale envisioned. On the positive side, the population supposedly benefited from the associated social programs and was largely protected from guerrilla intimidation. The program consistently disturbed or halted insurgent advances. While not as airtight as the Malayan experience, it far exceeded the effectiveness of that in Vietnam and was relatively humane alongside Algeria. In the long run, however, resettlement only bought time for the Portuguese and could not necessarily destroy the enemy. This interlude was valuable and might have been used to build the necessary local political participation for an autonomy that would have fully countered the nationalist arguments.

Self-Defense

It was in the area of village self-defense that the Portuguese had one of the greatest opportunities to frustrate the guerrilla contact with the population. More than anything else the population valued the products of their labors and wanted to be left in peace to enjoy them and to prosper. For this privilege the people would defend themselves. While the Portuguese did much to deliver these circumstances in a physical way, a ringing endorsement of trust came only reluctantly in some cases in the development of the village self-defense concept. In virtually every situation except the British in Malaya, counterinsurgency efforts required the full participation of large populations that were difficult to move out of reach of the enemy. Arriving at this realization belatedly, the Portuguese proceeded to develop and implement a village self-defense program in the form of local militia. At first one of the large drawbacks seemed to be an uncharacteristic reluctance to trust the black African population with weapons, when black troops had historically been armed in relatively large numbers.

Local militia were formed originally to mobilize the white colonists in Angola and later Mozambique under the banner of the OPVDC.[94] Only after the struggle matured toward 1968 were blacks widespread in this body. Its primary mission was defense and security, and it also served a secondary role in logistic aid and social operations. Equally important but less seriously regarded was the *Corpo Militar de Segunda Linha* (second line forces), which was organized as a militia largely to support the *aldeamento* program.[95] Members of this latter organization were the battlefield themselves, and if armed and trained properly, offered Portugal an opportunity to defeat the guerrillas by giving the population the choice of rejecting them on its own terms. These militia forces in Angola had reached a strength of 30,000 by the end of the war.[96]

In 1967 Ambassador William Colby espoused this point in Vietnam when he said that, as the security forces could not be omnipresent to protect the population from insurgent intimidation, village self-defense through a local citizens' militia was the considered answer not only for physical security but also as one of the best forms of political mobilization. Experience in Vietnam had shown that a disarmed village community could be entered and dominated by a five-man squad. If they met no opposition, they could harangue the population with their message, collect taxes and supplies, and recruit or conscript local youths. Even a modest local defense force could block this intrusion and allow villagers to resist the subversive intimidation. Automatic weapons were not required to present effective opposition, and vintage arms were found to be a sufficient deterrent.[97] This situation was no different in the three theaters.

Early on, it had become clear that the armed forces with their limited manpower could not maintain a presence in each village to protect it from possible insurgent attack. There was only one obvious solution: "suitably instruct and arm the population without regard to the color of its skin or the level of its education."[98] Thus in the east and north of Angola, in the north of Mozambique, and in all of Guiné it became routine to see the small villages with citizens ready to repel any terrorist attack in protecting that which was theirs. Like the itinerant medical program, the armed forces sought through training and arming villages to give the people a measure of self-sufficiency in protecting themselves.[99] The procedures were similar in each theater and were introduced in various styles.

In Guiné, General Spínola on his arrival in 1968 had directed the implementation of this concept in which each village or *tabanca* would have a militia for its self-defense.[100] This force was trained by the Army, reported to the village headman, and was equipped with radios to call for help from a local camp if a PAIGC attack threatened to overwhelm it.[101] Each village was defended by a series of earthworks and trenches, a barrier of barbed wire, and cleared fields of fire for 200 meters. Beer bottles and tinsel served as warning devices on the barbed wire. Anti-personnel mines were also used in the cleared approach areas to prevent a concentrated charge at the fortifications that could overwhelm militia firepower at a chosen point. The militia was equipped with an array of weapons, and training and weapon suites varied from village to village, depending on the availability of arms. Weapons ranged from light machine guns, Kalashnikov AK-47s, bazookas, and the Portuguese G-3 assault rifle to old Mauser bolt-action rifles.[102]

Not all programs in the theaters functioned on this model. In the north of Angola a similar pattern had developed in which the *aldeamentos* were in the vicinity of Army camps. During the day the inhabitants would work on their farms or on nearby plantations, and at dusk return to their settlements within the protective shadow of the Army. For resisting the terrorist overtures and refusing to cooperate, these people risked their lives and were thus given arms to protect themselves. For each *aldeamento* the Portuguese had organized a militia that consisted of a series of platoons under section leaders who reported to a Portuguese Army officer. If the settlement was attacked, the officer would direct its defense. This structure was necessary, as the majority of these people were refugees and often lacked leadership in the traditional headman. The Portuguese went to great lengths to emphasize the voluntary nature of the program, and Colonel Martins Soares, in a 1968 interview at Santa Eulalia, Angola, noted: "We do not give arms where they are not asked for—and then only when we are quite certain that they will be used for protective purposes."[103]

In northern Mozambique the population was relocated in *aldeamentos*, often forcibly. Because this operation imposed hardships on the people and was particularly unsettling to nomads, it created a degree of animosity that sometimes led to a reluctance in arming a resettled population. When they were armed, the weapons were generally the same as described above and may easily have been captured from FRELIMO. These weapons went largely to trusted village headmen, as over 82 had been murdered by FRELIMO and the remaining lived in fear of the same fate.[104] Ambassador Colby faced a similar situation in Vietnam and from the beginning was less reserved in his feeling on distributing arms to village militias. He felt that such action was an important show of government confidence in them with a commensurate benefit in enlisting the villagers' participation in resisting the Viet Cong. "Even if some of the weapons went astray, the net benefit in enlisting most of the people would be well worth it. My own estimate was that we would probably lose about 20 percent of the weapons but would gain 80 percent of the population—in my view a very good trade."[105] About 500,000 vintage weapons were distributed through Ambassador Colby's program to the Vietnamese villages over the

1967–1970 period with two effects, the loss of very few weapons and the increased participation of the villages in self-defense. Ambassador Colby explained that "losses were no more than 2 or 3 percent of those issued—far below the 20 percent I had anticipated."[106]

A similar "oil spot" method was used in the sparse areas of northern Mozambique to increase the participation of villages in self-defense. An official communiqué from the Commander-in-Chief stated that rural population groups organized under a self-defense system had increased by the end of 1972 to 230,000.[107] This figure was centered in the mobilization of Cabo Delgado (pop. 346,100), Niassa (pop. 285,300), and Tete (pop. 488,700), whose populations in 1970 totaled 1,120,100.[108] It thus represents a participation of about 21 percent of the people in the war districts and reflected the fact that "there was no shortage of volunteers for the village militia."[109] In 1969 the Vietnamese self-defense force rose to 2 million or about 20 percent of the population, of which 400,000 were armed. The Vietnamese program was successful in pacifying the Mekong Delta and reached as far north as Hué by the spring of 1971.[110] It had taken four years to reach this degree of success. The Portuguese self-defense mobilization in Mozambique, although quite similar, was slower and more tentative, having taken seven years to reach a similar level.[111]

The French in Algeria established local *maghzen* units for settlement self-defense. These were detachments of from thirty to fifty Algerian volunteers who were armed by the French Army and helped to protect the villages supported by SAS teams. Because of desertion incidents the European community had mixed feelings about arming Algerians. The practice drew a constant barrage of criticism from military quarters that were suspicious of arming any Algerian.[112] While such a force was necessary to protect the SAS and its projects from the guerrillas, it was always controversial and suffered from a low comfort level in the security forces. Its effectiveness suffered accordingly.

Portuguese implementation of village self-defense most resembled that of the United States in Vietnam. The British in Malaya had only to worry about the minority ethnic Chinese population as a source of support for the guerrillas. It was thus a far easier job to resettle and isolate this limited portion of the population than it was in any other insurgency. While Home Guards were an important part of the villages and their defense, their organization and loyalty were far easier to engineer than in Algeria, Vietnam, or Portuguese Africa, where entire populations were vulnerable.[113]

ASSESSMENT OF SOCIAL OPERATIONS

When General Spínola arrived in Guiné in 1968, he was disturbed about the overall deteriorating situation and implemented his Psychological Campaign for Recovery, in which the people and the Army would build a better Guiné with improved health, education, infrastructure, and commerce.[114]   This program was known as *Um Guiné Melhor* or "A Better Guiné," and directed substantial resources toward social operations on the premise that by attacking the fundamental needs of the people through deeds supported by an oral message, the promises of the PAIGC would be directly challenged.[115]   This theory proved to be valid, and the PAIGC saw the Portuguese program as potentially even more dangerous than General Spínola's devastatingly efficient helicopter assaults.[116]   Social problems were perceived to be the root of the insurgency problem in all of the theaters and their cure as critical to any hope of victory.

In Angola the war had been won by 1972, and this victory was perhaps 80 percent attributable to successful social operations.[117]   The population there was relatively secure.   In Mozambique many mistakes had been made; however, the situation was retrievable even in 1974 with the addition of resources and patient and skillful leadership.   The blueprint remained valid in that social operations were the key to any government success against the insurgents.   The Portuguese Army had entered the conflict largely prepared to fight a military engagement and adjusted to shouldering a great part of the civilian burden as well, as it came to understand counterinsurgency and its own Campaigns.   This shift in emphasis was the result of Portugal's search for the successful solution to its insurgency in accordance with its low-cost, long-haul strategy.

While many of the aspects of social operations were extremely positive, such as health, education, and infrastructure, the *aldeamentos* program remained controversial.   Resettlement led to the social and psychological insecurity of those affected, and an unhappy population was one vulnerable to guerrilla influence.[118]   While the *aldeamento* program was adequately successful to disrupt guerrilla intimidation of the population, it can be argued strongly that the pursuit of such a course is invariably a difficult and chancy policy decision in any counterinsurgency strategy.   On balance Portugal's social operations brought a distinct elevation in the standards of living of the indigenous populations throughout the theaters.   This aspect contributed effectively to keeping the conflict subdued through its substantive effort to gain the loyalty of the population and neutralize the insurgents.

NOTES

1. D. S. Blaufarb and George K. Tanham, *Who Will Win?: A Key to the Puzzle of Revolutionary War* (London: Crane Russak, 1989), 18.

2. Malyn Newitt, *Portugal in Africa: The Last Hundred Years* (London: C. Hurst & Co., 1981), 102.

3. Brigadeiro Renato F. Marques Pinto, interview by the author, 7 November 1994, Cascais.

4. Marques Pinto correspondence, 22 May 1995, Oeiras.

5. Peter Janke, "Southern Africa: End of Empire," *Conflict Studies*, no. 52 (December 1974): 5.

6. George A. Kelly, "Revolutionary Warfare and Psychological Action," in *Modern Guerrilla Warfare*, ed. Franklin Mark Osanka (New York: Free Press of Glencoe, 1962), 430.

7. Colonel Carlos da Costa Gomes Bessa, "Angola: A Luta contra a Subversão e a Colaboração Civil-Militar" [Angola: The Fight against Subversion and Civil-Military Collaboration], *Revista Militar* (August-September 1972): 435.

8. Ibid., 410.

9. Estado-Maior do Exército, *Resenha Histórico-Militar das Campanhas de África (1961-1974)* [Historical Military Report of the African Campaigns (1961-1974)] (Lisbon: Estado-Maior do Exército, 1989), Vol. II, 29.

10. Gomes Bessa, 416.

11. Ibid., 417.

12. Província da Guiné, *Prospectiva do Desenvolvimento Económico e Social da Guiné* [Prospectus for the Economic and Social Development of Guiné] (Lisbon: Junta de Investigações do Ultramar, 1972), 63-72.

13. Gomes Bessa, 418.

14. Ibid., 407.

15. Andrew F. Krepinevich, Jr., *The Army in Vietnam* (Baltimore: Johns Hopkins University Press, 1986), 217.

16. Newitt, 141.

17. Willem S. van der Waals, *Portugal's War in Angola 1961-1974* (Rivonia: Ashanti Publishing, 1993), 123.

18. Ministry of Foreign Affairs, *Portuguese Africa: An Introduction* (Lisbon: Ministry of Foreign Affairs, 1973), 56-57.

19. Ibid., 58.

20. van der Waals, 43; Colonel Guilherme Pires Monteiro, *População de Angola Tendo em Vista a sua Defesa* [Population of Angola Relative to Its Defense] (Lisbon: Instituto de Altos Estudos Militares, 1965), 5.

21. *Portuguese Africa: An Introduction*, 54-57.

22. *Prospectiva do Desenvolvimento Económico e Social da Guiné*, 188.

23. Neil Bruce, "Portugal's African Wars," *Conflict Studies*, no. 34 (March 1973): 15.

24. Comando-Chefe das Forças Armadas da Guiné, "Diretivo No. 65/69: Manobra Socio-Economica. Esforço no 'Chão' Manjaco" [Directive No. 65/69: Socioeconomic Operations. Work in the Manjaco "Sacred Lands"], 13 August 1969, Headquarters, Bissau, p. 3.

25. *Prospectiva do Desenvolvimento Económico e Social da Guiné*, 188.

26. Colonel Lemos Pires, interview by Al J. Venter in *Portugal's War in Guine-Bissau* (Pasadena: California Institute of Technology, 1973), 53.

27. Michael Calvert, "Counter-Insurgency in Mozambique," *Royal United Services Institute Journal for Defense Studies* (March 1973): 84.

28. Ibid., 85.

29. *Portuguese Africa: An Introduction*, 76.

30. Ibid., 70.

31. Newitt, 238.

32. Neil Sheehan, *A Bright Shining Lie: John Paul Vann and America in Vietnam* (New York: Random House, 1988), 522.

33. Alistair Horne, *A Savage War of Peace: Algeria 1954–1962* (Harmondsworth: Penguin Books, 1987), 61.

34. Ibid., 421

35. *Prospectiva do Desenvolvimento Económico e Social da Guiné*, 211.

36. *Portuguese Africa: An Introduction*, 50–51.

37. *Prospectiva do Desenvolvimento Económico e Social da Guiné*, 211.

38. *Portuguese Africa: An Introduction*, 52.

39. Colonel Luís Alberto Santiago Inocentes, interview by the author, 14 April 1994, London. Colonel Inocentes was Chief of Staff, Brigade Headquarters, Guiné, 1970–1972.

40. Inocentes correspondence, 15 July 1995, London.

41. Inocentes interview, 14 April 1994.

42. U.S. Marine Corps, *Professional Knowledge Gained from Operational Experience in Vietnam, 1967* (Washington: Headquarters, United States Marine Corps, 1969), 482.

43. Al Hemingway, *Our War Was Different* (Annapolis: Naval Institute Press, 1994), 112, 133.

44. Peter Paret, *French Revolutionary Warfare from Indochina to Algeria: An Analysis of a Political and Military Doctrine* (London: Pall Mall Press, 1964), 46–47.

45. Ministério do Exército, *Os Dez Anos do Batalhão de Engenharia da Guiné* [The Ten Years of the Engineering Battalion of Guiné] (Lisbon: Estado-Maior do Exército, 1974), 17–32.

46. *Portuguese Africa: An Introduction*, 73.

47. Colonel da Souza, interview by Al J. Venter in *The Terror Fighters: A Profile of Guerrilla Warfare in Southern Africa* (Cape Town: Purnell and Sons, 1969), 129.

48. Colonel (Engineers) Armando Girão, *10 Batalhãões de Engenharia em Angola...Antes da Subversão* [10 Engineering Battalions in Angola...Before the Subversion] (Lisbon: Instituto de Altos Estudos Militares, 1965), Annex.

49. *Os Dez Anos do Batalhão de Engenharia da Guiné*, 33.

50. Inocentes interview, 14 April 1994.

51. Vice Admiral Nuno Gonçalo Vieira Matias, interview by the author, 23 November 1994, Lisbon. Admiral Matias is a former detachment commander of *Fuzileiros Especiais* (Special Marines) in Guiné.

52. *Portuguese Africa: An Introduction*, 73.

53. Ibid.

54. Calvert, 83.

55. Girão, 33.

56. General Pedro Alexandre Gomes Cardoso, interview by the author, 29 March 1995, Lisbon.

57. Ibid.

58. *Os Dez Anos do Batalhão de Engenharia da Guiné*, 54.

59. Ibid., 52.

60. Ibid., 77.

61. Comando-Chefe das Forças Armadas da Guiné, *Plano Director para o Reordenamentos* [Plan Directive for Resettlements] (Bissau: Headquarters, Comando-Chefe das Forças Armadas da Guiné, 1969), 5.

62. Província da Guiné, *Ordenamento Rural e Urbano na Guiné Portuguesa* [Rural and Urban Resettlement in Portuguese Guiné] (Lisbon: Agência-Geral do Ultramar, 1973), 7–9.

63. Pedro Cardoso interview.

64. *Os Dez Anos do Batalhão de Engenharia da Guiné*, 78.

65. Marques Pinto interview, 30 March 1995, Oeiras.

66. *Ordenamento Rural e Urbano na Guiné Portuguesa*, Index.

67. Horne, 109.

68. Luiz F. Carreiro da Câmara, "Aldeamentos," *Jornal do Exército* (April 1970): 62.

69. Inocentes correspondence, 15 July 1995, London.

70. Edward Bradford Burns, *A History of Brazil* (New York: Columbia University Press, 1970), 29–30.

71. Gilberto Freyre, *The Masters and the Slaves*, trans. Samuel Putnam (Berkeley: University of California Press, 1986), 165.

72. van der Waals, 120.

73. Gerald J. Bender, *Angola under the Portuguese: The Myth and the Reality* (Berkeley: University of California Press, 1978), 165.

74. van der Waals, 200–201.

75. Bernard B. Fall, *The Two Vietnams* (New York: Frederick A. Praeger, 1963), 372.

76. Bender, 164.

77. van der Waals, 201.

78. Ibid., 232.

79. Thomas H. Henriksen, *Revolution and Counterrevolution: Mozambique's War of Independence, 1964–1974* (London: Greenwood Press, 1978), 155.

80. Miguel Artur Murupa, *Perspectivas da África Portuguesa* [Perspectives of Portuguese Africa] (Beira: Privately published, 1973), 35–37.

81. Duke of Valderano, interview by the author, 17 March 1995, London.

82. Henriksen, 158.

83. Inocentes interview, 14 April 1994.

84. Kaúlza de Arriaga, *Coragem, Tenacidade e Fé* [Courage, Tenacity and Faith] (Lourenço Marques: Empresa Moderna, 1973), 198, 200–201.

85. C. F. Villiers, "Portugal's War," *African Institute* (Bulletin), vol. 11, no. 6 (1973): 249.

86. Henriksen, 162.

87. Richard Clutterbuck, *The Long Long War: The Emergency in Malaya 1948–1960* (London: Cassell & Co., 1966), 60–61.

88. Fall, 372–373.

89. Ibid., 373.

90. Captain André Souyris, "Un Procédé de Contre-Guérilla: L'Auto-Défense des Populations," *Revue de Défense Nationale* (June 1956): 686–699.

91. Fall, 373.

92. William Colby, *Lost Victory* (New York: Contemporary Books, 1989), 102–103.

93. Horne, 338–339.

94. Douglas L. Wheeler, "African Elements in Portugal's Armies in Africa (1961–1974)," *Armed Forces and Society*, 2, no. 2 (February 1976): 241.

95. Douglas L. Wheeler, "The Portuguese Army in Angola," *Modern African Studies*, 7, no. 3 (October 1969): 432.

96. Bender, 161.

97. Colby, 99, 242. See also James Eliot Cross, *Conflict in the Shadows: The Nature and Politics of Guerrilla War* (London: Constable & Company Ltd, 1964), 82. The author argues that the simple shotgun remains as popular as ever in guerrilla warfare. "Most irregular fighting in thick country takes place at short or point-blank ranges where the accuracy of a military rifle is wasted even in the hands of a well-trained man. Furthermore, much of the fighting takes place in the dark of night when accurate aiming is impossible. Under these circumstances a shotgun blast is likely to be pretty effective." The British issued them extensively to auxiliary forces for village self-defense in Malaya, and Castro's guerrilla force in Cuba also used them in large numbers.

98. "Aldeamentos em Autodefesa," *Jornal do Exército* (April 1971): 62.

99. Ibid., 62–63.

100. Comando-Chefe das Forças Armadas da Guiné, "Diretivo No. 43" [Directive No. 43], 30 September 1968, Headquarters, Bissau.

101. Captain Manuel Medina Matos, interviewed by Al J. Venter in *Portugal's War in Guine-Bissau* (Pasadena: California Institute of Technology, 1973), 144–146.

102. Ibid.

103. Colonel Martins Soares, interview by Al J. Venter in *The Terror Fighters: A Profile of Guerrilla Warfare in Southern Africa* (Cape Town: Purnell and Sons, 1969), 16.

104. Calvert, 84.

105. Colby, 242.

106. Ibid., 243.

107. Commander-in-Chief of the Armed Forces of Mozambique, "Portuguese Armed Forces Communique No. 1/73," 29 January 1973, Headquarters, Nampula, p. 5.

108. Estado-Maior do Exército, *Resenha Histórico-Militar das Campanhas de África (1961–1974)* [Historical Military Report on the African Campaigns (1961–1974)] (Estado-Maior do Exército, 1989), Vol. IV, 27.

109. Edgar O'Ballance, *The Algerian Insurrection*, 1954–1962 (Hamden, Conn.: Archon Books, 1967), 87.

110. Colby, 313.

111. Henriksen, 154.

112. Alf Andrew Heggoy, *Insurgency and Counterinsurgency in Algeria* (Bloomington: Indiana University Press, 1972), 196.

113. Bruce Hoffman and Jennifer M. Taw, *Defense Policy and Low-Intensity Conflict, The Development of Britain's "Small Wars" Doctrine During the 1950s* (Santa Monica: Rand Corporation, 1991), 90.

114. Pedro Cardoso interview.

115. Pedro Cardoso, undated personal notes on psychosocial operations in Guiné from 1968 to 1973, pp. 30–31.

116. Patrick Chabal, *Amílcar Cabral: Revolutionary Leadership and People's War* (Cambridge: Cambridge University Press, 1983), 94.

117. Gomes Bessa, 407.

118. Bender, 195–196.

9

SELECTED ASPECTS OF LOGISTICAL OPERATIONS

Portugal faced the very formidable logistical challenge of delivering adequate goods and services to the three distant and differing war zones and distributing them locally to sustain the Campaigns. This chapter will identify selected problems that Portugal faced in moving and maintaining its forces, and describe the imaginative solutions devised to overcome the limitations encountered and to achieve the desired ends.

LIFEBLOOD OF WAR

Military activity is normally described in terms of strategy and tactics, and these arts of war make exciting accounts; however, the truly important activity lies outside of this narrow range. Field Marshal A. C. P. Wavell explained this broader perspective: "The more I have seen of war the more I realize how it all depends on administration and transportation (what our American allies call logistics). It takes little skill or imagination to see *where* you would like your army to be and *when*; it takes much knowledge and hard work to know where you can place your forces and whether you can maintain them there."[1] The Portuguese had a long history of military operations in the colonies and had developed an understanding of these principles early in their pacification operations. Their later experience with the Atlantic Alliance had refined and modernized their concept of logistic support, and as a result they had developed a cadre of logistically indoctrinated and trained personnel. The Portuguese armed forces, having shifted to the *Tipo Americano* or *TA* methodology in 1953, proceeded to send their officers to the major command and staff colleges in the United States, where they studied this logistic phenomenon. As a consequence, the U.S. and the similar NATO logistical doctrine and practices were reformulated and adapted in concept, principle, and practice by the Portuguese armed forces. When the uprisings of 1961 occurred, Portugal was thus theoretically prepared to apply what it had learned in supporting the wars in the *ultramar*.[2]

Unfortunately, at the onset of the wars Portugal had two reasons for concern in this area. The first was that despite the elaborate training and indoctrination in logistics for conventional war in Europe, the Ministry of the Army had written no doctrine or regulations regarding logistic support for counterinsurgency in the *ultramar*. The second paralleled the first in that a separate doctrine needed to be established for each of the three theaters, as they differed so much in their individual campaign requirements. These deficiencies were in reality strengths to the extent that while Portugal did not have a logistic system designed to support a war on the scale of the Campaigns, it began without the encumbrance of any inadequate doctrine or system. Thus Portugal proceeded to design and install the necessary procedures that pragmatically considered the characteristics and conditions of each of the theaters and that would also function with flexibility and responsiveness in supporting both military and social operations.[3]

ORGANIZING FOR WAR

At the beginning of the Campaigns in Angola in 1961, it was relatively easy to move troops to Luanda by air and transport them to the battlefield. There was, however, no logistic structure capable of effectively supporting these initial units and the subsequent ones that arrived by ship with increasing frequency and in increasing numbers. To address this problem the Military Region of Angola was forced to adapt quickly to the new situation.[4]

Because the fighting in these early years was concentrated in the northern most of the four tactical intervention zones, the bulk of the support was required there. As a consequence, Angola was divided into two logistic areas, the first covering the Northern Intervention Zone (ZIN) and the second covering the rest of the territory in the Central, Southern, and Eastern Intervention Zones (ZIC, ZIS, and ZIL). The area around Luanda was the logical center for resupply and support with its developed port, airport, and road infrastructure. The existence of this natural control point near the fighting meant that logistic support was de facto considered and administered from here in the context of the entire Military Region of Angola rather than the intervention zones individually.[5]

Most of the traditional arms of a logistical service did not exist in Angola in 1961. There was no commissariat, and it took the better part of 1961 to establish a functioning depot in Luanda that was capable of serving all of Angola. Matériel distribution and support were initially inadequate and had to be adjusted in size and scope to deliver and maintain matériel to units on the move. The Health Service was centered in the Military Hospital of Luanda, which was embryonic in 1961. By the beginning of 1962 it began to function with some efficiency. There was no transport service organized in 1961. Unloading ships and aircraft and directing cargo and personnel were inefficient, and progress was not made until a Transport Section was established in the 4th Division of the Headquarters, Military Region of Angola, in April 1962. Engineering support was propitiously in place and functioning, and required only the establishment of a depot for its supplies. Communication Battalion 361 did not arrive in Angola until the spring of 1962, and after its arrival communication support improved to wartime needs.[6] As the logistic system was designed, established, and refined, this managerial resource was replicated in Guiné and Mozambique and tailored to the specific requirements of each of these theaters.

Because the armed struggle did not begin in Guiné until 1963, it had the opportunity to benefit from much of the experience gained in Angola. The fundamental adjustments to the Angola-developed system were centered in moving from primarily a land-based operation to a maritime one. Guiné's small size, large fluvial system, and poor roads with mines dictated waterborne distribution as the most practical transportation solution. Another factor affecting logistics was the oppressive climate, which had an adverse effect on health, machinery maintenance, and radio operation. Tropical diseases and infections were constant problems, and thus required Health Service adjustments. The subsistence economy dictated the need to import foodstuffs for the armed forces rather than buying them locally. This situation contrasted markedly, for instance, with Angola, where in 1962 about 62 percent of logistic requirements by tonnage were met locally.[7] Bissau was the logistic hub and distribution center for Guiné. From there, in tonnage, 84 percent of all cargo moved over water, 14 percent by road, and 2 percent by air.[8] Airlift was reserved for cargo of the highest priority, including casualty evacuation and mail service.

The armed struggle did not begin in Mozambique until 1964, and thus there had been time to upgrade the logistic system. It paralleled that of Angola and was adapted to the peculiarities of Mozambique with its great length, lack of north–south communication routes, primary air and sea terminals located a great distance from the fighting, and civil infrastructure unable to support the war effort. From the beginning the logistic base system in Mozambique was considered inadequate with its single depot in Lourenço Marques some 1,000 kilometers from the war zone in the north. As a consequence depots were established in Beira, Nacala, and Porto Amélia, nearer the fighting. This new port network served as the basis for the logistic structure developed in Angola with identical organization and functions. It was further modified and refined to coordinate maritime transport along the coast with road and air delivery to the interior.[9]

In Mozambique logistic communications saw cargo and personnel arriving directly from the *metrópole* by ship at one of the several deep-water ports or by air to one of the five primary airfields capable of handling the large air transports and their cargo: Nacala, Tete, Lourenço Marques, Beira, and Nampula.[10] They would then be locally distributed by airlift, truck convoy, rail, or a combination thereof.

Portugal executed the logistical equation well, never allowing the guerrillas fully to isolate even small posts. This capability required the application of imagination, flexibility, and hard work. While most aspects of logistic communications were routine, there were three that deserve mention for their innovative thinking: airlift, ground transportation, and medical care. These will be explored in the following paragraphs.

Airlift

Prior to 1961 the Portuguese had for many years relied almost exclusively on their commercial maritime capability as a link with the three theaters, and this resource was used in the opening years of the Campaigns to move the bulk of the troops and matériel to Africa. This process became less and less attractive as the war progressed, for it was increasingly expensive to operate a ship compared with an aircraft, particularly in moving people. It cost about £5,000 per day for a chartered vessel under way and £2,700 per day alongside the pier.[11] The troops were unable to perform their duties while on a voyage, and for a nation pressed for manpower and cash, it made less and less sense to have an unusable manpower pool hostage to an expensive transit process. An aircraft could transport troops and priority cargo far more efficiently when all associated costs were considered.

For instance, the approximate cost of transporting personnel to the theaters in chartered ships and commercial aircraft in 1970 was £4,534,038 (312,000 contos). The approximate cost of transporting matériel in commercial ships in the same year was £653,948 (45,000 contos), or a total of £5,187,986 (357,000 contos). After 1971, with the substitution of Portuguese Air Force Boeing B-707 aircraft for the chartered vessels, the cost of shipping by sea was reduced to £1,634,150 (115,000 contos) per year, about 32 percent of the preceding year's cost.[12] While ocean shipping expenses were reduced by shifting to aircraft, the aircraft were also comparably less expensive than vessels.

This shift came relatively late in the Campaigns. The Portuguese began the war with a modest airlift capability centered in the Douglas DC-6A (cargo) and DC-6B (passenger) model aircraft, which were purchased from Pan American World Airways. Ultimately Portugal operated a fleet of 10 DC-6s. Because of the mechanical nature of piston-engine aircraft and their consequent high maintenance requirements, availability never exceeded six aircraft at any one time. The DC-6 series could carry only about 50,000 pounds of cargo, and thus this small fleet had a limited impact on the overall logistic picture. The Portuguese were always short of spare parts to maintain the aircraft, and while there were measures taken to skirt this problem, such as chrome-plating the engine cylinders to retard wear, the situation never improved significantly. These measures were important, nevertheless, in that the aircraft were operated safely at very high utilization rates and never had an accident. Round trips to the theaters were flown two or three times per week from Lisbon to

Mozambique and took forty-eight hours. These missions always required relief crews stationed en route to maintain the schedule. Thus with its limited cargo and passenger capacity and its slow speed, the DC-6 series was outdated even by airlift standards of the day.[13]

In 1971 the Portuguese Air Force purchased the last two B-707 models produced by Boeing Aircraft Corporation. These were purpose-built aircraft with a strengthened undercarriage and a mixed cargo and passenger cabin. Flown according to Pan American operating standards, they ultimately realized in Portuguese hands the highest utilization of any B-707 worldwide, a fact confirmed by Boeing. One of the two aircraft was always on a mission, and the reliability and flexibility of the plane made a dramatic difference in the logistic picture. In 1973 the two B-707s together flew 299 missions alongside 209 missions for the entire fleet of 10 DC-6s.[14] The DC-6s had by then been relegated to the shorter missions to Guiné, the Azores, Madeira, and Europe, and the B-707s were serving Luanda and Mozambique. The B-707 typically left Lisbon at 1130 hours, flew to Luanda, was unloaded, serviced, and loaded, and returned to the *metrópole* by 2230 hours the same day.[15] According to Portuguese Air Force records in 1972, transporting passengers and their luggage by B-707 instead of by ship saved the armed forces £4,207,469 (266,633 contos). In 1973 comparable savings were £4,437,355 (267,633 contos). These savings over two years paid for the two B-707s.[16]

Intratheater airlift was shouldered primarily by the Noratlas aircraft, originally conceived in 1955 by Nord Aviation for this purpose in the French and West German air forces. The Noratlas fleet performed well and served Portugal's needs. Other intratheater support was performed by a variety of aircraft, including the Douglas DC-3 (C-47), DC-4, and DC-6. This assortment was necessary to accommodate the various site limitations. For instance, by 1964 Angola had 403 airfields and Mozambique had 216, with the following capabilities:

Table 9.1
Airfield Capability by Theater

Field Capability	Angola[17]	Mozambique[18]	Guiné[19]
DC-6/Super Constellation/B-707/DC-8	12	5	1
C-54	5	10	
Noratlas	6	15	
DC-3/C-47	11	30	
Lesser fields (some permit DC-3)	369	156	20
Totals	403	216	21

The majority of the landing strips were so primitive that only helicopters or very light aircraft, such as the Dornier DO-27 or Harvard T-6, could be accommodated. Nevertheless, the airlift capability, as embodied in the numerous fields throughout the theaters, extended as a logistical communication link to virtually every base of the Portuguese armed forces.

While the Portuguese began their counterinsurgency operations some twelve years after the Berlin Airlift (June 1948–September 1949), the lessons in this application of logistic power were an integral part of their thinking. The Berlin Airlift had shown that given the machines and bases, air transport was more than a prop for short-term logistic emergencies. The intensive operational techniques developed there showed the way to a sure alternative to surface transport, providing the procedures and infrastructure were in place. General Arriaga, then the Subsecretary of State for Aeronautics, had established the infrastructure in the 1950s, and Portugal proceeded to graft these lessons onto its airlift operations.[20]   Except for U.S. operations in Vietnam, other governments fighting comparable insurgencies seemed less attuned to these airlift calculations. Malaya was the most comparable in distances and troop numbers, and here the British made no such effort. There was an endless stream of British troopships arriving in Singapore to support the war, and one newly commissioned subaltern described this expensive and leisurely process, in which "We spent hours eating huge P. and O. meals, and then more hours after them recovering in deckchairs, watching waves sliding past the ship, endlessly, without pause...."[21] This process was anything but a focused preparation for counterinsurgency warfare or a rapid insertion into the local environment. The Portuguese thus sought the rapid and cost-effective avenue of air transport to move troops and critical supplies, a choice that improved the sustainability of the Campaigns. The shift from high-profile troopships arriving and departing with fanfare to the more subtle aircraft reinforced the low-key nature of the Campaign.   The low profile of routinely arriving and departing aircraft providing timely deliveries and a rapid response to needs in the theaters fit the tenor of the Campaigns.

Ground Transportation and Mine Countermeasures

Portugal had military posts established throughout all of the theaters that had to be supplied by truck, as there was no other practical means to deliver heavy items. Rail lines were restricted by the route that they took, and airlift by weight limitations. If Portugal was to win its war, then the trucks with their supplies must reach their destinations in sufficient numbers to provide for the soldiers. Truck passage had to negotiate not only an enemy but also some of the most primitive and daunting territory in the world, and thus travel by truck could be a slow and grueling process in most areas. Paved roads were easy routes but tended to connect only the principal towns, not the villages and the more remote sites, outposts that were important in keeping the insurgents separated from the population. Delivering supplies to the more remote areas required a fleet of supply vehicles negotiating not only the paved highways but poor roads, tracks, and trails. In many cases these latter *pistes* could degenerate into rutted tracks through deep sand. Vehicles could and did become stuck in these primitive roads, requiring hours to extricate. During the rainy season unpaved roads became quagmires of soft mud and sand, and were virtually impassable. In the dry season they remained a problem, although the dry riverbeds baked hard and provided a solid roadway. Some of these trails could follow a dry watercourse for as much as 50 kilometers.[22]

Trucks traveled these routes generally by convoy when enemy contact was expected. The convoy might be all military or a combination of commercial haulers and military. When entering an area of known or probable insurgent presence, the trucks would be assembled, and the drivers briefed on convoy procedure for driving, being ambushed, or hitting a mine. Mines were used increasingly in all of the theaters as the war progressed. Initially the guerrillas were inept in using them, but their proficiency improved over time, as they acquired the skill of safely handling and effectively placing the devices. Eventually their use far exceeded that in other insurgencies.[23] Mining of the road system was the easiest way for the insurgents to disrupt the Portuguese ground logistic system and create an opportunity for the ambush of a truck convoy almost at their discretion.[24] Widespread mining prompted the Portuguese to adopt a series of countermeasures in the modification and operation of their vehicles and in demining procedures.

The two vital items for a Portuguese soldier were his water and his ammunition, and these held true for the insurgent as well. The insurgent was generally forced to bring his munitions with him from his sanctuary country, and with a limitation on what he could carry, so there was a consequent restriction on his offensive potential. He might have increased this potential, had he built an arms cache that had remained undiscovered by the Portuguese. The average anti-vehicular mine weighed five kilograms, and after the insurgent had carried this weight the considerable distance from his sanctuary at substantial danger, he wanted a commensurate return for his risk. Consequently, the mine was planted where it would be activated within a relatively short wait, giving a nearly immediate effect and instant gratification. Because the insurgent minelaying capability was constrained by these logistics, there was no real pattern either to the minefield or to its associated operations. The mine may have been laid singly or as part of a group. It may have been employed with an ambush, in a hit-and-run tactic, or simply as an isolated threat. All of these eventualities had to be addressed in Portuguese countermeasures.[25]

First, the trucks were made as safe as possible in the event that they contacted a mine in the roadway. The Berliet truck was designed and built for resupply. Its wheels were well in front of the cab, so that the mine would be detonated ahead of the driver and passenger, with the engine providing protection from the blast. The hood and the metallic top of the driver's cab were removed. The hood could act as a guillotine, decapitating the driver and passenger in a mine explosion. The force of the explosion would also throw them both upward against the cab roof with severe injury, if it were not removed. The floor and bed of the truck were laid with sandbags to protect the occupants against shrapnel from the explosion. It was also important for occupants to keep their arms and legs inside the vehicles to achieve maximum protection from the sandbags.[26]

Convoy organization and truck operating procedures were adjusted to accommodate the danger of mines. The lead vehicle was traditionally a Berliet "mine crasher" truck followed by a Mercedes Benz Unimog troop carrier with 50 meters' standard separation. The remainder of the convoy followed. On sandy roads convoy drivers followed immediately in the tracks of the vehicle ahead to be certain of a safe and tested path. Troop carriers were positioned throughout the convoy, and a Berliet concluded the train. Progress was generally irregular, depending on what obstacles the escort found in the road. There could be debris, a suspicion of a mine, or a broken truck. When night came, the vehicles would form a laager, then were on the road again at first light. The convoys would travel at night only if they met an oncoming convoy that had cleared the road ahead. It would then be important to cover the sanitized route as quickly as possible, before the insurgents had the opportunity to plant new mines. The road tarring program made mining much more difficult for the insurgents. Planting mines under a hard-surfaced road meant carefully removing a section of pavement, digging a hole for the mine, and then replacing the section over the explosive. The pavement section had to be retarred artfully to conceal its lethal charge. While no road was thus fully immune, the insurgents preferred the sandy tracks.[27]

Convoys along the highways employed a lookout who assessed the situation in the road ahead. If he felt that there was a risk of mines, then the convoy would halt, and a team of four to eight men would alight from the trucks. These men would begin a line-abreast search in the path of the vehicles, using pointed probes called *picas*. These were wooden rods about 2 meters long with a metallic 50-centimeter point, the name of which was derived from the lance used in bullfighting. These *picadores* or "trailblazers" were rotated every twenty minutes, with all soldiers detailed to the convoy taking a turn. The job was tedious as well as dangerous, and required uninterrupted concentration. Once a mine was discovered, a combat knife was gently used to clean sand and earth from the device. If the charge appeared to be booby-trapped, it was destroyed in place. If, however, a mine could be recovered intact without exploding it, it was valuable for study. Most mines were destroyed in situ.[28]

Often antipersonnel mines were employed with the antivehicular type, placed either around it or in the roadside next to it. The purpose of this pattern was to frustrate convoy procedures where personnel would abandon the trucks and seek shelter on the shoulder of the road to avoid the effects of an ambush. By freezing the personnel in their vehicles with the threat of antipersonnel mines, the insurgents would increase their chances for a successful ambush or whipping burst of gunfire known as a *flagelação*. Antipersonnel mines also had the effect of confusing the situation for the *picadores* and making demining more difficult. Mines also were planted in chains, where raising one would cause the others to explode.   Under these conditions progress was limited, and eighteen–twenty kilometers a day was not considered inordinately slow.   During the rainy season from October to April, the roads were a quagmire, and it took a convoy about ten days to go eighty kilometers.   Rain made the job even more hazardous.   For the driver it would become almost impossible to follow the tracks of the vehicle ahead, increasing the chances of contacting a mine.   For the mine detection squad the job would become suicidal.   One method of accelerating the process was the use of captured insurgents.   They rarely resisted helping, and they knew where the devices were planted because they had laid them.[29]

Electronic detectors were tried, but never proved as effective as *picas*.   They were not considered reliable because of the nonmetallic mine casings and the presence of metal debris in the road.   In the case of wooden-cased mines, termites would often have eaten the wooden casings and only loose explosives remained in the soil.   The Portuguese found that the *pica* in the hands of an experienced *picador* was the most effective and reliable method of locating mines.   It was also the most cost-effective.   Specially trained dogs were valuable aids in detection but were by no means as reliable as the *picadores*.   Many mechanical road flagellation systems were also tested, but they were cumbersome and expensive, and none matched a team of four experienced *picadores*.   The task of demining was always in a state of flux, as the insurgents constantly adopted new techniques.   Consequently, it was the human factor that could adjust most readily to these changes.   The magnitude of the demining problem was reflected in an unofficial record held by a team of four *picadores* who discovered fifty-two mines in a single day.[30]

Thus mine detecting and destruction were raised to a high art to meet the threat.   As the U.S. Marine Corps noted in 1969, in Vietnam, a conflict characterized by mines and booby traps: "Although a great many detection means, ranging from intricate electronic devices to specially trained dogs, have been developed, experience has shown that an alert Marine, aware of what to look for and where to look, is the most effective detection device."[31]   The procedures that the Portuguese developed were an important element in subsequent demining operations by the South African security forces in its border war (1966–1989).

Evacuation and Hospitalization

While the advent of modern medical care for the population in the theaters was important, it was relatively mundane.   The most dramatic effort occurred in the care of war casualties.   Although the Portuguese soldier was largely uncomplaining and took danger in stride, the presence of an excellent health service with hospitalization and evacuation capabilities not only represented an important morale factor but also served as a practical measure.   Historically armies have suffered more from poor hygiene and sickness than from enemy action.   As Colonel P. D. Foxton, a logistician with the British Army, explained, "Every seven days an armoured division (about 14,000 men) is on exercise it can expect to have up to 500 soldiers report sick as a result of infection, routine disabilities and accidents. An efficient medical service is, therefore, vital to any army embarking on operations."[32] Angola represents the best starting point, as that is where the Campaigns began.

Portugal designed its medical care and evacuation around certain principles for handling casualties. The first was the "Six Hour Rule," in which a casualty has the greatest chance of surviving if he can receive the proper medical treatment for his wounds within six hours. The primary difficulty lay in moving the wounded to a proper treatment site within the critical period. While many of the combat casualties occurred in remote theaters, the combat forces maintained radio contact with headquarters, and help could be summoned. Initial treatment was more often than not from nonmedically trained personnel, a fact that highlights the importance of first aid and casualty training. Whether by truck or helicopter or a combination thereof, the first treatment by a doctor was most likely at company headquarters, although medical personnel did go with a patrol irregularly. In Angola, in addition to first aid stations (*postos de socorros*), it was mandated that an infirmary (*enfermaria de estacionamento*) of at least ten beds be established at company headquarters to make best use of the local medical personnel. Depending on where the unit action had taken place, the casualties could receive treatment here or at the sector-level infirmary, which had at least a thirty-bed capacity (*enfermaria de sector*). These sector infirmaries also served as recuperation sites for those treated at the company-level infirmaries whose condition did not warrant evacuation to a hospital. In both of these instances available civilian hospitals could be used as an alternative. The Military Hospital of Luanda, which had an 800-bed capacity, could treat virtually any case, and served as the ultimate evacuation site for Angola.[33]

Once a casualty had had initial surgery, the "Ten Day Rule" came into effect. This guideline, based on experience gained in treating casualties generally, suggested that the chances of a casualty surviving surgery increased markedly if he was given ten days to rest before he was moved. The number of infirmaries and the beds in each were based on the number of anticipated casualties, the "Six Hour Rule," and the "Ten Day Rule." These calculations accounted for the likelihood that once casualties had been received at an infirmary and surgery had been performed, they would not be moved for ten days. There was consequently a sense of urgency to evacuate the sick and wounded from the forward areas so that the medical facilities there could accommodate new casualties. This process called for the cooperation of both service and combat personnel in executing a prompt move of patients to the general hospital, where the long-term nursing and rehabilitation could begin. Accordingly, the movement schedule for recuperating personnel was established in Angola, and these guidelines applied throughout the other theaters, being promulgated by the appropriate authorities:

At the unit-level infirmaries	10 days
At the sector infirmaries	20 days
At the civilian hospitals	30 days
At the Military Hospital of Luanda	60 days.[34]

In Guiné there was the Military Hospital of Bissau with 320 beds and the capabilities of a general hospital. There was also the network of unit infirmaries and first aid stations, but because Guiné was such a small theater, the intermediate facility of the sector infirmary was omitted and the hospital in Bissau served this purpose. In Mozambique there were three hospitals. The primary was the Military Hospital of Lourenço Marques with 340 beds and the capabilities of a general hospital. The secondary hospitals were the Military Hospital of Beira and the Military Hospital of Nampula, with the capabilities of regional hospitals. The Beira facility had 75 beds with a surge capability of 120 beds. The Nampula facility had 240 beds. Like Angola, Mozambique had a network of sector and unit infirmaries and first aid stations.[35] Given the casualties of the Campaigns, these beds were adequate to allow every case during the war fifty-one days of recuperation in Guiné, seventy-eight days in Angola, and sixty-one days in Mozambique without evacuation to the metrópole.[36] With the exception of the Republic of South Africa and Rhodesia, there was no better medical care anywhere in Africa.

In certain cases of orthopedic corrective surgery, skin grafts for burn victims, or other complicated specialties, arrangements were made with the South African Defense Force for treatment at the military hospital in Pretoria.[37] There was a small ward of about fifty patients from late 1972 until the end of the Campaigns, largely blacks. It was the policy to evacuate all whites to the metrópole, where they could recuperate with their families. There were nine military hospitals on the mainland with a total of 2,615 beds and a surge capability of 2,955 beds.[38] The exception to this general policy was burn cases and other extreme trauma casualties. These were flown to the Portuguese Air Force Hospital at Air Base No. 4 on the Island of Terceira in the Azores. This 100-bed facility was separated from the mainland and thus removed the wounded from any use as pawns in the antiwar movement.[39]

The effectiveness of Portuguese medical care compared with that of other conflicts is shown in Table 9.2. The highest success rate for medical attention lay with the United States, whose vast resources overcame most complications. Portuguese medical care was the next best, with one chance of dying for every 5.4 men wounded. While these figures are a general indicator, they are also influenced by such factors as medical advances since the beginning of World War II, the intensity of the conflict, and climatic conditions. In Malaya helicopter evacuation was embryonic, and the jungle conditions posed a problem even for those not wounded. In the Falklands the conditions were filthy and the fighting intense, a difficult environment for wounded. Nevertheless, the Portuguese figure stands as a substantial achievement and carries a message that

Portugal was sensitive to the health and morale of its troops, particularly in the context of its manpower shortage.

Table 9.2
Ratios of Deaths to Wounds

Conflict	Proportion
Vietnam	1 to 5.6
Portuguese African Campaigns	1 to 5.4
Algeria	1 to 4.7
Korea	1 to 4.1
Falkland Islands	1 to 3.8
World War II	1 to 3.1
Malaya	1 to 2.4

Paranurses

The Portuguese soldier knew that while his diet in the bush might be meager, the tropical conditions oppressive, and danger lurking in his next step, his Army would go to great lengths to speed him to a hospital should he be wounded. Every available resource was sought, and in an era of traditional female roles, one of the most important and unique aspects of this effort was Portugal's paranurses. In the field of medical care, the Portuguese had observed that the presence of a woman in the early stages of a physical trauma did much to improve the morale of a soldier, particularly one who had been under the stress of combat conditions for an extended period of time. The Portuguese lesson came from the limited French use of nurses in combat in Indochina and Algeria. In 1937 the French Red Cross had originally sponsored the use of three nurses to be inserted into areas of public calamity for relief of the injured. Following World War II, the French brought this program under military sponsorship, and in the period from 1949 until the program was closed in 1962, recruited forty women as paranurses. There were only about fifteen active at any one time, and of this group only five served in Indochina and seven volunteered for Algeria. While the deployment of paranurses demonstrated the benefits of such a program, it remained largely a French experiment because of its modest size.[40]

Following World War II and the widespread troop demobilization, women assumed a token role in armed forces generally with the exception of Israel, which was always short of manpower.[41] There was a resurgence in the Korean conflict in which the various U.S. military nurse corps were increased to a strength of 5,400 through a recall of reservists, and 500 to 600 of these served in the combat zone but were not routinely exposed to fire.[42] For the remainder of the 1950s and the early 1960s the various U.S. services downplayed women, calling them "typewriter soldiers" because of their circumscribed roles. The token female recruiting of the U.S. Marine Corps was even based on beauty as late as 1964, a reflection of the narrow attitude within the U.S. military.[43] The

British and French were no more adventurous, although there were small numbers of nurses serving in Malaya, Algeria, and Indochina. In the latter theater there were even some female liaison pilots. Consequently, when women were introduced into the Portuguese Air Force in 1961 with the thought of putting them in harm's way, it was considered avant-garde, particularly in a society where a woman's role was so strongly defined in the tradition of homemaker.

With the establishment of the Portuguese Air Force, it was easier to introduce innovative fighting concepts. There was little opposition in this new service, where hidebound tradition had not been established and where there was little resistance to change. The Air Force established its own battalion of parachutists in 1955 and in 1961 created a cadre of five officers and one sergeant from female volunteers who were designated as a part of the Air Force Health Service (Nursing).[44] These six, whose given names were all Maria, were the first graduates of the program and became known as the "six Marias." Dr. Salazar had originally had some concerns about the nurses serving in isolated environments surrounded by men; however, General Arriaga, then the Subsecretary of State for Aeronautics, assured him that all volunteers would be selected from nursing schools run by the Roman Catholic Church and would thus be imbued with a strong morality. Indeed, the sisters who ran the schools were very supportive of the plan and were invited to award the distinctive green beret to their former students on their graduation from military training.[45] During the fourteen years that the program existed there were nine courses graduating a total of forty-eight paranurses, all of whom operated in a combat environment.[46]

This number may not seem significant alongside later figures; however, the only country to mobilize women on any scale prior to the end of the Campaigns in 1974 was the United States. The British in 1975 accorded women equal pay status with men, and by 1976 about 4 percent of its armed forces were women. Between 1976 and 1977 women were placed in a combat role with their assignment to the Ulster Defense Regiment in Northern Ireland. France severely restricted women until 1971, and in 1973 only 2 percent of its 513,000 troops were female.[47] The U.S. military had remained closed-minded in this area until 1967, when it had a manpower shortage for Vietnam. By June 1970 there were slightly more than 5,000 Army nurses on active duty, and by the end of the U.S. involvement in Vietnam 5,000 to 6,000 women had been rotated through the combat zone. The theater level was about 300 from 1967 onward. These women were frequently assigned to duty at remote firebases and conducted MEDCAP with other personnel.[48] So when the Portuguese Air Force began recruiting and in 1961 deploying its nurses in the combat environment, it represented the forefront in seeking women to ease its manpower shortage and recognizing that there are some things a woman can do better than a man, particularly in providing a link between the wounded and normal life outside of combat.

This effective aspect of trauma care in the Campaigns is a clear example of the careful thought that extended not only to the comforting support and the medical care of the sick and wounded but also to the overall message of personal concern that the Portuguese were attempting to deliver to the people throughout the theaters. While the French had had a heroic but small and virtually experimental program, the Portuguese had adopted and expanded on the principles of this small success to meet their own requirements for trauma care in the field. The uniqueness of this program lay in the Portuguese commitment to an important medical concept and its implementation in the face of traditional social roles for women and interservice resistance to innovation. Conversely, it is interesting to note that the PAIGC subscribed to the same thinking and on a very limited basis used female nurses in combat for identical reasons. One such nurse, Sofia Biaia from the Base de Morés in Guinea, was captured in Operation "Titão." This PAIGC practice was not thought to be widespread, nor were others encountered in Angola or Mozambique.[49]

COMPARATIVE COUNTERINSURGENCIES

Long before the wars Portugal saw the growth and development of transportation as the key to conducting a counterinsurgency campaign in the *ultramar*. It developed the fundamental road, airfield, and port infrastructure well ahead of the trouble in 1961 and proceeded to expand on this earlier work as the shape of the conflict became more apparent. It also began the Campaigns with a trained cadre of logisticians and expanded this group in the years immediately after 1961. It had developed solutions to the problem of great distances between the *metrópole* and the theaters, and it had successfully avoided France's tight situation in Indochina, where the logistic lines of communication from Europe were overstretched. France had also struggled with a local infrastructure too rudimentary to support an extensive counterinsurgency campaign and with no resources to improve it. Portugal had foreseen this problem and addressed it in its strategy.

In logistical operations Portugal was quick to shed the troop transport after the initial surge in favor of aircraft, although it was less quick to upgrade this decision to jet transports. This move contrasted with the British in Malaya, who clung to the troopship for moving personnel even though the fastest of them had become obsolete. In 1957 it cost £120 per person for sea passage to Singapore. The comparable contract airfare was £45. This reluctance to change was inconsistent for a country that had in 1950 developed the first propeller-jet airliner, the Vickers Viscount, and the first turbojet airliner, the DeHavilland Comet, two years later. It was even more puzzling in that travel by sea separated a soldier from his proper duties for perhaps three weeks, compared with forty-eight hours by air.[50]

In making the transition from the primary airheads and ports of the theaters to local distribution, Portugal developed an elaborate ground-transportation system based on a wide network of roads, protected convoys, and tested demining procedures. These measures were designed to defeat the guerrilla attempts at disruption and to sustain Portuguese troops. Portugal's medical response ranked among the best of post–World War II conflicts, exceeding all efforts except that of the U.S. involvement in Vietnam. It had applied the proper resources imaginatively to produce these results, and collaterally to provide health care to the population. Sound innovations in this field, such as employing helicopters and paranurses in medical evacuation, increased the effectiveness of this care. In summary, the Portuguese were able to overcome the threat of having the *ultramar* wilt at the end of slow-moving sea lines of communication. They established a system responsive to the conflict and flexible enough to ensure a high degree of sustainability. The Commission on the Study of the Campaigns (1961–1974) established by the General Staff of the Army observed in its report: "All who participated in the Campaigns, whatever the Theater of Operations, agreed that never did they lack a ration, a medication, a piece of uniform, a munition, a weapon. There would be no great needs and great abundances, but the essentials, the fundamentals, would never lack...."[51] There were shortages in some remote areas from time to time because of guerrilla action against the road convoys; however, in no case was this disruption more than an inconvenience. Portuguese logistics were timely and tailored in their delivery, and the result of this effectiveness was a sustainable military capability.

NOTES

1. Archibald C. P. Wavell, *Speaking Generally* (London: Macmillan, 1946), 78–79.

2. Estado-Maior do Exército, *Subsídios para o Estudo da Doutrina Aplicada nas Campanhas de África (1961–1974)* [Aid to the Study of Doctrine Applied in the Campaigns of Africa (1961–1974)] (Lisbon: Estado-Maior do Exército, 1990), 193–194.

3. Ibid., 198.

4. Estado-Maior do Exército, *Resenha Histórico-Militar das Campanhas de África (1961–1974)* [Historical-Military Report of the African Campaigns (1961–1974)] (Lisbon: Estado-Maior do Exército, 1989), Vol. I, 439.

5. Ibid., 439–440.

6. Ibid., 440–443.

7. Chief of the 4th Division of the Military Region of Angola, Logistic Report/Directive 100 of 15 August 1963, Annex G.

8. *Subsídios para o Estudo da Doutrina Aplicada nas Campanhas de África*, 312.

9. *Resenha Histórico-Militar das Campanhas de África (1961–1974)*, Vol. I, 475.

10. Colonel Ivo Ferreira, *Transportes Estratégicos entre as Províncias de Angola e Moçambique* [Strategic Transport Between the Provinces of Angola and Mozambique] (Lisbon: Instituto de Altos Estudos Militares, 1964), 9.

11. Colonel Luís Alberto Santiago Inocentes, interview by the author, 14 April 1994, London.

12. *Resenha Histórico-Militar das Campanhas de África (1961–1974)*, Vol. I, 449. In 1970 the average exchange rate for a conto was £14.53; in 1971, £14.21; in 1972, £15.78; and in 1973, £16.58.

13. General Tomás George Conceição Silva, interview by the author, 3 April 1995, Lisbon. General Conceição Silva was Chief of Staff of the Portuguese Air Force from 1988 to 1991, and had extensive airlift experience in Africa.

14. Commander, 1st Air Region, "Resumo Estatístico das Missões Realizadas e Passageiros Transportados (Ida e Volta), 1972 e 1973" [Statistical Résumé of Missions Flown and Passengers Transported (Round Trip), 1972 and 1973], 30 September 1974.

15. General Rui Tavares Monteiro, "Transporte Aéreo na FAP, Do zero aos 707" [Air Transport in PoAF, from Zero to the 707], *Mais Alto*, No. 283 (1993): 7.

16. Commander, 1st Air Region, "Resumo Estatístico das Missões Realizadas e Passageiros Transportados (Ida e Volta), 1972 e 1973."

17. Ferreira, 9.

18. Ibid.

19. Colonel António Fernandes Morgado, *Apoio Logístico na Guiné 1973–1974* [Logistical Support in Guiné 1973–1974] (Lisbon: Instituto de Altos Estudos Militares, 1979), 9–11.

20. Kaúlza de Arriaga, *Sínteses* [Synthesis] (Lisbon: Privately published, 1992), 190. General Arriaga served as the Subsecretary of State for Aeronautics from 1955 to 1962.

21. Oliver Crawford, *The Door Marked Malaya* (London: Rupert Hart-Davis, 1958), 13–14.

22. Colonel (Engineers) Luís Valença Pinto, interview by the author, 15 November 1994, Tancos. Colonel Valença Pinto is the Commandant of the Portuguese Army Practical School of Engineering in Tancos and has extensive experience with demining operations in Angola (1971–1972) and Cabinda (1973–1974).

23. Thomas H. Henriksen, *Revolution and Counterrevolution: Mozambique's War of Independence, 1964–1974* (London: Greenwood Press, 1978), 43.

24. Valença Pinto interview.

25. Ibid.

26. General José Manuel de Bethencourt Rodrigues, interview by the author, 9 November 1994, Lisbon.

27. Valença Pinto interview.

28. Ibid.

29. Inocentes interview.

30. *Subsídios para o Estudo da Doutrina Aplicada nas Campanhas de África*, 176.

31. U.S. Marine Corps, *Professional Knowledge Gained from Operational Experience in Vietnam, 1969, Special Issue, Mines and Boobytraps* (Washington: Headquarters, United States Marine Corps, 1969), 2.

32. P. D. Foxton, *Powering War: Modern Land Force Logistics* (London: Brassey's, 1994), 69.

33. Headquarters, Military Region of Angola, 4th Division (Logistics), Luanda, "General Plan of the Standard Operating Procedures Issued by the 4th Directorate," 15 August 1963, section on "General Rules on Hospitalization."

34. Ibid.

35. Colonel Lourenço de Sousa Pereira, "A Integração da Função Evacuação/ Hospitalização nos Três Ramos das Forças Armadas" [Integration of the Evacuation/ Hospitalization Function in the Three Branches of the Armed Forces], lecture given at the Instituto de Altos Estudos Militares, Lisbon, 1968–1969 session of the Course for Senior Command, 19–20.

36. Joaquim da Luz Cunha, et al., *África: A Vitória Traída* [Africa, Betrayed Victory] (Lisbon: Editorial Intervenção, 1977), 70–71. Based on figures for sick and wounded from all causes in Guiné of 27,790, in Angola of 48,465, and in Mozambique of 38,950; and days of combat in Guiné of 4,016, in Angola of 4,746, and in Mozambique of 3,647.

37. Inocentes interview, 14 April 1994. Colonel Inocentes was the Portuguese Military Attaché to the Republic of South Africa from 1972 to 1975.

38. Sousa Pereira, fig. 6.

39. Conceição Silva interview.

40. Colonel Luís A. Martinho Grão, interview by the author, 2 April 1995, Tomar, Portugal. Colonel Martinho Grão, a former parachutist, is presently writing a history of the Portuguese paranurses.

41. Martin Binkin and Shirley J. Bach, *Women in the Military* (Washington: Brookings Institution, 1977), 134. Women in the predecessor to the Israeli Defense Force made their first substantial appearance in 1936 in the guerrilla war between the Arabs and the Jews. By the end of World War II, one in five frontline troops was female.

42. Major General Jeanne Holm, USAF (Retired), *Women in the Military: The Unfinished Revolution* (Novato, Calif.: Presidio Press, 1982), 228.

43. Ibid., 181. Each prospective female Marine had to submit four photographs (front, back, right and left views), and the hiring decision was made at the unusually high level of Head of Recruiting.

44. Decree Law No. 42 073 of 31 December 1958; and its modifying Decree No. 43 663 of 5 May 1961.

45. Martinho Grão interview. The schools were *Escola de Enfermagem Franciscana Missionárias de Maria* and *Escola de S. Vincente de Paulo*.

46. Luís A. Martinho Grão, "Os Filhos de Belerofonte" [The Sons of Bellerophon], *Boina Verde*, Supplement (April–June 1993): 24.

47. Binkin and Bach, 117.

48. Holm, 227.

49. Martinho Grão interview.

50. Kenneth Macksey, *For Want of a Nail: The Impact on War of Logistics and Communications* (London: Brassey's, 1989), 158–167.

51. *Subsídios para o Estudo da Doutrina Aplicada nas Campanhas de África*, 198.

10

THE PORTUGUESE WAY

The preceding chapters have argued that there was a specific Portuguese approach to counterinsurgency which successfully drew on its strengths and which devolved from a national strategy of husbanding its limited resources. Portugal translated this parsimony into policies and practices at the campaign and tactical level that permitted it to conduct a sustained and lengthy war in the *ultramar* between 1961 and 1974. A review of the record reveals that Portugal fashioned a style of counterinsurgency that was distinct from that of other countries and that enabled it to overcome its major geographical challenges and resource limitations and to grind the nationalist movements to a halt. This Portuguese way focused on a subdued, low-tempo style of fighting that was a function of its constrained resources and low technology. Portugal knew from the beginning that it was going to have to fight a long war, and thus it would have to fight well and cheaply to sustain the conflict.

In the implementation of this strategy Portugal's activities fell into two primary categories, the management of human and material resources and the specific tactical adaptations for fighting counterinsurgency. The sum of these two areas reflected the Portuguese achievement of fighting a subdued war with minimal resources for a protracted period. Portugal had acknowledged from the beginning that there would be no immediate solutions to its situation in Africa and had proceeded to favor strengths and avoid weaknesses. While it lost its colonies, it did not lose them because of military reasons. Central to the Portuguese military achievement was the recognition that the role of the military in a counterinsurgency was to buy time to match the guerrilla concept of protracted war, and it was this goal that dictated a long-haul, low-cost strategy. This aim reflected the generally accepted principle that if the tempo of the conflict could be contained in all of its dimensions—geographical extension, populations affected, technology employed, domestic and international public opinion voiced–then the cost of the war could be made acceptable.[1]

This Portuguese way of fighting focused on maintaining an overall low-intensity conflict with its implied low cost. Portugal developed its doctrine to achieve this end after having assiduously studied the French and British experiences and gleaned the lessons that they held for Portuguese Africa. It followed this doctrine in educating and training its troops in the methods of conducting such a conflict. It did so through the establishment of counterinsurgency-specific training and then moving it to the *ultramar* to provide a more effective acclimatization to the fighting environment. It reorganized its Army into small light-infantry units. This type of force was the most effective and proven in counterinsurgency campaigning, as it could maintain the all-important contact with the population while fighting small, company-sized bands of guerrillas. Light infantry is also the most basic type of military force in its simplicity and low firepower capability, and as such it has remained relatively inexpensive to equip, train, and deploy. It is also less likely to terrorize the population and alienate this target audience with any massive use of firepower. This force structure embodied Portugal's policy of conducting a subdued, low-tempo, affordable war.

Portuguese infantry not only hunted the enemy but befriended the population. It concomitantly participated in social projects to elevate the people's standard of living and provide a tangible alternative to insurgent promises. This initiative, which included the redressing of grievances, was supported by psychological operations that promoted these benefits. These operations ranged from troop instruction in the purpose of the war and the individual soldier's importance in Portugal's African mission to the strong promotion of social benefits targeted to selected civilian audiences. These actions, too, were part of the implementation of Portuguese strategy for a low-intensity war, in that undermining the will of the enemy and strengthening the will of the armed forces and the population through communication was less expensive than a military offensive. Social projects were also benign and inexpensive alongside military operations and demonstrated a commitment by Portugal to its African citizens. Promoting these benefits through psychological operations enhanced their effectiveness through a broad understanding and appeal to the population.

Further, the local people were enlisted to fight in very significant numbers. This Africanization of counterinsurgency served to remove recruiting pressure from the *metrópole*, reduce transportation costs, and engage the local populations in their own defense. Again, Portuguese strategy was supported with this reduction of costs and mobilization of the African population, which helped to dampen domestic public pressure in Portugal and provide sustainability to the conflict. Finally, the Portuguese through the use of turned guerrillas, infiltrators, spies, and refugee troops created adverse diplomatic pressure and debilitating internal friction within the nationalist organizations. Initiating these relatively inexpensive disruptions to the guerrilla capability to organize offensives reduced pressure on the fighting forces. It also reduced guerrilla intimidation of the population by undermining enemy initiative.

Portugal sought to use relatively simple methods and equipment that could be easily understood and employed by its forces, matching the guerrillas low technology. High technology was not required to counter the guerrillas and employing it in counterinsurgency increased the cost of fighting exponentially with only a small marginal gain in effectiveness. The Portuguese mastered these principles, and the depth of this understanding was reflected in the comparative management of their resources and direction of their military forces alongside those of other powers similarly engaged.

One of the best comparative indicators in the management of human resources is the number of casualties absorbed in relation to troops deployed in this and other similar conflicts. In terms of deaths in the Campaigns the overall level of intensity was low. The measure of this intensity is normally taken by comparing deaths for the entire conflict based upon an average per day of war per thousand combatants.

Table 10.1
Combat Deaths per Day of War per Thousand Combatants for Selected Conflicts[2]

Malaya	0.0017
Portuguese African Campaigns	0.0075
Algeria	0.0107
Vietnam	0.0365
Indochina	0.0691
World War II	0.1400

Malaya was by far and away the least intense, followed by the Portuguese Campaigns. The French and U.S. experiences were more costly and intense. The figures follow generally the style of warfare. The French conducted their reoccupation of Indochina as if it were a conventional conflict, as did the United States. in its subsequent involvement in Vietnam, and both experienced a high rate of combat deaths for troops deployed because of the intensity. The French *guerre révolutionnaire* as applied in Algeria was military in nature, and this approach, while an improvement over Indochina, still exceeded the intensity of the Portuguese experience. The World War II experience is the classic high-intensity conventional conflict and is included as a contrasting reference.

The total number of Portuguese deaths from all causes in the three theaters for the entire war was 8,290, of whom 5,797 were recruited from the *metrópole* and 2,493 were recruited from the colonies.[3] The French forces in Algeria (1954–1962) counted 17,456 dead from all causes in eight years.[4] The United States experienced 58,135 deaths in Vietnam from 1961 to 1973, a period of twelve years. Between the years of 1964 and 1969, Portugal's years of heaviest fighting, average annual deaths per thousand deployed troops was 2.23 and was its highest in 1966 at 2.69.[5] In Vietnam the United States experienced between 1964 and 1972 an average annual rate of 14.7 deaths per thousand troops deployed, with a maximum rate of 23.5 in 1968 at the height of the fighting.[6] Portugal in the Great War, its most recent previous combat experience, deployed troops and fought on three fronts: France, the south of Angola, and the north of Mozambique. In France there were 57,000 Portuguese combatants, and in the two African colonies there were 32,000 plus 25,000 local troops, a total of 114,000 men under arms. The war for Portugal lasted two years. The number of deaths was a staggering 7,908, for a death rate per thousand per year of approximately 34.68.[7]

On balance, then, the death rate during the 1961–1974 period was substantially less than either of the two similar contemporary insurgencies in Vietnam and Algeria and in Portugal's last conventional war experience of 1914–1918. The fact that the Portuguese armed forces from 1961 had fewer deaths in a decade than the French in Algeria had in a single year reinforces the achievement of Portuguese policy.

Low casualty rates in conflicts are generally attributed to thorough training, good leadership, and a sound battle plan that is understood by all parties. The Portuguese constantly sought to improve their counterinsurgency training, and moving much of it to the theaters from 1968 onward made it very effective, in that it thoroughly acclimatized the troops to the African battlefield environment. Spirited military leadership was evident in Guiné from 1968 under General Spínola and in Angola from 1970 under Generals Costa Gomes and Bethencourt Rodrigues. Building on earlier foundations, General Spínola introduced an effective counterinsurgency battle plan in his "A Better Guiné," which combined military and social action both to check the guerrillas and to provide a viable alternative to the PAIGC promises. Similar plans were introduced in Angola by General Costa Gomes and in Mozambique by General Arriaga. Implicit in these plans was the restrained use of firepower to avoid terrorizing the population and the mix of social action with military protection. Except for the Angola uprisings of 1961 there was no guerrilla army, as in Indochina, Algeria, and Vietnam, that massed troops and employed them in conventional ways. The Portuguese dealt largely with small bands, as embodied in the PAIGC *bi-grupo* of twenty-six men. An insurgent force of as many as 200 men was rare. As the territories were sparsely inhabited and had difficult—and also, in Angola and Mozambique, vast—terrain, finding guerrillas was a considerable challenge. Where they were encountered, fights were generally brief affairs with limited casualties. The style of war simply would not produce the volume of casualties inherent in a more conventional grinding battle of attrition with massed troops and massive firepower. The intent of the Portuguese to conduct a long-haul, low-cost conflict was well appreciated and borne out in the casualty figures.

The financial cost of war is a relative measure, and Portugal's experience must be seen in the context of its economy and alongside that of other similar conflicts. It is estimated that the Campaigns cost approximately £1,461,846,750 over thirteen years, or £112.5 million per year.[8] In Malaya the cost from June 1948 until Independence Day on 31 August 1957 was an estimated at £700 million, or £77.8 million per year.[9] The cost of the French reoccupation of Indochina from 1946 to 1954 was put at £3.6 billion plus another £335 million from the United States, or about £491.8 million per year total.[10] The war in Algeria for military action alone cost an estimated £4 billion and social operations an additional 25 percent, or about £667.7 million per year total.[11] By comparison the U.S. involvement in Vietnam is estimated to have cost £50,220,000,000, or £5,580 million per year. Again from these figures it is apparent which belligerents elected to use a low-cost, long-haul counterinsurgency strategy. Malaya, the least expensive engagement, and the Portuguese Campaigns were both relatively inexpensive and sustainable. The French reoccupation of Indochina and the subsequent U.S. involvement in Vietnam were many times more expensive, as they were both conducted on a largely conventional basis.[12] Algeria, a highly militarized counterinsurgency, cost as much as a conventional conflict. It is readily apparent that the cost of a counterinsurgency is directly related to its tempo and the type of strategy and tactics that are employed to yield this rhythm. This principle was embodied in the Portuguese approach, allowing its armed forces to sustain the war effort in step with the guerrilla strategy of protracted conflict.

This burden also appeared reasonable when viewed from the overall perspective of the Portuguese national budget; however, there was a cost in increased political dissent. During the period of the Campaigns the expenditures for national defense as a portion of state expenditures ranged between a high of 23 percent in 1961 and a low of 17.1 percent in 1973.[13] In absolute terms defense spending increased fivefold from 1960 to 1975. These increases, while they remained a declining percentage of the overall national budget, were part of an increasing public financing burden that was funded through increased taxes and inflation, factors that aggravated public dissent as time went on. Comparatively, in France in 1965, a period of peace following Algeria, defense expenditures represented 20 percent of the national budget.[14] Despite the apparent reasonableness of Portugal's expenditure, its political fabric was wearing thin. This situation was beyond the generals to repair, and while it was the duty of the politicians, they were failing.

Nevertheless, the human and economic cost of the war was a powerful burden for Portugal. No matter how contained the conflict and how reasonable its cost financially, the burden on the population after thirteen years was telling. In addition to the 8,290 deaths, Portuguese wounded and mutilated totaled 27,919.[15] Social services in the *metrópole* were unprepared for the magnitude of this rehabilitation task. The youth of Portugal had been mobilized in one of the largest and most arduous military conscriptions in the world.[16] The troops required for this ambitious venture had stretched Portugal's capacity. Only conscription first of the *metrópole* population and later of that in the *ultramar* would support a broad occupation of the colonies to maintain order, the momentum of the social initiative, and the flexibility of mobile reserves. While this strategy resulted in one of the largest uses of indigenous troops in any modern counterinsurgency, an important element in the Portuguese way, the *metrópole* was still adversely affected. The burden was extreme in that despite the low casualty figures showing that the military was executing its plans as envisioned, Portugal's force level in Africa in relation to its population was five times higher than the U.S. commitment in Vietnam.[17] Deaths from all causes were, on a percentage basis relative to the population, about three times as great for Portugal than for the United States in its Southeast Asia involvement. This situation created a problem of diminishing public support that was outside of the military's control no matter how effectively troops were deployed. As a result annual emigration had risen to 170,000 in 1971. Over the period of the Campaigns an estimated 1.5 million emigrants reduced the workforce to 3.5 million, and the total population to 8.6 million.[18] Inflation by 1974 was running at 20 percent per year, and the population was increasingly voting with its feet to avoid the economic and social penalties of the war.[19]

Another approach to measuring the Portuguese way is an examination of the execution of its doctrine. The Portuguese Army made the most important initial step in establishing doctrine before the conflict. It sought to achieve the twin goals of avoiding the cost of relearning the lessons of other militaries that had fought counterinsurgencies, and of committing forces ignorant of how victory would be attained. In the first instance the Portuguese delved into the literature on guerrilla wars and the doctrinal manuals on the counterinsurgencies of others. They sent missions to French, British, and U.S. schools and on operations relating to the pertinent aspects of "small wars," and sought the voices of experience in counsel with veterans. They found that little had been written on modern counterinsurgency. In the majority of instances there was no easily transmitted doctrine, and security forces in earlier conflicts had been largely left to feel their way along. The literature that was belatedly written for the British action in Malaya, for instance, was only by chance transmitted to Kenya, and neither of the volumes on these two experiences had been well known to the troops in Cyprus.[20] France in Indochina and in the first two years of Algeria was similarly unfocused. The Portuguese assembled counterinsurgency information painstakingly, reduced it to a plan for the defense of their colonies, and committed it to a written doctrine for the Campaigns, *O Exército na Guerra Subversiva*.[21] This work described for the entire army the nature of the enemy and the methods to be used to defeat him. The instruction was unusual in that the British and the French only belatedly committed their counterinsurgency doctrine to writing after they had been fighting for some time.

Portuguese soldiers were sent into battle from the start knowing how victory was supposed to be achieved. Although the doctrine was fresh from its writing and had been neither taught nor tested in the field, it was available and served as a guide in its raw form. In the modern counterinsurgencies of Britain, France, and the United States, initial hostilities went without the benefit of such guidance. Assembly of the Portuguese doctrine and its transmission had presented a challenge, but the importance of understanding the opposition and its methods in advance was thought to be vital to success. Adjustments were needed when teething problems arose in the early years of the conflict, and Portugal made them in the areas of training and organization and a relaunched social initiative supported by psychological operations. In doing so it defined the Portuguese character of counterinsurgency in the shape of its forces, their education, and their deployment.

In addition to the timely development of Portuguese doctrine, the Portuguese Army converted itself on a wholesale basis into a counterinsurgency force. The magnitude of this conversion cannot be understated. The upheaval of changing an army from one trained and organized to fight a conventional war in Europe to one primarily structured in small infantry units for counterinsurgency in Africa was cathartic. This adjustment was frustrated further by a great influx of conscripts whose ambitions were far different from those of the professional soldiers. Nevertheless, the entire Army did change, and its training was adjusted to address the threat. No such wholesale change was either tried or effected in any other counterinsurgency. While Britain, France, and the United States were always short of manpower to conduct their counterinsurgencies, and indeed had to rely on conscription to do so, they never regarded these conflicts in the same light as Portugal and consequently did not feel compelled to convert their entire armies to the task.[22] Their counterinsurgencies, while important, diverted resources from their primary military focus, which was a conventional war in Europe against the Red Army. For Portugal the African Campaigns were its main conflict.

Emphasizing the tactical flexibility demonstrated by the British as well as their PAIGC opponents, the Portuguese redefined the use of small infantry units and specialized troops. Portugal changed the training of its infantry forces to emphasize in-theater indoctrination and instruction to make them more familiar with the local combat environment and their adaptation to it more facile. These changes had the effect of shaping the conflict to one of low intensity and of keeping it that way. The French in Indochina and Algeria and the United States in Vietnam never sought a truly subdued engagement.[23]

Intelligence in counterinsurgency drives military operations and troop employment, and so to support these actions Portugal developed an efficient political and military intelligence apparatus in the use of agents and informers, police, and air and ground reconnaissance patrols. The information from all sources was processed through a system of intelligence coordination centers and disseminated to support operations. This organization was copied from the British system in Malaya and adapted to Portuguese Africa with reliable results. Portugal also struggled to coordinate its military efforts with those of the civil sector in an effort to overawe the enemy through its social programs. It sought to present a very tangible alternative of peace and social advancement opposite the promises of the insurgents. Every aspect of the Portuguese organization for war and deployment of its troops was constructed on the British premise of minimal force, as demonstrated in Malaya, which kept the Campaigns subdued and affordable within the limits of Portugal's resources.

In the final analysis, while Portugal fought an imaginative campaign to retain its colonies in an anticolonial era, no amount of military verve could overcome the political problem of Portugal's legitimacy in Africa. Because of this circumstance, Portugal lost the war and ultimately its colonies despite its enormous sacrifices. This development reinforced the point that wars are largely resolved politically. General Spínola, in writing his book *Portugal e o Futuro* [Portugal and the Future] in 1971, acknowledged this principle and saw no point in continuing to expend resources at the expense of the overall good of the country in pursuing a dead-end strategy.[24] In a counterinsurgency, military action can be used only to support political and social measures. It cannot replace them. By 1971 in all theaters the military had given Portugal credibility and was prepared to provide further time for a negotiated disengagement. By 1970 General Spínola had checked the PAIGC momentum and generated a stalemate through spirited leadership and his "A Better Guiné" social program. This stalemate began to slip in 1973 as the military realized the needed political solution was not in sight. By 1971 Generals Costa Gomes and Bethencourt Rodrigues were producing a military victory in Angola that remained intact through the end of the war. In Mozambique the nationalist movements were contained until 1970, the conflict having been relatively quiescent until then. After 1970 the situation began gradually to deteriorate from the northern border with Tanzania southward. This fraying could have been corrected with an application of additional troops and matériel under spirited leadership. Military force could not, however, end the war. No amount of imaginative campaigning could have done so. General Spínola and all of the Portuguese armed forces were aware of this fact. Portugal's political leadership, however, remained shortsighted and removed from reality. The true hope for the regeneration of Portugal lay in releasing its colonies to resolve both domestic and international dissent and to embrace the European prosperity then under way. Portugal's position in Africa had been untenable from the start, and the military had recognized this fact. Portuguese military leadership had proved farsighted in both its planning and its conduct of the war. It had conducted a sophisticated campaign in three theaters a long way from home. It had successfully addressed its problems within the context of its limited resources and fashioned a style of warfare that ground the enemy to a halt. It had skillfully managed the use of Portuguese lives and treasure. When the politicians failed to provide the necessary complementary support, it was the military that intervened on 25 April 1974 and provided the political solution that not only freed the colonies but ultimately liberated Portugal and made possible a transition to democracy.

NOTES

1. Sir Robert Thompson, *Lessons from the Vietnam War*, Report of a seminar held at the Royal United Services Institute in London, 12 February 1966, 18.

2. Neil Sheehan, *A Bright Shining Lie: John Paul Vann and America in Vietnam* (New York: Random House, Inc., 1988), 172; Alistair Horne, *A Savage War of Peace: Algeria 1954–1962* (Harmondsworth: Penguin Books, 1987), 538; Alf Andrew Heggoy, *Insurgency and Counterinsurgency in Algeria* (Bloomington: Indiana University Press, 1972), 175; Joaquim da Luz Cunha, et al., *África: A Vitória Traída* [Africa: Betrayed Victory] (Lisbon: Editorial Intervenção, 1977), 70–71; Harry Miller, *Jungle War in Malaya: The Campaign Against Communism 1948–60* (London: Arthur Barker, 1972), 17; and *Statistical Abstract of the United States* (Washington: U.S. Department of Commerce, 1994), 362.

3. Estado-Maior do Exército, *Resenha Histórico-Militar das Campanhas de África (1961–1974)* [Historical Military Report of the African Campaigns (1961–1974)] (Lisbon: Estado-Maior do Exército, 1988), Vol. I, 264–266.

4. Horne, 538.

5. Luz Cunha, 74–75.

6. *Statistical Abstract of the U.S. 1975* (Washington: U.S. Department of Commerce, 1976).

7. Luz Cunha, 73.

8. Ibid., 63. Imputed from General Luz Cunha's figures in contos and converted to sterling.

9. Robert Jackson, *The Malayan Emergency: The Commonwealth's Wars 1948–1966* (London: Routledge, 1991), 115.

10. Bernard B. Fall, *Hell in a Very Small Place: The Siege of Dien Bien Phu* (New York: Harper & Row, 1967), viii.

11. Horne, 538–539.

12. Andrew F. Krepinevich, Jr., *The Army and Vietnam* (Baltimore: Johns Hopkins University Press, 1986), 258–260.

13. *Resenha Histórico-Militar das Campanhas de África (1961–1974)*, Vol. I, 513.

14. Luz Cunha, 62.

15. Ibid., 70–71.

16. Willem S. van der Waals, *Portugal's War in Angola 1961–1974* (Rivonia: Ashanti Publishing, 1993), 244.

17. Ibid.

18. Ibid.

19. António de Spínola, *Portugal e o Futuro* [Portugal and the Future] (Lisbon: Editora Arcádia, 1974), 37–38, 41.

20. Thomas R. Mockaitis, *British Counterinsurgency, 1919–60* (London: Macmillan, 1990), 184.

21. Estado-Maior do Exército, *O Exército na Guerra Subversiva* [The Army in Subversive War] (Lisbon: Estado-Maior do Exército, 1963).

22. Krepinevich, 127.

23. Ibid., 192.

24. Spínola, 42–43.

SELECTED BIBLIOGRAPHY

PORTUGUESE GOVERNMENT OFFICIAL AND SEMI-OFFICIAL PUBLICATIONS AND DOCUMENTS

Ministries of the Colonies, of the *Ultramar*, and of Foreign Affairs

Martins, E. A. Azambuja, Colonel, Portuguese Army. *O Soldado Africano de Moçambique*. [The African Soldier of Mozambique]. Lisbon: Agência Geral do Colónias, Ministério das Colónias, 1936.

Ministry of Foreign Affairs. *Portuguese Africa: An Introduction*. Lisbon: Ministry of Foreign Affairs, 1973.

Moreira, Adriano, Professor. *Estudos de Ciências Políticas e Sociais, No. 1, Política Ultramarina*. [Studies in Political and Social Science, No. 1, *Ultramar* Policy]. Lisbon: Junta de Investigações do Ultramar, Centro de Estudos Políticos e Sociais, 1961.

Pinheiro, Joaquim Franco, Jaime de Oliveira Leandro, and Hermes de Araújo Oliveira. *Estudos de Ciências Políticas e Sociais, No. 62, Subversão e Contra-Subversão*. [Studies of Political and Social Science, No. 62, Subversion and Counter-Subversion]. Lisbon: Junta de Investigações do Ultramar, Centro de Estudos Políticos e Sociais, 1963.

Província da Guiné. *Ordenamento Rural e Urbano na Guiné Portuguesa*. [Rural and Urban Plan for Portuguese Guiné]. Lisbon: Agência-Geral do Ultramar, 1973.

_____. *Prospectiva do Desenvolvimento Económico e Social da Guiné*. [Prospectus for the Economic and Social Development of Guiné]. Lisbon: Junta de Investigações do Ultramar, 1972.

Teixeira da Mota, A. *Monografias dos Territórios do Ultramar: Guiné Portuguesa*. [Monographs of the Overseas Territories: Portuguese Guiné]. Lisbon: Agência Geral do Ultramar, Ministério do Ultramar, 1954.

Portuguese Army

Estado-Maior do Exército. *Resenha Histórico-Militar das Campanhas de África, Vol. I, Enquadramento Geral.* [Historical Military Report of the African Campaigns, Vol. I, General Framework]. Lisbon: Estado-Maior do Exército, 1988.

_____. *Resenha Histórico-Militar das Campanhas de África, Vol. II, Dispositivo das Nossas Forças Angola.* [Historical Military Report of the African Campaigns, Vol. II, Disposition of Our Forces in Angola]. Lisbon: Estado-Maior do Exército, 1989.

_____. *Resenha Histórico-Militar das Campanhas de África, Vol. III, Dispositivo das Nossas Forças Guiné.* [Historical Military Report of the African Campaigns, Vol. III, Disposition of Our Forces in Guiné]. Lisbon: Estado-Maior do Exército, 1989.

_____. *Resenha Histórico-Militar das Campanhas de África, Vol. IV, Dispositivo das Nossas Forças Moçambique.* [Historical Military Report of the African Campaigns, Vol. IV, Disposition of Our Forces in Mozambique]. Lisbon: Estado-Maior do Exército, 1989.

_____. *Subsídios para o Estudo da Doutrina Aplicada nas Campanhas de África (1961-1974).* [Aid to the Study of the Doctrine Applied in the Campaigns of Africa (1961-1974)]. Lisbon: Estado-Maior do Exército, 1990.

_____. *O Exército na Guerra Subversiva.* [The Army in Subversive War]. Lisbon: Estado-Maior do Exército, 1963.

_____. *Guia para o Emprego Táctico das Pequenas Unidades na Contra Guerrilha.* [Guide to the Tactical Employment of Small Units in Counter-Guerrilla Operations]. Lisbon: Estado-Maior do Exército, 1963.

Private Authors

Cardoso, Pedro Alexandre Gomes, General, Portuguese Army. *As Informações em Portugal.* [Intelligence in Portugal]. Lisbon: Instituto da Defesa Nacional, 1980.

Duarte Silva, Joaquim Miguel de Mattos Fernandes. *Lourenço.* [Lawrence]. Lisbon: Privately printed, 1980.

Felgas, Hélio. *África: A Evolução Política de 1956 a 1970.* [Africa: The Political Evolution from 1956 to 1970]. Lisbon: Estado-Maior do Exército, Colecção Cadernos Militares, 1970.

Ribeiro Villas, Gaspar do Couto, Colonel, Staff Corps, Portuguese Army. *As Tropas Coloniais na Vida Internacional.* [Colonial Troops in International Affairs]. Lisbon: Sociedade de Geografia, 1924.

INTERVIEWS AND CORRESPONDENCE

Almeida Santos, Dionísio de, Colonel, Portuguese Army (Retired). Former liaison officer to the pro-Tshombe (Tschambe) Katanganese gendarmes who fled to eastern Angola in 1967. Interview by the author, 30 March 1995, Porto.

Bethencourt Rodrigues, José Manuel de, General, Portuguese Army (Retired). Chief of Staff, Angola (1961-1964); Military Attaché, London (1964-1967); Commander, Eastern Military Zone, Angola (1971-1973); and Commander-in-Chief, Armed Forces, and Governor of Guiné (1973-1974). Interview by the author, 9

November 1994, Lisbon.

Brochado de Miranda, Jorge, General, Portuguese Air Force (Retired). Chief of Staff, Portuguese Air Force (1984–1988). Interviews by the author, 21 November 1994 and 3 April 1995, Lisbon.

Canêlhas, José Luís Almiro, General, Portuguese Army (Retired). Chief of Psychological Operations (5th Division) in Mozambique (1969–1971). Interview by the author, 3 April 1995, Lisbon.

Cardoso, Óscar, Inspector, Polícia Internacional e de Defesa do Estado (PIDE) and its successor, Direcção Geral de Segurança (DGS), from 1965 to 1974. Interview by the author, 1 April 1995, Azaruja, Portugal. Correspondence with the author, 22 April 1995, Azaruja.

Cardoso, Pedro Alexandre Gomes, General, Portuguese Army (Retired). General Secretary of Guiné (1968–1972). Interviews by the author, 17 November 1994 and 29 March 1995, Lisbon.

Conceição Silva, Tomás George, General, Portuguese Air Force (Retired). Cargo airlift pilot (1966–1969) and Chief of Staff, Portuguese Air Force (1988–1991). Interview by the author, 3 April 1995, Lisbon.

Duarte Silva, Joaquim Miguel de Mattos Fernandes, General, Portuguese Army (Retired). Former liaison officer for the UPA defector, Alexandre Taty, and his *Tropas Especiais* (1966–1967). Interview by the author, 3 April 1995, Lisbon.

Fabião, Carlos, Colonel, Portuguese Army (Retired). Army liaison for *militia* troops in Guiné in 1971. Interview by the author, 31 March 1995, Lisbon.

Felgas, Hélio, Brigadeiro, Portuguese Army (Retired). Battalion commander in Guiné (1963–1965), and on staff of General Spínola (1968–1969). Interview by the author, 22 November 1994, Lisbon.

Gomes Bessa, Carlos da Costa, Colonel, Staff Corps, Portuguese Army (Retired). Executive Director, *Revista Militar*, and former staff expert responsible for the liaison between the military and civil government. Interview by the author, 18 November 1994, Lisbon.

Inocentes, Luís Alberto Santiago, Colonel, Cavalry, Portuguese Army (Retired). Operations officer, Headquarters Military Region Mozambique (1962–1966); Military Attaché, Rhodesia (1966–1969); Chief of Staff, Brigade Headquarters, Guiné (1970–1972); and Military Attaché, Republic of South Africa (1972–1975). Interviews by the author, 18 March, 9 April, 14 April, 30 August, 2 September, 5 September, and 22 October 1994, and 17 March 1995, London. Correspondence with the author, 10 August 1994, London; 7 October 1994, Lisbon; 18 November 1994, 10 December 1994, 1 February 1995, 7 February 1995, 15 February 1995, 4 March 1995, 18 April 1995, 5 June 1995, 14 July 1995, and 15 July 1995, London.

Mano, César Augusto Rodrigues, Colonel, Cavalry, Portuguese Army (Retired). Commander of an Armored Reconnaisance Company (1963–1965), Operations Officer of a Cavalry Battalion (infantry role) (1967–1969), Commander of a Cavalry Battalion (infantry role) (1972–1973), and Commander of the Grupo de Dragões de Angola (1973–1974). Interview by the author, 10 November 1994, Oeiras.

Marques Pinto, Renato Fernando, Brigadeiro, Portuguese Army (Retired). Chief of Military Intelligence, Angola (1963–1965); Director of Serviço de Centralização e Coordenação das Informações (Angola) (1965–1968); Chief of Intelligence,

Army (1968–1970); Military Attaché, London (1970–1974); Chief of Staff, Army, Mozambique (1974–1975); and Chief of Intelligence, Armed Forces (1975–1977). Interviews by the author, 7 November 1994, Cascais; 30 March 1995, Oeiras; and 3 April 1995, Lisbon. Correspondence with the author, 23 February 1995, Oeiras; 22 May 1995, Oeiras; 26 June 1995, Lagos; 18 July 1995, Oeiras; 9 August 1995, Oeiras; 6 September 1995, Oeiras; and 13 November 1995, Oeiras.

Martinho Grão, Luís António, Colonel, Paratroops, Portuguese Air Force (Retired). Historian for the Portuguese Paratroops. Interview by the author, 2 April 1995, Tomar. Correspondence with the author, 15 April 1995, Tomar.

Matias, Nuno Gonçalo Vieira, Vice Admiral, Portuguese Navy, Superintendent of Material Services. Former commander of a detachment of *fuzileiros especiais* in Guiné under General Spínola. Interview by the author, 23 November 1994, Lisbon.

Menezes, Manuel Amorim de Sousa, General, Portuguese Army (Retired). Chief of Staff, Armed Forces, Mozambique (1970–1975). Interviews by the author, 17 November 1994 and 29 March 1995, Lisbon. Correspondence with the author, 17 July 1995, Caxias.

Valderano, Duke of, formerly Colonel Ronald Waring, British Army. Professor of English Language from 1956 to 1974 at the Instituto de Altos Estudos Militares, Lisbon. Served before and during World War II with the King's Royal Rifle Corps and the Royal Hampshire Regiment. Interview by the author, 17 March 1995, London. Correspondence with the author, 21 April 1995, London.

Valença Pinto, Luís, Colonel, Engineers, Portuguese Army, Commandant of the Practical School of Engineering, Tancos. Interview by the author, 15 November 1994, Tancos.

BACKGROUND LITERATURE

Abshire, David M., and Michael A. Samuels. *Portuguese Africa: A Handbook.* London: Pall Mall Press, 1969.

Bender, Gerald J. *Angola Under the Portuguese: The Myth and the Reality.* Berkeley: University of California Press, 1978.

Birmingham, David. *Frontline Nationalism in Angola and Mozambique.* London: James Currey, 1992.

Bruce, Neil. *Portugal: The Last Empire.* London: David and Charles, 1975.

Clarence-Smith, W. Gervase. *The Third Portuguese Empire 1825–1975.* Manchester: Manchester University Press, 1985.

Duffy, James. *Portugal in Africa.* Harmondsworth: Penguin Books, 1962.

_____. *Portuguese Africa.* Cambridge, Mass.: Harvard University Press, 1961.

Isaacman, Allen F. *The Tradition of Resistance in Mozambique.* London: Heinemann Educational Books, 1976.

Kay, Hugh. *Salazar and Modern Portugal.* London: Eyre & Spottswoode, 1970.

Livermore, H. V. *A New History of Portugal.* Cambridge: Cambridge University Press, 1966.

Minter, William. *Portuguese Africa and the West.* Harmondsworth: Penguin Books, 1972.

_____, ed. *Operation Timber: Pages from the Savimbi Dossier*. Trenton, N.J.: African World Press, 1988.

Moreira, Adriano. *Portugal's Stand in Africa*. Translated by William Davis and others. New York: University Publishers, 1962.

Newitt, Malyn. *Portugal in Africa, The Last Hundred Years*. London: C. Hurst & Co. Ltd.,1981.

Norton de Matos, José Mendes Ribeiro. *A Província de Angola*. [The Province of Angola]. Porto: Edição de Maranus, 1926.

_____. "O Exército em Angola." [The Army in Angola]. *Revista Militar* (March 1924): 83-85.

O'Meara, F. *Report on Economic and Commercial Conditions in Angola (Portuguese West Africa)*. London: Department of Overseas Trade, 1937.

Robinson, Richard A. H. *Contemporary Portugal*. London: George Allen & Unwin, 1979.

Salazar, António de Oliveira. *Doctrine and Action: Internal and Foreign Policy of the New Portugal 1928-1939*. Translated by Robert Edgar Broughton. London: Faber & Faber, 1939.

LITERATURE ON THE PORTUGUESE AFRICAN CAMPAIGNS, 1961-1974

Abbott, Peter, and Manuel Ribeiro Rodrigues. *Modern African Wars(2): Angola and Moçambique 1961-1974*. London: Osprey, 1988.

Alberts, Donald J. "Armed Struggle in Angola." In *Insurgency & Terrorism, Inside Modern Revolutionary Warfare*, ed. Bard O'Neill, William Heaton, and Donald Alberts, 235-267. Washington: Brassey's, 1990.

Arriaga, Kaúlza de. *Guerra e Política*. [War and Policy]. Lisbon: Edições Referendo, 1987.

_____. *The Portuguese Answer*. London: Tom Stacy, 1973.

_____. "A Defesa Nacional Portuguesa nos Últimos 40 Anos e no Futuro." [Portuguese National Defense During the Last 40 Years and in the Future]. Lecture delivered at a conference by the same name in Lisbon, 20 October 1966.

Beckett, Ian F. W. "The Portuguese Army: The Campaign in Mozambique, 1964-1974." In *Armed Forces and Modern Counter-Insurgency*, ed. Ian F. W. Beckett and John Pimlott, 136-162. London: Croom Helm, 1985.

Bender, Gerald J. "The Limits of Counterinsurgency: An African Case." *Comparative Politics*, 4, no. 3 (April 1972): 331-360.

Biggs-Davison, John. *Portuguese Guinea: Nailing a Lie*. London: Congo Africa Publications, 1970.

Bruce, Neil. "Portugal's African Wars." *Conflict Studies*, no. 34 (March 1973).

Cabral, Amílcar. *Unity and Struggle*. Translated by Michael Wolfers. London: Heineman Educational Books, 1980.

Caetano, Marcello. *Depoimento*. [Deposition]. Rio de Janeiro: Distribuidora Record, 1974.

Caio, Horácio. *Angola: Os Dias do Desespero*. [Angola: The Days of Desperation]. Lisbon: Editorial Minerva, 1966.

Calvão, Guilherme de Alpoim. *De Conakry ao M.D.L.P.: Dossier Secreto*. [From Conakry to the M.D.L.P.: Secret Dossier]. Lisbon: Editorial Intervenção, 1976.

Calvert, Michael, Brigadier, British Army (Retired).   "Counter-Insurgency in Mozambique." *Royal United Services Institute Journal for Defense Studies* (March 1973): 81–85.

César, Amândio. *Guiné 1965: Contra-Attaque.* [Guiné 1965: Counterattack]. Braga: Livraria Editora Pax, 1965.

Chabal, Patrick. "Emergencies and Nationalist Wars in Portuguese Africa." *Journal of Imperial and Commonwealth History*, 21, no. 3 (September 1993): 235–249.

_____. *Amílcar Cabral: Revolutionary Leadership and People's War.* Cambridge: Cambridge University Press, 1983.

Chaliand, Gérard. *Armed Struggle in Africa: With the Guerrillas in "Portuguese" Guinea.* Translated by David Rattray and Robert Leonhardt. New York: Monthly Review Press, 1969.

Coelho, João Paulo Borges. *O Início da Luta Armada em Tete, 1968–1969: A Primeira Fase da Guerra e a Reacção Colonial.* [The Beginning of the Armed Struggle in Tete, 1968–1969: The First Phase of the War and the Colonial Reaction]. Maputo: Arquivo Histórico de Moçambique, 1989.

Davidson, Basil. *In the Eye of the Storm.* Garden City, N.Y.: Doubleday, 1972.

_____. *The Liberation of Guiné.* Harmondsworth: Penguin Books, 1969.

Felgas, Hélio. *A Luta na Guiné.* [The Struggle in Guiné]. Lisbon: Academia Militar, 1970.

_____. "Os Movimentos Subversivos do Ultramar Português." [Subversive Movements in the Portuguese *Ultramar*]. *Revista Militar* (January/February 1970): 33–62.

_____. "Papel do Helicóptero na Guerra da Guiné." [Role of the Helicopter in the War in Guiné]. *Jornal do Exército* (August 1968): 32–33.

_____. *Os Movimentos Terroristas de Angola, Guiné e Moçambique.* [The Terrorist Movements of Angola, Guiné and Mozambique]. Lisbon: Privately printed, 1966.

_____. "Angola e a Evolução Política dos Territórios Vizinhos." [Angola and the Political Evolution of the Neighboring Territories]. *Revista Militar* (December 1965): 705–736.

_____. *Guerra em Angola.* [War in Angola]. Lisbon: Livraria Clássica Editora, 1961.

Ferrand d'Almeida, António, Lieutenant Colonel, Cavalry, Portuguese Army. "Recordações de um «Dragão de Angola»." [Recollections of a "Dragoon of Angola"]. *Revista Militar* (October/November 1985): 689–719.

Gann, L. H. "Portugal, Africa, and the Future." *Journal of Modern African Studies* (March 1975): 1–18.

Gomes Bessa, Carlos da Costa. "Angola: A Luta Contra a Subversão e a Colaboração Civil-Militar." [Angola: The Fight Against Subversion and Civil-Military Collaboration]. *Revista Militar* (August/September 1972): 407–443.

Henriksen, Thomas H. "Lessons from Portugal's Counterinsurgency Operations in Africa." *Journal of the Royal United Services Institute for Defense Studies* (June 1978): 31–35.

_____. *Revolution and Counterrevolution: Mozambique's War of Independence, 1964–1974.* London: Greenwood Press, 1978.

_____. "Portugal in Africa: Comparative Notes on Counter-insurgency." *Orbis* (Summer 1977): 395–412.

_____. "Some Notes on the National Liberation Wars in Angola, Mozambique, and Guinea-Bissau." *Military Affairs* (February 1977): 30–36.

_____. "People's War in Angola, Mozambique, and Guinea-Bissau." *Journal of Modern African Studies*, 14, no. 3 (1976): 377–399.

Hipólito, Abel Barroso, Brigadeiro, Portuguese Army. *A Pacificação do Niassa: Um Caso Concreto de Contraguerrilha*. [The Pacification of Niassa: A Concrete Case of Counterguerrilla Warfare]. Lisbon: Privately printed, 1970.

Humbaraci, Arslan, and Nicole Muchnick. *Portugal's African Wars*. New York: The Third Press, 1974.

Janke, Peter. "Southern Africa: End of an Empire." *Conflict Studies*, no. 52 (December 1974).

Luz Cunha, General Joaquim da, General Kaúlza de Arriaga, General José Manuel de Bethencourt Rodrigues, and General Silvino Silvério Marques. *África: A Vitória Traída*. [Africa: Betrayed Victory]. Lisbon: Editorial Intervenção, 1977.

Maciel, Artur. *Angola Heróica: 120 Dias com os Nossos Soldados*. [Heroic Angola: 120 Days with Our Soldiers]. Amadora: Livaria Bertrand, 1963.

Maier, F. X. *Revolution and Terrorism in Mozambique*. New York: American African Affairs Association, 1974.

Marcum, John A. *The Angolan Revolution, Volume I: The Anatomy of an Explosion (1950–1962)*. Cambridge, Mass.: MIT Press, 1969.

_____. *The Angolan Revolution, Volume II: Exile Politics and Guerrilla Warfare (1962–1976)*. Cambridge, Mass.: MIT Press, 1978.

Mondlane, Eduardo. *The Struggle for Mozambique*. London: Zed Press, 1969.

Negrão, Joaquim Vito Corte-Real, Captain, Pilot Aviator, Portuguese Air Force. "Subsídios para o Reconhecimento Aéreo Visual." [Aid to Visual Aerial Reconnaissance]. *Boletim do Estado-Maior da Força Aerea* (December 1962): 30–43.

Pélissier, René. *Le Naufrage des Caravelles: Etudes sur la Fin de l'Empire Portugais (1961–1975)*. [The Shipwreck of the Caravels: Studies on the End of the Portuguese Empire (1961–1975)]. Orgeval: Editions Pélissier, 1979.

_____. *La Colonie du Minotaure: Nationalismes et Révoltes en Angola (1926–1961)*. [The Colony of the Minotaur: Nationalist Movements and Revolts in Angola (1926–1961)]. Orgeval: Editions Pélissier, 1978.

_____. "Private War." *The Geographical Magazine* (November 1971): 78–80.

Porch, Douglas. *The Portuguese Armed Forces and the Revolution*. Stanford: Hoover Institution Press, 1977.

Rocha, Nuno. *Guerra em Moçambique*. [War in Mozambique]. Lisbon: Editora Ulisseia, 1969.

Silva Cunha, Joaquim Moreira da. *O Ultramar, a Nação e o "25 de April."* [The Overseas Provinces, the Nation and the "25th of April"]. Coimbra: Atlântida Editora, 1977.

Spínola, António de. *Portugal e o Futuro*. [Portugal and the Future]. Lisbon: Editoria Arcádia, 1974.

_____. *Por uma Guiné Melhor*. [For a Better Guiné]. Lisbon: Agência-Geral do Ultramar, 1970.

van der Waals, Willem S. *Portugal's War in Angola 1961–1974*. Rivonia, South Africa: Ashanti Publishing, 1993.

Venter, Al J. "Why Portugal Lost Its African Wars." In *Challenge: Southern Africa Within the African Revolutionary Context*, ed. Al J. Venter, 224–272. Gibraltar: Ashanti Publishing, 1989.

_____. *The Zambesi Salient*. London: Robert Hale & Co., 1974.
_____. *Portugal's Guerrilla War: The Campaign for Africa*. Cape Town: John Malherbe, 1973.
_____. *Portugal's War in Guiné-Bissau*. Pasadena: California Institute of Technology, 1973.
_____. *The Terror Fighters: A Profile of Guerrilla Warfare in Southern Africa*. Cape Town: Purnell and Sons, 1969.
Waring, Ronald (Duke of Valderano). "The Case for Portugal." In *Angola, a Symposium: Views of a Revolt*, ed. Philip Mason. Oxford: Oxford University Press, 1962.
Wheeler, Douglas L. "African Elements in Portugal's Armies in Africa (1961-1974)." *Armed Forces and Society*, 2, no. 2 (February 1976): 233-250.
_____. "The Portuguese Army in Angola." *Modern African Studies*, 7, no. 3 (1969): 425-439.
_____, and René Pélissier. *Angola*. London: Pall Mall Press, 1971.

LITERATURE ON COUNTERINSURGENCY WARFARE AND COMPARATIVE CAMPAIGNS

Blaufarb, D. S., and George K. Tanham. *Who Will Win?: A Key to the Puzzle of Revolutionary War*. London: Crane Russak, 1989.
Callwell, Colonel C. E. *Small Wars: A Tactical Textbook for Imperial Soldiers*. London: Her Majesty's Stationery Office, 1896; reprint, London: Lionel Leventhal, 1990.
Clutterbuck, Richard. *The Long Long War: The Emergency in Malaya 1948-1960*. London: Cassell & Co., 1966.
Colby, William. *Lost Victory*. New York: Contemporary Books, 1989.
Crawford, Oliver. *The Door Marked Malaya*. London: Rupert Hart-Davis, 1958.
Cross, James Eliot. *Conflict in the Shadows: The Nature and Politics of Guerrilla War*. London: Constable & Co., 1964.
Crozier, Brian. *The Rebels*. London: Chatto and Windus, 1960.
Fall, Bernard B. *The Two Vietnams: A Political and Military Analysis*. New York: Frederick A. Praeger, 1963.
Foxton, P. D. *Powering War: Modern Land Force Logistics*. London: Brassey's, 1994.
Galula, David. *Counter-Insurgency Warfare: Theory and Practice*. London: Pall Mall Press, 1964.
Green, T. N., ed. *The Guerrilla and How to Fight Him*. New York: Frederick A. Praeger, 1962.
Harmon, Christopher C. "Illustrations of 'Learning' in Counterinsurgency." *Comparative Strategy* (January-March 1992): 29-48.
Heggoy, Alf Andrew. *Insurgency and Counterinsurgency in Algeria*. Bloomington: Indiana University Press, 1972.
Hoffman, Bruce, and Jennifer M. Taw. *Defense Policy and Low-Intensity Conflict: The Development of Britain's "Small Wars" Doctrine During the 1950s*. Santa Monica: Rand Corporation, 1991.
Horne, Alistair. *A Savage War of Peace: Algeria 1954-1962*. Harmondsworth: Penguin Books, 1987.

Jackson, Robert. *The Malayan Emergency: The Commonwealth's Wars 1948–1966.* London: Routledge, 1991.

Kitson, General Sir Frank. *Bunch of Five.* London: Faber and Faber, 1977.

_____. *Low Intensity Operations: Subversion, Insurgency and Peacekeeping.* London: Faber and Faber, 1971.

Krepinevich, Andrew F., Jr. *The Army and Vietnam.* Baltimore: Johns Hopkins University Press, 1986.

McCuen, John J. *The Art of Counter-Revolutionary War.* London: Faber and Faber, 1966.

Metz, Steven. "Victory and Compromise in Counterinsurgency." *Military Review* (April 1992): 47–53.

_____. "Counterinsurgent Campaign Planning." *Parameters* (September 1989): 60–68.

Miller, Harry. *Jungle War in Malaya: The Campaign Against Communism 1948–60.* London: Arthur Barker, 1972.

Mockaitis, Thomas R. *British Counterinsurgency, 1919–60.* London: Macmillan, 1990.

O'Ballance, Edgar. *The Algerian Insurrection, 1954–1962.* Hamden, Conn.: Archon Books, 1967.

Oliveira, Hermes de Araújo. *Guerra Revolucionária.* [Revolutionary War]. Lisbon: Privately printed, 1960.

Osanka, Franklin Mark, ed. *Modern Guerrilla Warfare.* New York: Free Press of Glencoe, 1962.

Paget, Julian. *Counter-Insurgency Campaigning.* London: Faber and Faber, 1967.

Paret, Peter. *French Revolutionary Warfare from Indochina to Algeria: The Analysis of a Political and Military Doctrine.* London: Pall Mall Press, 1964.

_____, and John W. Shy. *Guerrillas in the 1960's.* New York: Frederick A. Praeger, 1962.

Pustay, John S. *Counterinsurgency Warfare.* New York: The Free Press, 1965.

Rice, Edward E. *Wars of the Third Kind: Conflict in Undeveloped Countries.* Berkeley: University of California Press, 1988.

Royal United Services Institute. *Lessons from the Vietnam War.* Report of a seminar held at the Royal United Services Institute in London, 12 February 1966.

Sheehan, Neil. *A Bright Shining Lie: John Paul Vann and America in Vietnam.* New York: Random House, 1988.

Stubbs, Richard. *Hearts and Minds in Guerrilla Warfare: The Malayan Emergency 1948–1960.* Oxford: Oxford University Press, 1989.

Thompson, Robert. *Peace Is not at Hand.* London: Chatto & Windus, 1974.

_____. *Defeating Communist Insurgency: Experiences from Malaya and Vietnam.* London: Chatto & Windus, 1972.

_____. *Revolutionary War in World Strategy 1945–1969.* London: Martin Secker & Warburg, 1970.

Trinquier, Roger. *Modern Warfare: A French View of Counterinsurgency.* Translated by Daniel Lee. London: Pall Mall Press, 1964.

INDEX

About the Author

JOHN P. CANN, a former naval flight officer and retired captain, served both on the staff of the Assistant Secretary of Defense for Special Operations and Low-Intensity Conflict and subsequently on that of the Under Secretary of Defense for Policy. He holds a Ph.D. in war studies from King's College, University of London, and has published articles on counterinsurgency and military funding.

ISBN 0-313-30189-1

90000>

EAN

9 780313 301896

HARDCOVER BAR CODE